African Cultures, Memory and Space:
Living the Past Presence in Zimbabwean Heritage

Edited by
Munyaradzi Mawere
&
Tapuwa R. Mubaya

Langaa Research & Publishing CIG
Mankon, Bamenda

Publisher
Langaa RPCIG
Langaa Research & Publishing Common Initiative Group
P.O. Box 902 Mankon
Bamenda
North West Region
Cameroon
Langaagrp@gmail.com
www.langaa-rpcig.net

Distributed in and outside N. America by African Books Collective
orders@africanbookscollective.com
www.africanbookcollective.com

ISBN: 9956-792-97-7

© Munyaradzi Mawere & Tapuwa R. Mubaya 2014

List of Contributors

Munyaradzi Mawere is Associate Professor at Universidade Pedagogica-Gaza, Mozambique. Before joining this University, Mawere was lecturer at the University of Zimbabwe. He has written and published more than fifteen books and over fifty papers in scholarly journals.

Tapuwa Raymond Mubaya is a Lecturer at Great Zimbabwe University, Faculty of Culture and Heritage. Before joining Great Zimbabwe University, Mr. Mubaya worked for National Museums and Monuments of Zimbabwe for eight years as the Senior Curator of Archaeology and Head of the Great Zimbabwe Conservation Centre.

Jacob Mapara is a Professor of Indigenous Knowledge and African Languages and Literature. He is currently with the Centre for Indigenous Knowledge and Living Heritage at Chinhoyi University of Technology, Zimbabwe. Dr. Mapara's other interests are in onomastics, the Shona novel and short story.

Farai M. Chabata is Senior Curator of Ethnography with the National Museum and Monuments of Zimbabwe. He obtained his MA in African History with the University of Zimbabwe. His research interests include heritage management, intangible cultural heritage and collections management.

Henry Chiwaura is currently a PhD Candidate in Heritage with the University of KwaZulu-Natal, South Africa. He obtained his MA in Heritage Studies from the University of Zimbabwe. He is working as Lecturer in Archaeology, Museums and Heritage Studies, Great Zimbabwe University, Zimbabwe. His research interests includes but not limited to, heritage management, museology and public archaeology.

Thomas Panganayi Thondhlana is currently the Director of the School of Culture and Heritage Studies at the Great Zimbabwe University. He holds a PhD in Archaeology from the University College of London.

Jane Sigauke is incumbent Teaching Assistant in the Department of Archaeology, Heritage and Museum Studies at Great Zimbabwe University. Her research interests are in the area of sustainable heritage management, traditional methods of managing heritage and museology. She obtained her BA Honours in Archaeology, Cultural Heritage and Museum Studies from Midlands State University.

Shadreck Dzingayi: Assistant Lecturer at Great Zimbabwe University, Faculty of Culture and Heritage.

Lesley Hatipone Machiridza is currently a PhD candidate registered with the University of Pretoria in South Africa. Machiridza has worked for the National Museums and Monuments of Zimbabwe (NMMZ) and the Midlands State University before joining the Faculty of Culture and Heritage Studies at the Great Zimbabwe University. His interest in the Rozvi stretches as far back as 2004 when he started interrogating their archaeological past. Over the years, that research interest has blossomed as evidenced by his sustained intriguing academic contributions to the subject.

Francis Muchemwa is a Lecturer at Great Zimbabwe University, Faculty of Culture and Heritage Studies. He worked for National Museums and Monuments of Zimbabwe based at the Great Zimbabwe World Heritage site for thirteen years as a cultural heritage interpreter/ presenter to the visiting tourists before joining Great Zimbabwe University.

Genius Tevera is an Assistant Lecturer at Great Zimbabwe University, Department of Heritage Studies, Faculty of Culture and Heritage Studies, Zimbabwe.

Table of Contents

Whither African cultures? An introduction

Introduction

While issues related to culture are inexorably complex to address in their entirety in one volume, they are worthy of concentrated interrogation particularly in culturally diverse and historically fragile milieus like those of Zimbabwe; contexts where fieldwork observations and case studies examined in this book emerge. In these culturally diverse contexts, the inscrutable amalgam of a complex history of skewed colonial education with its social vestiges, vices and anomalies and where most of the vices and anomalies are persistent even today, a rigorous academic excursion of emerging vibrant forces such as globalisation are befitting and more relevant now than ever.

Globalisation, for instance, offers the latest episode in the development of approaches to culture studies, connecting cultures with all possible geographical landscapes. Yet, some cultures, for example, in Africa are essentially enduring given the spiteful experiences they have gone through since the colonial period to the present as a result of large scale processes such as westernisation. Globalisation comes to the fore as an actor that potentially offers new approach(es) towards the recognition that issues of culture transcend national and even regional boundaries that call for mutual understanding, respect and common approach to appreciate different societies. Unfortunately for Africa and other so-called 'subaltern' world societies, more often than not, it is the latter actor [globalisation] that imperial countries in the West and Americas capitalise on to impose their 'nefarious' values – culture-wise or otherwise – on other societies in the name of globalisation. This introductory chapter reflects on the material and analyses presented in the contributions of this diverse, impeccable collection and explore what the future may have in store for the previously disadvantaged and marginalised world societies as those of Africa and in particular Zimbabwe.

Objectives of the book

The more than 10 authors contributed to this book are drawn from across different disciplines and institutions. They all speak in their own independent voices, and with interesting glimpses of their respective fieldwork and case studies, on topical themes ranging from folklore, traditional dances, traditional medicines, colonialism, globalisation, ethnicity and identity in relation to the contemporary cultures of Zimbabwe. This is done without looking at the referred themes from a disciplinary knowledge perspective as the authors believe that although "disciplinary knowledge provides an important foundation for understanding different aspects of live reality [...] on their own, disciplines are limited in their ability to grasp the full complexity of what was, is and might be *the case*" Moser 2013: 37; emphasis original). The thrust of the book, thus, is inter-, trans-, and multi-disciplinary approach grounded in a multifaceted engagement to the study of culture. This thrust has been embraced following the contributors' realisation that viewing a single issue from different and multidisciplinary vantage point has the merit that it provides deep, rich and nuanced understanding of complex and dynamic issues that may in turn help to inform and influence policy formulation, especially in contexts where there are people from different cultural backgrounds.

As such, this book has as one of its objectives, to influence research around large-scale processes such as globalisation as well as policy-making on the same [culture] at national, regional and international levels. This implies that at another level, the present book aims to mobilise the wider academic community (from all disciplines concerned with culture and society) to engage more effectively and seriously in their study of culture so as to develop a more integrated and transformative research around present day topical issues such as globalisation and westernisation among others, that have impacted on culture in varying degrees. Integrated and transformative research guarantees openness to other ways of viewing and studying world processes. It also ensures that new and different kinds of questions that emerge from different disciplines and people from different societies across the world will be appreciated in the joint search for that which is good for the human society – the common good and global peace – now and for the future generations.

Reflections on the book chapters

As already been pointed out in the section above, this chapter is a synthesis of all the contributions that constitute this book. It is an exploration of the main themes that run from the first to the eleventh chapter of this cherished collection.

In chapter 1, Thomas Thondhlana grapples with the critical but often highly controversial issue of diversity and ethnicity in Zimbabwe. While Thondhlana acknowledges that ethnicity, which in Zimbabwe is the springboard of identity, is normally linked to blood ties it is the people's common history that also binds and sometimes define them as a people. Thondhlana, thus, argues: "people from different backgrounds can end up identifying themselves with particular ethnic groups as a result of historical factors irrespective of the lack of blood ties. Ethnic identities are socially created and constructed; they are sometimes very fluid *and* situational". Yet, while ethnicity is important in tagging identities, Thondhlana observes that they are also detrimental to socio-economic and political development in the historically and ethnically diverse modern states such as that of Zimbabwe. In view of this observation, Thondhlana concludes that the issue of ethnicity should not be taken seriously when it comes to nation building as it promotes "lobby groups and ethnic movements".

Chapter 2 by Munyaradzi Mawere takes up the issue of European colonialism in Africa and how it has impacted on the African people's lives and worldviews even today. Mawere, thus, argues:

Colonialism has always had perennial bearing on the African people's lives and worldviews. This is premised on the fact that colonialism differed from other episodes of domination in *world history in* that it involved a different mode of production (capitalism) and technology (industrialisation) on a virtually global scope.

In fact for Mawere, colonialism unlike previous forms of imperialism and domination such as racial slavery, has had perennial impact on the lives of Africans for the major reason that it targeted at dominating and eliminating other societies' religio-cultural norms and values as well as modes of production, replacing these with Western/European particularities thereby conquering the Africans in totality. In short, colonialism was a process of elimination of other peoples' cultures and histories. For Mawere, this is an unequal or asymmetrical relationship (between Africa and Europe) that has persisted even to date. In view of this observation, Mawere concludes his chapter by (re)constructing a unified compendium through which he calls for a reversal of the imperial gestures in a dialogic and reflexive way that promotes social justice, equality and global peace.

In chapter 3, Tapuwa Raymond Mubaya and Henry Chiwaura tussle head on with legislation and management of landscapes to locate their locus in Zimbabwe. They note that most of the problems in the legislation and management (such as the exclusion of local communities) of cultural landscapes in Africa and particularly in Zimbabwe were inherited from the colonial government. Mubaya and Chiwaura lament lack of participation in the legislation and management of heritage sites in the country which in their view has a negative impact on the overall protection and wellbeing of the sites. Mubaya and Chiwaura, thus, argue with Muringaniza (1998) that:

> Legislation pertaining to the management and protection of heritage in the country only recognises NMMZ as the sole custodian. Resultantly, local communities have developed an indifference towards the country's heritage. The negative attitude by local communities in Zimbabwe towards their cultural and natural heritage emanates from the alienating

legislation, which has not undergone significant changes since the attainment of independence in 1980 to accommodate local aspirations.

Mubaya and Chiwaura conclude their chapter by calling for the government to seriously consider all stakeholders, especially local communities, in the legislation and management of heritage sites in Zimbabwe.

Farai M. Chabata and Henry Chiwaura's chapter 4 expands Mubaya and Chiwaura's concern on heritage sites protection and management in Zimbabwe. Using a case study of the heritage site, Chitungwiza chaChaminuka Shrine in Zimbabwe, Chabata and Chiwaura show the kind of conflicts and contestations (by different stakeholders) surrounding many heritage sites in the country in terms of ownership and management. For Chabata and Chiwaura, these conflicts and contestations are normally a result of the memories and histories that a people attach to particular spaces, which in fact, were largely disturbed by colonialism and subsequently the post-colonial government which failed to attend to such issues. Yet while Chabata and Chiwaura's piece provides a lot of insights on issues of memory, history and space, it could have been richer had it provided concrete solutions to conflicts and contestations that normally arise around management and protection of heritage sites.

Drawing on his wealth experience of lectureship and research, Jacob Mapara's luminary work (in chapter 5) takes up the issue of folktale which he argues is one of the most enduring aspect, and indeed the intangible heritage, of the Bantu people and in particular the Shona of Zimbabwe. Yet, Mapara does not only consider folktale as one of the most enduring component of the Bantu folklore, but as a source of inspiration, entertainment and a deductive tool for the Bantu people. He notes with concern that although huge strides have been taken by the government of Zimbabwe to recognise the resilience and value (moral or otherwise) of folklore, in some schools across the country, students are unfortunately taught that folklore is a waning and indeed moribund art on the brink of extinction. Mapara, thus, argues: "Contrary to what is taught to some students studying Shona at Advanced Level and those studying oral literature in colleges and universities in the country, the folktale is not a dying art but has shown resilience." Mapara's observation of what is being taught in most of the learning institutions across Zimbabwe with regard to folktale, is a fiasco to appreciate and understand the dynamism and evolutionary nature of folktale, which he thinks should be realised by those concerned with the teaching and studying of the subject.

In chapter 6, Jane Sigauke, Henry Chiwaura and Munyaradzi Mawere target an important niche of traditional medicine, one of the chief constituent of the cultural heritage that has been bequeathed to the Zimbabwean people (and those beyond) from its progenitors. While the realm of traditional medicine is inestimable, Sigauke, Chiwaura and Mawere focus specifically on the use and efficacy of the medicine in child bearing mothers whom the trio refer to as the connoisseurs of traditional medicine. From their findings, the trio note the resilience of traditional medicine amidst the sad pejorative histories that the medicine has suffered since the dawn of colonialism in Zimbabwe. Given the locally availability and efficacy of the medicine, Sigauke, Chiwaura and Mawere argue for the full recognition of traditional medicine by the Zimbabwean government and those in the mainstream medical fraternity, besides the need for Western medicine and traditional medicine to work together to complement or enrich one another.

Tapuwa R. Mubaya and Shadreck Dzingayi's chapter 7 makes a conscious, concerted endeavour to unpack the niceties envisaged potentials of traditional dance and music, intangible heritage, that ever since the beginning of history of the Shona people of Zimbabwe has been used as a source of inspiration and entertainment. Mubaya and Dzingayi blame globalisation and rapid urbanisation in the recent years for the fast disappearing of traditional dance and music from the Zimbabwean scene especially in the urban settings. The duo, thus, argue:

Different forms of dance and music have been negatively affected by the strong tide of globalisation which has strongly swept through the country particularly in the 21st century ... majority of the people have abandoned *their dancing groups* in preference of Christianity, an appendage of colonialism and globalisation. It is also disheartening to note that traditional music and dance have not been spared by rural to urban migration.

Mubaya and Dzingayi lament the fast disappearing of traditional dance and music in Zimbabwe as this has a negative impact on the country's socio-economic development especially in tourism industry and human socialisation. Thus, owing to their importance as identity marks, socialising tools and 'boosters' for the tourism industry, Mubaya and Dzingayi argue for the continued upholding of the traditional dances and music in Zimbabwe.

In chapter 8, Lesley Hatipone Machiridza provides an eloquent, nuanced narrative of the dialectics of the Shona people (of Zimbabwe) and in particular the traditions of the Rozvi ethnic group that identified the latter as a people and one of the most prominent ethnic groups in the history of Zimbabwe. For Machiridza, the Rozvi identities were culturally, situationally and systematically constructed from the local Shona communities such that they became unique and true to themselves. While a plethora of the Shona institutions were readily adopted by the Rozvi people to suit their needs and changing society, Machiridza makes the important point that the institutions of marriage, totemism and taboos were mainly manipulated as these helped to shape and reshape the social and political landscapes of the Rozvi people. Machiridza's historic chapter is significant in that it shows how the dynamics of power among the Rozvi, as in many other Shona ethnic groups, were played out. Yet, the chapter could have been even richer had the author demonstrated how other Shona ethnic groups benefitted from the Rozvi people's institutions.

Chapter 9 by Tapuwa R. Mubaya and Munyaradzi Mawere focuses on heritage typologies and organisation in Zimbabwe, particularly in terms of questions and insights as well as policy issues that arise from the typologies and organisation. While acknowledging some huge strides by the Zimbabwean government towards addressing the problems affecting heritage, Mubaya and Mawere note that a lot more is still desired to be done especially in view of local communities who have always been the custodians of heritage resources across the country. In the light of this realisation, the authors of this chapter offer incisive analysis and questioning of the current heritage typologies and organisation with a view to (re)shape and influence policy.

Francis Muchemwa, Tapuwa R. Mubaya and Munyaradzi Mawere's chapter 10 tackles head on the question of theory of culture. While the trio acknowledge that there are a myriad of theories that have been advanced in attempt to interpret culture, they marshal three theories of culture namely cultural relativism, cultural determinism and ethnocentrism in relation to the Zimbabwean context. As noted by Muchemwa, Mubaya and Mawere, the choice of the aforementioned theories is premised on their observation that the chief characteristics of these theories are not only applicable but observable in many cultures around the country. The strength of this chapter lies in its recognition of difference and uniqueness between different cultures while at the same time advocate mutual and symmetrical relationships of the cultures.

In chapter 11, Genius Tevera and Tapuwa Raymond Mubaya grapple with the culturally volatile question of marriage in contemporary Zimbabwean society plagued with social uncertainty about tradition, cultural fragilities and social ambiguities imposed by the controversial process of globalisation. Tevera and Mubaya acknowledge that the issue of marriage has been discussed extensively in literature. Nevertheless, they observe that the relationship between marriage and globalisation has not been fully discussed in literature, yet the impact of the latter is observable throughout Zimbabwe. In view of the changes observable in the institution of marriage, Tevera and Mubaya argue for need to restore the intrinsic value of marriage transaction and institution as that meant to foster relationships between families and not as a trade where women are sold and purchased. On this note, Tevera and Mubaya caution us to treat the force of globalisation in a way that does not undermine our culture, traditions and dignity as a people.

From the foregoing, I should underline that an exploration of all the aforementioned chapters that constitute this volume reveals that globalisation is at the center of cultural changes in most (if not all) societies. Yet, as is revealed in most of the contributions in this volume, globalisation is essentially a politically driven process whose contribution to world societies, especially the previously disadvantaged and marginalised ones is often negative or rather controversial.

Globalisation and the promise for global peace, harmony and oneness

Typically, protagonists of [inclusive] globalisation have presented globalisation as a win-win process for both peoples in the global north and global south – imperial countries and the previously disadvantaged countries – and to safeguard social equity, human dignity and well-being for all as well as for economic development, global resource conservation, international peace-building, economic integration and development. There is need, therefore, to understand why globalisation, though associated with these *super* objectives, still meet with controversy and criticism especially by academics and members of the public in previously disadvantaged and marginalised societies.

Due to its association with the different limitations discussed in different chapters that constitutes this book, globalisation emerges as a zone of competing claims and opportunities for world peace building, economic development, and mutual understanding between people of different societies. In respect of values to be embraced globally (by the world as a whole), the legal status and mandate to manage them is, for example, frequently bestowed on America and the Western imperial countries with media channels (e.g. television channels) created by and accountable only to the aforementioned countries (America and the Western countries). This can never go well with countries in the global south making the future of globalisation straddling on the edge, as one of increased conflict, marginalisation and subjugation of previously disadvantaged societies or as one of increasing interaction while offering fresh opportunities for the previously disadvantaged. It is no doubt that globalisation may give rise to diverse world culture-based enterprise that enrich the lives of both those in the global north and global south. The bottom line, however, is how globalisation as a process is initiated and with what benefits to all stakeholders – all the cultures of the world? Most of the contributors to this volume have argued that as long as globalisation is dictated from the global north and the Americas and other societies are made 'backseaters' or what I call "flat actors" it is bound to fail. By flat actors I mean those actors (in this case, societies in the global south or the subaltern) that are considered by imperial countries as lacking the ability and power to offer anything meaningful to the world: they can only receive without question that which comes from 'above' – those societies that consider themselves as superior to all others. This kind of globalisation, which in fact is never inclusive, will fail because it will never be able to yield positive results for all. In fact, the long-term future of globalisation as a process that wins the hearts of all is likely to be compromised, if not threatened to annihilation as was the case with colonial administration, unless it supports the lives and interests of the previously marginalised and disadvantaged societies or at most privilege different perspectives, arguments and contexts. This is to say that while globalisation may function as a driver for peace and oneness of the world (the so-called global village), its role as a connoisseur may also depend on its negotiating tactics and ability to foster mutuality, equity, and fairness. People would always question about the incentives or benefits of globalisation to their societies and progeny, hence most of the chapters in this book have largely cautioned the imperial countries of the world to seriously consider the plight of the previously disadvantaged in (re)negotiating globalisation as a unifying force.

On one hand, the above discussion raises questions about the nature and role of the current force of change – globalisation – and also about the need to investigate the reasons for indifference, scepticism and denialism of that 'force' in many parts of the world. On the other hand, the discussion entails the need for concerted action to safeguard social equity, human dignity and well-being for all. This book, thus, picks up this challenge by issuing an urgent appeal to both the so-called developed and developing countries to form a symmetrically united front with a common vision and goal oriented towards sustainable globalisation.

Obstacles to sustainable globalisation

As highlighted in the preceding section and also most of the chapters in this book, globalisation has met with serious controversies and criticisms over the years mainly due to its support and promotion of those values that colonialism (or the Western imperialists and subsequently Americans) advanced directly or otherwise. Put differently, the major charge against the present day globalisation has been that it is being dictated by the so-called developed countries from the West and the Americas. In fact, it is beyond reasonable doubt that most of the values, theories and/or ideas that dominate the world today are from the West and the Americas. Unfortunately, those values and ideas have failed to capture the attention, relationships, interactions, imagination, belief systems and thinking of the more traditional and marginalised societies of the world. Unless this is reversed, such a scenario will always pose a great threat and consequences to all other societies. Also, the anxiety, social discontent and distrust of those institutions previously entrusted with fostering global peace will continue growing. As a result, globalisation as a process geared towards positive change in world relations has failed to appeal to and embraced by all societies across the world.

New opportunities and solutions to make-up for the failures of globalisation

The realisation that globalisation has met with serious criticisms as a largely failed process calls for new strategies that can offer better promises for global peace and good international relations, or at least a new invigorated form of globalisation that will seriously consider and recognise different practices, perspectives, cultural values, beliefs, knowledge systems, interactions, relationships, and institutions across the world. I call this new invigorated form of globalisation "global unification". I believe this new force of change – global unification – though seemingly too ambitious will effectively integrate efforts from across disciplines and societies of the world as a whole. It will, in this thrust, mark significant progress in creating new opportunities for the marginalised and influence relations and interactions at a global scale.

Overall, the book offers a highly readable account of cultural heritage, social structures, thought-processes, social knowledge, spacio-histories, and modes of communication of different ethnic groups across Zimbabwe. The book is primarily an invaluable asset that renders penetrating insights for cognoscenti, policy makers and educators in the fields of Heritage Studies, Social Anthropology, African Studies, social/political ecology and Sociology.

Munyaradzi Mawere

References

Hackmann, H. and Moser, S. 2013. Social sciences in a changing global environment: General introduction, In *World Social Science Report, 2013: Changing Global Environments*, UNESCO Publishing, Paris.

Muringaniza, J. S. 1998. *Community participation in archaeological heritage management in Zimbabwe*: The case of Old Bulawayo, Unpublished Mphil thesis, University of Cambridge.

Chapter 1

Ethnicity in Zimbabwe: The peopling of the modern nation-state

Thomas Panganayi Thondhlana

"On a particular Wednesday I may spend most of my time highlighting my role as a professor at a liberal arts college. The following Saturday, I may spend all day playing the role of a loving daughter for my mother's birthday celebration, an occasion at which the fact that I am a professor may be more or less irrelevant" (Fought 2006: 20).

Introduction

The modern day nation-state of Zimbabwe is home to at least twelve million people from diverse backgrounds. Owing to its complex and dynamic past Zimbabwe is a melting pot of many cultures and people of different ethnic backgrounds. Linguistically, Zimbabwe has a multifaceted ethnolinguistic makeup comprising of at least twenty language varieties (Hachipola 1998; Ndhlovu 2009). It is thus important to generate information that fosters unity in this diversity. As human beings, we always find comfort in belonging and sometimes people identify us with certain groups of people. These identities are created and sometimes they are very situational. These identities can take many forms like race, gender, class, ethnicity, nationality and religion among others (Machiridza 2013: 206). Moreover, the construction of identities by individuals or a group of people is a very complex process. The quotation from Fought (2006) given at the beginning of this chapter highlights how an individual's roles and identity can change in different contexts. Ethnicity is one of the central concepts in humanities and social science inquiry (Bolaff *et al.* 2003). This chapter seeks to give a very brief, but comprehensive, overview of ethnic groups that cover the landscape of Zimbabwe. Each of the ethnic groups has a unique history and customs but

1

collectively they form what some scholars prefer to view as 'Zimbabwean culture'. However, this phrase should not be confused with the 'Zimbabwe Culture' used by archaeologists (Caton-Thompson 1931; Pikirayi 2001). As an archaeological phenomenon, the 'Zimbabwe Culture' is synonymous with the building of dry-stone monuments like Great Zimbabwe, Khami, Danangombe and Naletale. Although Zimbabwe is made up of people with diverse backgrounds they have lived side by side both in times of peace and conflict, for several centuries. Indigenous African people have embraced each other during the different time periods.

Terms such as 'tribes', 'ethnic group' and 'ethnicity' are frequently found in literature that deals with the discourse of group identities. Current scholarship has reservations with the use of the term 'tribe' which is seen as derogatory with stereotypes of groups that are primitive; as such these terms, ethnic group and ethnicity will be used in this chapter. Since this chapter discusses the ethnic makeup of Zimbabwe it is imperative to first explore the meaning of the term ethnicity. Ethnicity is a very complex, elusive, contested and loaded term. According to Fought (2006: 4), scholars across the disciplines generally agree that ethnicity is a socially constructed group identity marker that is constantly defined and redefined. There is usually a misconception and limited view that ethnic identity is determined by one's language. It is a fact that language does play a critical role in the creation of ethnic identities but ethnicity is much more complex than this (Fought 2006). Fought (2006) actually argues that in some cases ethnicity is imposed on a group of people by others whilst sometimes it is self-selected. According to Barker (2012: 255) ethnicity is a cultural concept centred on the sharing of norms, values, beliefs, cultural symbols and practices. It is a process of boundary formation that is constructed and maintained under specific socio-historical conditions (Barker 2012: 256). The simple definition of an 'ethnic group' adopted in this chapter is that it is a group of people of common descent or ancestry who share similar customs. An ethnic group usually shares unique cultural values and individuals in that group are brought together by historical commonalities. Ethnic groups are usually tied together by collective memory of previous colonisation or migration whilst membership to a particular ethnic group does not always imply strong blood ties (Fought 2006: 8). As will be demonstrated in this chapter people from different backgrounds can end up identify themselves with particular ethnic groups as a result of historical factors even if they lack of blood ties. Ethnic identities are socially created and constructed; they are sometimes very fluid and situational. These identities are sometimes strong or hard or in some cases weak or soft (MacGonagle 2007: 2).

It is emphasised right from the beginning that ethnic labels outlined in this chapter, were and are still very fluid. The reader should appreciate that ethnicity is not static. According to Machiridza (2013: 199) pre-colonial Zimbabwe is characterised by the creation of new identities, their transformation, negotiation and accommodation. Ethnic groups discussed in this chapter are a result of fusion, assimilation, intermarriages which have occurred over a long period of time. Over the centuries there was acculturation of some groups as a direct result of political domination by other groups. The reader should also be made aware that some scholars vigorously reject regional ethnic identities like the ones presented in this chapter (e.g. Chimhundu 1992; Ranger 1985). They argue that, in the case of Zimbabwe, it is highly questionable that such identities are actually deeply rooted, immemorial and natural (Chimhundu 1992: 91). These scholars view ethnic identities as a recent construction of Western colonial culture which was non-existing prior to the coming of Europeans to Africa. This view, in the discourse of ethnic studies, is known as constructivism (Msindo 2012: 2-3). Constructivists vigorously argue for the abolishment of terms like 'tribe', 'ethnicity' or 'ethnic group'. On the other hand, we have primordialism as a theory which views ethnic identities as a natural and immutable (Mhlanga 2013; Msindo 2012: 10). Primodialists view ethnic identities as deep rooted in African culture; they trace these ethnic identities to the pre-colonial era. The major criticism of the constructivism theory in the study of ethnicity is that it gives the impression that Africans

3

are not active agents in the creation of their own group identities (Msindo 2012: 12).

The sentiments of constructivists may better be understood within the context of the post-colonial era. Modern nation-states are a relatively recent invention (Barker 2012: 259). Generally as nation-states emerge from colonialism one of their top priorities is to create national identity based on collective memory and history (see Holtorf 2011; Ucko 1994). Emphasis on national identity is much favoured over ethnic identities by the ruling class. As a result nation-states have a tendency to move more towards cultural homogeneity and suppression of distinctiveness, cultural diversity or regional cultures. Most post-colonial countries will go to greater lengths to try to mask cultural plurality through the process of foregrounding nationals as ethnically homogenous populations (Ndlovu-Gatsheni 2009). Subconsciously the original title of this chapter was "Introduction: an overview of Zimbabwean culture". The initial idea was to foreground the 'Zimbabwean culture' as a strong collective identity. However, it was later discovered that this is problematic because it assumes that there is cultural homogeneity. According to Barker (2012: 260) national identity is a way of unifying cultural diversity. For the nation-states emphasis on regional, cultural, and ethnic identities can result in the revival of strong cultural sentiments and the quest for self-determination. According to Ucko (1994: 266) support for local cultural activities may result in more localised and introverted ethnic revivalism. It is for this reason that in 1981, soon after the protracted war for independence, government officials encouraged Zimbabweans to lose out their ethnic identities in order to suit within the context of the national identity (Ucko 1994: 264). Wuriga (2012: 208) correctly notes that such national cultures demand uniformity and conformity.

Our knowledge of Zimbabwe's past, by extension ethnohistories, comes from written documents. Unfortunately, in southern Africa written documents were a product of European maritime expansion from the fifteenth century, and most of these reports are limited to the encounters that took place on the coastal areas. It took some

4

more centuries for Europeans to penetrate into the interior. The majority of the documents of European encounters in the interior only became prevalent in the nineteenth-century. These early documents are notably laden with racial prejudice. For the reconstructions of Zimbabwe's pre-colonial past we also have to rely on oral traditions that are notably selective, concentrating mostly on political or mythical events to validate present day political arrangements (Mitchell 2002: 3). For a deeper time-resolved insight of history of people with a much greater antiquity in the country we have to rely on archaeology and linguistic reconstructions. These various sources inform us that various groups of people moved into various parts of the country at different times in the past. The information provided in this chapter is based on the substantial work that has been published by other scholars on the origins of the major ethnic groups in Zimbabwe. The chapter should therefore be viewed as a synthesis of work that has been done on the subject matter.

A brief guide to the geography of Zimbabwe

Zimbabwe's physiographic background information provides a suitable base upon which one can contextualise population dynamics and cultural differences. The various groups of people that are discussed in this chapter were lured to the Zimbabwean plateau and adjacent lowlands by various resources located therein. Geographically, Zimbabwe is a landlocked country that is located in the southern African region. The natural boundaries of Zimbabwe are the Zambezi River, which forms the northern frontier, Limpopo River, which forms part of the southern frontier and the eastern highlands, which demarcate boundaries with Mozambique, only its western parts are defined by artificial boundaries. The country is largely dominated by a large plateau with few low lying outliers as one approach the Zambezi Valley and Limpopo River. The eastern highlands are the highest parts of the Zimbabwe plateau with mountains over 2000 meters in altitude. Whilst about 20% of the country consists of the low veldt under 900 meters. The neighbours of Zimbabwe are South Africa, Botswana, Zambia and Mozambique. The current boundaries of Zimbabwe were first spelt out in the 1889 Royal Charter that was granted to Cecil John Rhodes by Queen Victoria of England (Nyathi 2006: 1). However, it is only in 1895 that this vast territory, covering an area of 390 757 square kilometres, in southern Africa was named Rhodesia after Cecil John Rhodes.

The greater parts of the Zimbabwe plateau are dominated by granite rocks. These granite rocks form a crucial part of the cultural landscape of Zimbabwe. They were utilised to build unique dry-stone monuments like Great Zimbabwe by the ancestral Karanga people. Exposed granite rocks tend to fracture under successive heat and cold cycles to form flat sheets of rocks (Beach 1984: 8). Archaeological studies have revealed that the location for some pre-colonial settlements was partly determined by the presence of granite rocks. On the other hand, the adjacent lowland regions of the country have always been very hot and were largely considered unhealthy for both humans and domestic stock by the first European settlers. Archaeological investigations in semi-arid lowland regions of Zimbabwe have shown that these perceived 'uninhabitable' landscapes were actually occupied on a permanent basis for centuries by indigenous Africans (Pwiti 1996; Manyanga 2006). It should be acknowledged that rainfall is very low in the adjacent Lowveld as such rain-fed agriculture is sometimes problematic. However, it has to be noted that traditional cultigens of southern Africa, such as sorghum and millets, are drought-resistant crops that thrived in the regions (Manyanga 2006: 38). The agriculture remains the backbone of the economy of the modern nation-state of Zimbabwe.

Climatically, the country experiences two distinct seasons namely the summer rain season from mid-September to May and dry cold winter season, from June to mid-September. December, January and February are usually the wettest and hottest months, whilst the months June, July and August are the driest and coldest. The country does not experience any snow, except for frost, which normally occurs in the morning during the winter season. Rainfall patterns are largely dictated by the altitude, where the highveld Zimbabwe plateau experiences more favourable climatic conditions than the adjacent Lowveld regions.

Zimbabwe is endowed abundantly with fauna; as a result, large tracts of land in the country have been designated either as sanctuaries for wildlife and nature reserves. Some of the large game reserves include Hwange National Park, Gonerezhou National Park, Mana Pools National Park, Matobo National Park, Nyanga National Park, Matusadonha National Park, Zambezi National Park and Chizarira National Park. These parks are home to Africa's Big Five dangerous wildlife game in the form of elephants, lions, buffalos, rhinoceros and leopards. In the past, this diverse faunal community would have given an endless source of ivory and skins bound for Asia during the so-called 'Iron Age' period. Some of these wild animals were actually a major source of protein through meat consumption as has been established by archaeologists (Pwiti 1996).

Zimbabwe is also richly blessed with mineral resources that have attracted different groups of people to settle in this country throughout history. In some cases mining and metallurgy were exclusive pulling factors for human settlements in some regions during the pre-colonial and colonial periods. The evidence of several pre-colonial mines attests the importance of these mineral resources to various groups of people (Swan 1994). Metals and metal artefacts often take on material and symbolic expressions of identity since they can be used as social markers of wealth, status, ethnicity (Knapp 1998: 2). Capital-intensive mining during the colonial era also saw the establishment of mining towns which further attracted people from regions outside the then Rhodesia. It is against this brief guide of the Zimbabwean geographic landscapes and its resources that we have to appreciate the diverse groups that currently occupy the country.

Abridged history of Zimbabwe

The history of Zimbabwe is complex as such it is beyond the scope and requirements of this chapter to provide a detailed outline of this history. For a much comprehensive coverage of the pre-

7

colonial history of Zimbabwe the reader is referred to Beach (1984), Mlambo (2014) and Mlambo and Raftopolos (2009). However, in order to contextualise the histories and origins of the different ethnic groups discussed in this chapter it is necessary to give a brief outline of the country's past. Our knowledge of early human settlement history during the 'Stone Age' period in Zimbabwe remains sketchy. The information that we know about this period comes from the evidence of stone tools and rock art sites. The greatest density of the 'Stone Age' sites has been reported in the Matopos area (Walker 1995).

Archaeologists generally accept that groups of people with different modes of subsistence from the hunter-gatherers moved into the southern African landscape from at least the first millennium AD (Maggs and Whitelaw 1991). It is largely accepted that these groups brought with them the practice of agriculture, rearing of livestock and metal production. The settlement history and cultural sequence of this 'Iron Age' period has been developed using ceramic typologies combined with stratigraphic information and radiocarbon dates (Pikirayi 2001). The vanguards of the first millennium 'Early Iron Age' (c. CE 100- 1000) migrations into Zimbabwe have been associated with Kadzi, Ziwa and Gokomere ceramics (Pwiti 1996). The 'Middle Iron Age' (c. CE 1000 – 1300) and 'Late Iron Age' (c. CE 1300 – 1880) saw the establishment of state-oriented societies who notably constructed dry-stone walls found across the Zimbabwean plateau and neighbouring countries. These sites have been linked to ancestral Shona people.

The recent history and population dynamics of the late second millennium CE are associated with the Shona, Ndebele, Nambya, Venda, Tonga, Remba, Hlengwe and settlers of Euroasian descent. The late 1880s witnessed British settlement and eventually imposition of their administration on the landscape of Zimbabwe. After being granted the Royal Charter to occupy the Zimbabwean landscape in 1889 Cecil John Rhodes and the British South African Company (BSAC) moved in, by 1890 they had established a permanent settlement in Salisbury (presently Harare). This was followed by the

8

establishment of colonial institutions. As a result of Christian missionary, activities and education were established during this period hence the majority of Zimbabweans are now Christians. In 1923 Rhodesia was granted permission to be a self-governing colony of the British Empire. Following years of a protracted war for independence (1965-1979) Zimbabwe was granted its independence on the 18th of April 1980.

Zimbabwean ethnic groups: temporal and spatial variations

Zimbabwe is presently home to people of diverse ethnic and linguistic backgrounds. Genealogies, oral accounts of major events, migration and interaction have been very useful in the reconstruction of the history and origins of the various indigenous African groups. These groups include the Shangaan, Shona, Ndebele, Tonga, Kalanga, Nambya, Venda, Xhosa, Remba and Hlengwe among others. Some of these ethnic groups have been systematically excluded from the narratives of the modern nation-state (see Fig 1). It is believed that the Tonga, Shona and Kalanga groups have a much greater antiquity in the country when compared to other groups (Ncube 2004). The second millennium CE saw the establishment or settlement of other groups in the country. The late nineteenth to early twentieth century saw the influx and settlement of immigrants of European and Asian descent. Eurasian descent ethnic groups are excluded in this chapter. This section of the chapter will outline the brief history of these various ethnic groups and also establish the core areas that they occupy. This section outlines the temporal and spatial variations in the ethnic groups found in the country. Some in-depth information about these various ethnic and linguistic groups can be gleaned elsewhere (Hachipola 1998; Ncube 2004; Nyathi 2006; Owomoyela 2002). For an in-depth view about cultural practice associated with these groups the reader is referred to other chapters in this book and other sources (see Bourdillon 1998; Nyathi 2001). However, some distinct and unique features of these ethnic groups will be highlighted where necessary.

9

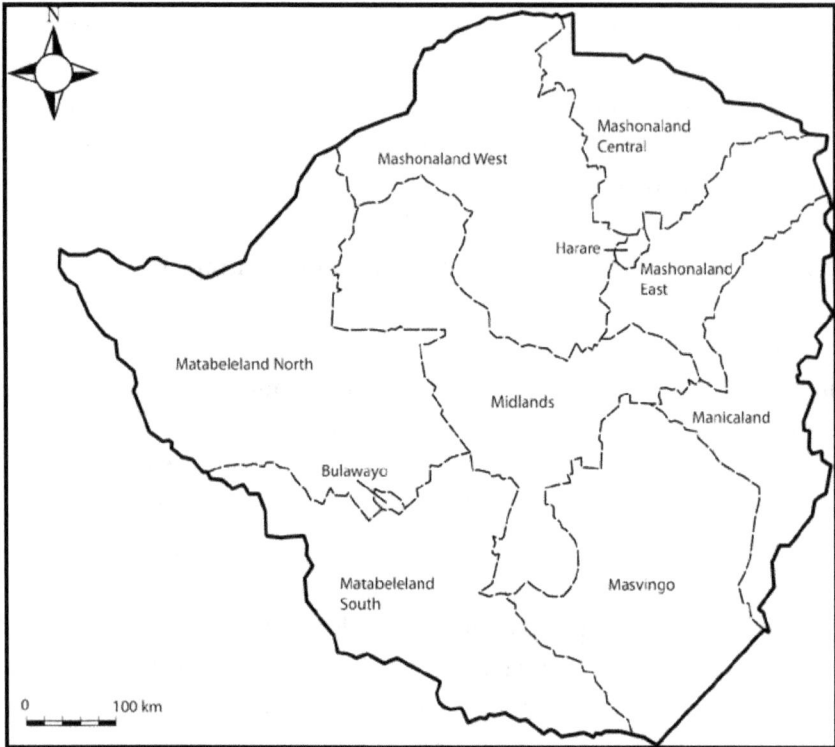

Figure 1: Map of Zimbabwe showing the nomenclature of Provinces which gives prominence to the Shona and Ndebele together with the elimination of other ethnic groups on the national landscape

Diverse as they are, the indigenous Zimbabwean ethnic groups are unified by common elements of the African culture (Nyathi 2006: 1). The majority of the African indigenous people in southern Africa belong to the Bantu stock or race, whilst it must be acknowledged that there are few who belong to the Khoi-San race. The original inhabitants of the Zimbabwean landscape were hunter-gatherers or simply the Khoi-San people. Khoi-San communities in Zimbabwe are now hard to identify but some can be found in the Tsholotsho District of Matabeleland North near the border of Botswana (Fisher 2010: 137). Unfortunately, their language and customs have slowly vanished whilst the few Khoi-San people usually conceal their identity by using Ndebele and Kalanga names. Conventional reconstructions of southern Africa region suggests that between 200 BCE and 300 CE there was a transition from hunting and gathering way of life which was a direct result of the coming of the Bantu speaking people. Historical linguistics suggests that these Bantu originated from West Africa particularly Nigeria and Cameroon (Beach 1984: 10). Bantu groups eventually absorbed the Khoi-San people.

The Shona people are the largest ethnic group in the modern nation-state of Zimbabwe. They make up at least 75% of the total population of the country. The Shona people can be divided into at least five sub-ethnic groups (dialects) namely Karanga, Korekore, Manyika, Ndau and Zezuru (Ndhlovu 2009: 48). From the oral reconstructions and archaeological sources it has been suggested that the Shona people have been on the Zimbabwean landscape for more than a thousand years (Nyathi 2006: 82). In the past the Shona people were renowned builders better known for their unique dry-stone architecture. Settlements that were occupied by the proto-Shona people can be identified using evidence of dry-stone structures. Based on archaeological reconstructions the ancestral Shona people can trace their origins to Mapungubwe, an early second millennium CE site which is found in the Limpopo Province of South Africa (Huffman 2000; Huffman 2009). However, information that has been gathered from oral traditions is incompatible with archaeological conclusions. The oral narratives unanimously suggest that the Shona people arrived on the Zimbabwean landscape from their initial homeland that was located in the North (Nyathi 2006). The Shona people occupy more than half of the Zimbabwe plateau.

The north-western part of Zimbabwe has been home to the Tonga people. Unfortunately there are no oral traditions about the origins of the Tonga people but based on archaeological evidence these people have great antiquity in this part of Zimbabwe (Burrett 1998). The majority of the earlier Tonga settlements were established in the Zambezi Valley. The Tonga language and customs are closely

11

related to the ones practised by groups found in Zambia and Democratic Republic of Congo (Nyathi 2006: 63). The major difference between the Tonga culture and that of other ethnic groups in Zimbabwe is that they operate from a matrilineal framework (Ncube 2004: 6). For example, they trace their descent and inheritance matrilineally through their mother's folk. This is in contrast to the rest of the other ethnic groups in Zimbabwe that are patriarchal. The Tonga people were initially spared from the impact of European colonisation because the settlers regarded their region unsafe because of tsetse flies and other vectors that caused sickness. According to Ncube (2004: vii), the area that was occupied by the Tonga people was initially viewed as economically marginal compared to the main Zimbabwe plateau. Unlike the Zimbabwe plateau the north-western region of Zimbabwe does not have mineral resources like gold and the soils are marginal. The Tonga people were, however, uprooted from the Zambezi Valley ancestral homeland to make way for Lake Kariba during the late 1950s. They were forcibly relocated and resettled in Binga, Hwange, Lupane, Gokwe North and Nyaminyami, Mount Darwin, Chirundu and Kariba Districts (Ndhlovu 2009: 54).

The south-western and western region of Zimbabwe is the homeland to the Kalanga (Tjikalanga) people (Msindo 2012). The Kalanga ethnic group has been staying in the part of the country for over a thousand years (Nyathi 2006: 104). Linguistically, Kalanga has its own dialects in the form of Lilina, Talawunda and Jawunda. With the appearance of the Ndebele people in 1839 the area of the Kalanga people started to diminish. With time the majority of the Kalanga were assimilated into the Ndebele communities. During the colonial era Kalanga people were evicted from their ancestral homelands such as Figtree, Morula and Soluswe to Bulilima-Mangwe, Tsholotsho, Matobo and Kezi districts (Nyathi 2006: 104). Today the Kalanga people of Zimbabwe have lost their language and customs as most of them now speak Ndebele as a result of the education and language policies that were created during the colonial and post-colonial period.

There is also an interesting ethnic group of people who prefer to call themselves Mwenye, but are popularly known as the Lemba or VaRemba, who are also found in various parts of Zimbabwe. The Lemba people have several non-Bantu characteristics and customs which tally very well with Semitic customs. Members of this group trace their ancestry to the Middle East (Asia) and prefer to see themselves as Jews (*see* Wuriga 2012). However, some scholars view them as descendants of intermittent Arab or Muslim traders (Mazarire 2009: 28). It is largely believed that the Lemba hailed from Judea, in Israel, but once settled in Sena Yemen, before they eventually came to southern Africa in search of gold and ivory (Wuriga 2012: xi). Although the time that they left Yemen cannot be ascertained it has been suggested that they came to southern Africa some few centuries at the beginning of the Common Era (Wuriga 2012: 3). After settling in the coastal areas of the country of Mozambique they established families with African wives. The Lemba eventually moved inland into the Zimbabwean landscape. There are traditions which claim that the Lemba also participated in the construction of the famous Great Zimbabwe between 1250 CE and 1400 CE (Wuriga 2012: 22). In Zimbabwe the majority of the Lemba people are found in the Midlands Province in areas like Zvishavane and Mberengwa. Lemba people are also present in the Soutpansberg area of the Limpopo Province of South Africa. They largely prefer ethnic purity and have largely been able to withstand the pressure of assimilation caused by globalisation and colonisation (Wuriga 2012: 14). To remain pure the Lemba people discourage marriages between non-Lemba and Lemba people. However, they lost their language through several centuries of social interaction with other groups in southern Africa. They speak Bantu languages that are spoken by their neighbouring communities as a result the Lemba people of Zimbabwe are usually classified as Shona and in South Africa they are viewed as Venda (Wuriga 2012: 212). Lemba people remain self-conscious about their distinct ethnic identity which they express through unique cultural expressions, strict dietary laws and ritual practices. What is highlighted by the Lemba case is that although language plays a critical role in the construction of ethnic identities it is not always an important ingredient in this process.

Apart from the Tonga people, the north-western region of Zimbabwe is also home to the Nambya ethnic group. A concise history of the Nambya (Nambiya) people has been published by other scholars (see Ncube 2004; Nyathi 2006). The Nambya people are a breakaway of the Changamire Rozvi state (Ncube 2004: 8). Initially they spoke one of the dialects of Shona. The Nambya people are closely related to the Karanga people of the south eastern part of Zimbabwe (Ndhlovu 2009: 54). Their oral traditions suggest that sometime in the 18th century a certain Rozvi group under the leader named Sawanga (later Hwange) migrated into the Deka and Matetsi Valleys which were occupied by the Tonga people. As a result of interaction between the Leya (Tonga people) and Rozvi under Sawanga distinct language and customs emerged (Ncube 2004: 1). The Nambya initially established their capital, with a stone-walled enclosure, at Shangano Hill in the Bhale area. It was at Shangano that the Rozvi under Sawanga created a new identity called Nambya. The Nambya eventually incorporated other groups, for example the Leya and some of Kalanga, into their ethnic group. The citadel of the Nambya people was later moved from Shangano to the Bumbusi area in Upper Deka Valley between 1834 and 1860 (Nyathi 2006: 125). At Bumbusi the Nambya people exhibited their dry-stone building prowess by building a Zimbabwe-type site. At the height of the *Mfecane* invasions from Zululand in present day South Africa the Nambya state was under the rule of Hwange Lusumbami. During the colonial era in 1963 the Nambya people were moved from Hwange to create space for Wankie Colliery and Game Reserve. Today Nambya people are found in Hwange district, and some parts of Tsholotsho, Nyamadhlovu and Victoria Falls districts of Matabeleland North.

The south and western parts of Zimbabwe are dominated by the Ndebele people. The Ndebele people established themselves as a migrant ethnic group starting from 1821. The origins of the Ndebele people can be traced to the Nguni states which included the Zulu,

14

Ndwandwe, Mthetwa and Swazi. The group emerged under the leadership of Mzilikazi Khumalo who was a son of Matshobana. Mzilikazi and his group of less than 500 people were the last to leave Zululand, south eastern seaboard of South Africa, during the time of *mfecane* (Nyathi 2006: 5). As this group, he trekked northwards it incorporated Sotho/Tswana and Pedi people who had settled in the Gauteng, Limpopo and Mpumalanga Provinces of the modern Republic of South Africa. Whilst in South Africa, between 1821 and 1839, Mzilikazi and his people managed to establish three settlements. It should be highlighted that when Mzilikazi left Zululand in 1821 he was just a military commander and leader not a King. It was only after he had incorporated more people in other parts of South Africa that he consolidated the Ndebele ethnic group (Mathema 2013: 35). As a result of constant raids and conflict with the Griqua and Boers, the Ndebele people under King Mzilikazi were forced to move northwards into what is now south-western Zimbabwe. By the time that the Ndebele people arrived on the Zimbabwean plateau, in 1839, they were about 20 000 in number (Beach 1984: 5). They finally established their citadel at Old Bulawayo in the south-western part of Zimbabwe. Prior to this the region was home to the Rozvi state which had been weakened by Queen Nyamazana's Swazi. When King Mzilikazi arrived in the region Queen Nyamazana Dlamini was presiding over a state named Mthwakazi. Queen Nyamazana got married to King Mzilikazi and eventually the king took over the state of Mthwakazi (Nyathi 2006: 6). In the south-western part of Zimbabwe the Ndebele further incorporated more people, including the Rozvi and Kalanga, into their ethnic group. As a result there are Ndebele people who actually trace their ancestry to other ethnic groups in the country. Mzilikazi was later succeeded by his son, Lobengula after a bloody civil war. The reign of King Lobengula was curtailed by the violent colonisation of Mthwakazi by Europeans. During this colonial era racist land tenure laws that were passed resulted in the eviction of the Ndebele people to reserves namely Nkayi, Lupane and Tsholotsho (Nyathi 2006: 6). In terms of their culture, the Ndebele are still very close to the Zulu, Xhosa and Swazi since they are all part of the Nguni people (Nyathi 2001). Today at least 16% of the people in Zimbabwe, second largest ethnic group, consider themselves Ndebele (Ndhlovu 2009: 49).

In the southern lowveld and south-eastern parts of Zimbabwe there are groups of people who are known as the Shangaan or Shangani. This group of people trace their origins to the Ngunis of South Africa (MacGonagle 2007). The Shangaan people left their homeland, currently KwaZulu-Natal, under the leadership of Soshangane in the 1820s after they were defeated by Shaka Zulu just like the Mzilikazi's Ndebele group discussed in the preceding paragraph. This group left for the modern day country of Mozambique where they eventually established the Gaza kingdom. The sphere of influence of Soshangane was extended into the Zimbabwean landscape, especially Chimanimani Mountains and Chipinge area, after he managed to conquer the Ndau people during the 1830s. Unlike the Ndebele who maintained their customs and most elements of their original Nguni language the majority of the Shangaan people were actually acculturated by the groups that they had surmounted. The Shangaan people in the Chipinge area now speak Ndau. Today Shangaan speaking people are largely concentrated in the Beightbridge, Mwenezi and Chiredzi Districts were they core exist with other ethnic groups. According to Earle *et al.* (2006) today there is an estimated 122, 000 Shangaan people in Zimbabwe.

Venda people are also found in the south-eastern parts of Zimbabwe and they also dominate in the Limpopo Province of South Africa. The Venda language has many Shona elements with some obvious influences of Sotho-Tswana (Nyathi 2005: 131). Archaeological reconstructions and oral traditions suggest that during the last half of the eighteenth century some Shona migrants from the Zimbabwe Plateau moved into the northern part of modern day South Africa. After crossing the Limpopo River these Shona people adopted a new identity as a result of intermarriages and social interaction with the Sotho-Tswana people who had settled in the

16

region earlier on (Loubser 1989). They eventually established their capital at Dzata which became the citadel of the Venda kingdom. The Venda people were however forced again to cross the Limpopo River into present day Zimbabwe as a result of the arrival of Mzilikazi's Ndebele in the northern parts of South Africa. Today the cultural heartland of the Venda people is the Nzhelele Valley, Soutpansberg Range, Limpopo Valley and Thoyandou area (Pikirayi 2001: 217). On the Zimbabwean side the Venda speaking people are largely concentrated in the Beitbridge District, Gwanda and Plumtree. It has been estimated that there are at least 81 000 Venda people who reside inside Zimbabwe (Earle *et al.* 2006). It is unfortunate that Venda like many other minority languages has been systematically excluded from national space in Zimbabwe (Nyota 2013).

There is also a group of Xhosa (Amafengu) people who occupy parts of western Zimbabwe. This group has been in the country since the last 100 years. The Zimbabwe Xhosa people trace their origins the south-eastern part of South Africa. Originally they belonged to the Hlubi ethnic group of Kwazulu-Natal, but during early nineteenth century upheavals this group sought refuge among Xhosa, hence their name amaFengu (which means to beg or ask for a place to settle) (Nyathi 2006: 58). During their stay among the Xhosa people in the Western Cape province of South Africa they were acculturated and ended up embracing the Xhosa language and customs. The Zimbabwean Xhosa were brought in by Cecil John Rhodes as reinforcement to subdue the Ndebele uprising against settler occupation. The Zimbabwean Xhosa have managed to preserve their language and cultural practice. Today this group is found in Mbembesi area in south-western Zimbabwe.

In Zimbabwe, there are group of people who came to the then Southern Rhodesia from Northern Rhodesia (presently Zambia) and Nyasaland (presently Malawi) during the 1950s (Ndhlovu 2009). In Malawi there are at least seven ethnic groups which include Yao, Lomwe, Sena, Chewa, Ngoni, Nyakyusa and Tonga. They came into the country as labour migrant workers to service in the capital-intensive mines, plantations and commercial farms. Today these people are largely labelled as Chewa although some of them do not prefer to be identified as such. The Chewa people are scattered in the old townships of Harare, Bulawayo, Kwekwe, Chegutu, and Kadoma. They also dominate in the major mining towns that were established during the colonial era like Shamva. It is estimated, based on information from Hachipola (1998), that their population in Zimbabwe is not less than half a million (Ndhlovu 2009: 67). Due to intermarriages and the language policy implemented in post-colonial Zimbabwe the Chewa people have been assimilated by the major ethnic groups in the areas that they settled.

Conclusion

As concluding remarks, this chapter has highlighted that the history of the Zimbabwean people is complex. Identities were constantly created as people moved from one settlement to the next. According to Chimhundu (1992: 89) as populations multiplied the chiefdoms kept on multiplying by creating new ethnic identities and the solution was moving into new territories to accommodate each other politically and socially. This, therefore, highlights the fact that ethnicity does not denote a static category but a very fluid one. I have often heard colleagues at work labelling me Shangaan or Ndau because of my surname. Whilst I am Shangaan in terms of ancestry, by acculturation and linguistically I am Karanga because I was born and bred in the Midlands Province of Zimbabwe where the dominant group is Karanga. I am quite aware of my Shangaan ancestry; however, I cannot communicate in Xichangana. My mother is Zezuru and whilst my wife is Ngoni, of Malawian origin, and she speaks Chewa. It is only my surname and totem that identifies me as Shangaan. As a result of population movements, emphasis, thus, should be more on hybrid identities. The point that I am trying to highlight here is that group identities in Zimbabwe have over the centuries become complex. Assimilation and integration processes have been happening since time immemorial. According to Ucko (1994: 263), cultural change is and always has been, omnipresent and inevitable. Nonetheless, "Zimbabwe is diverse, but Zimbabwe is one" (Mathema 2013: 3).

In the face of forced resettlement schemes during the colonial era various groups of people were dispossessed of their territories to make way for the game reserves, mines and farms. Recent rural to urban migration and the recent move into the diaspora further complicates identities based on ethnicity. The history of Zimbabwe outlined in this chapter shows that ethnic groups are not static, conservative, closed or a homogenous social unit (Machiridza 2013). It is now difficult to come by insular communities that are bound together by common ancestry and culture today (Chirikure and Pwiti 2008). The identification of people with certain groups in Zimbabwe is no longer that easy because different people have developed close ties as a result of intermarriages and social intermingling. This is aptly captured by Mathema (2013: 3) who envisages that there is no province in Zimbabwe without a Tonga, without a Zezuru, without Karanga, without Shangaan, without Sotho, without Manyika, without Kalanga, without San, without Nambya, without Korekore, without Ndau. Zimbabwean people have always co-existed through intermarriages and other forms of social interaction. It has also been highlighted that modern nation-states usually view ethnic labels as detrimental to nation building because they promote lobby groups and ethnic movements. Nationalists would, thus, be more comfortable with an ethnically homogenous nation and the use of modern day national identities rather than local identity.

References

Barker, C., 2012. *Cultural Studies: Theory and Practice,* 4th ed. Los Angeles: Sage Publications.

Barth, F., ed., 1969. *Ethnic Groups and Boundaries,* Boston: Little Brown.

Beach, D. N., 1984. *Zimbabwe Before 1900,* Gweru: Mambo Press.

Bolaff, G., Bracalent, R., Braham, P. and Gindro, S. eds., 2003. *Dictionary of Race, Ethnicity and Culture,* London: Sage Publications.

Bourdillon, M. F. C., 1998. *The Shona Peoples: An Ethnography of the Contemporary Shona, with Reference to their Religion,* 3rd ed. Gweru: Mambo Press.

Burrett, R. S., 1998. *Shadows of Our Ancestors: Some Preliminary Notes on the Archaeology of Zimbabwe,* Harare: Texel Desktop Publishing.

Caton-Thompson, G., 1931. *The Zimbabwe Culture: Ruins and Reactions,* Oxford: The Claredon Press.

Chimhundu, H., 1992. Early missionaries and the ethnolinguistic factors during the 'invention of tribalism' in Zimbabwe, *Journal of African History,* 33(1), pp. 87-109.

Chirikure, S. and Pwiti, G., 2008. Community involvement in archaeology and cultural heritage management, *Current Anthropology,* Volume 49, pp. 467-485.

Cohen, R., 1978. Ethnicity: problem and focus in anthropology, *Annual Review of Anthropology,* Volume 7, pp. 379-403.

Crowell, A. L., 2011. Ethnicity and periphery: the archaeology of identity in Russian America, In: S. K. Croucher and L. Weiss, eds. *The Archaeology of Capitalism in Colonial Contexts: Postcolonial Historical Archaeologies,* New York: Springer, pp. 85-104.

Earle, A., Goldin, J., Machiridza, R., Malzbender, D., Manzungu, E., and Mpho, T., 2006. *Indigenous and Institutional Profile: Limpopo River Basin,* Colombo, Sri Lanka: International Water Management Institute.

Fisher, J. L., 2010. *Pioneers, Settlers, Aliens, Exiles: The Decolonisation of White Identity in Zimbabwe,* Canberra: The Australian National Univeristy E Press.

Fought, C., 2006. *Language and Ethnicity: Key Topics in Sociolinguistics,* Cambridge: Cambridge University Press.

Gat, A. and Yakobson, A., 2013. *Nations: The Long History and Deep Roots of Political Ethnicity and Nationalism,* Cambridge: Cambridge University Press.

Hachipola, S. J., 1998. *A Survey of the Minority Languages of Zimbabwe,* Harare: University of Zimbabwe Publications.

Hastings, A., 1997. *The Construction of Nationhood: Ethnicity, Religion and Nationalism,* Cambridge: Cambridge University Press.

Holtorf, C., 2011. The changing contribution of cultural heritage to society, *Museum International,* 63(1-2), pp. 8-16.

Huffman, T. N., 2000. Mapungubwe and the origins of the zimbabwe culture, *Goodwin Series,* Volume 8, pp. 14-29.

Huffman, T. N., 2009. Mapungubwe and Great Zimbabwe: The origins and spread of social complexity in southern Africa, *Journal of Anthropological Archaeology,* 28(1), pp. 37-54.

James, P. W., 2006. *Globalism, Nationalism, Tribalism: Bringing Theory Back,* London: SAGE Publications.

Jones, S., 1997. *The Archaeology of Ethnicity: Constructing Identities in the Past and Present,* London: Routledge.

Knapp, A. B., 1998. Social approaches to the archaeology and anthropology of mining. In: A. B. Knapp, V. C. Pigott and E. W. Herbert, eds. *The Archaeology and Anthropology of Mining,* London: Routledge, pp. 1-24.

Lancanster, C. S., 1974. Ethnic identity, history and "tribe" in the Middle Zambezi Valley. *American Ethnologist,* Volume 1, pp. 707-730.

Lentz, C. and Nugent, P. eds., 2000. *Ethnicity in Ghana: The Limits of Invention,* London: MacMillian Press Ltd.

Loubser, J. H. N., 1989. Archaeology and early Venda history, *Goodwin Series,* Volume 6, pp. 54-61.

MacGonagle, E., 2007. *Crafting Identity in Zimbabwe and Mozambique,* New York: University of Rochester Press.

Machiridza, L. H., 2012. *Material Culture and Dialects of Identity and Power: Towards a Historical Archaeology of the Rozvi in South-Western Zimbabwe,* Pretoria: Unpublished MA Archaeology Dissertation, Department of Archaeology and Anthropology, University of Pretoria.

Machiridza, L. H., 2013. Insights into the meaning of Nyai, Rozvi and Torwa: a historical archaeology approach to identities, In: M. Manyanga and S. Katsamudanga, eds. *Zimbabwean Archaeology in the Post-Independence Era,* Harare: Sapes Books, pp. 199-212.

21

Maggs, T. and Whitelaw, G., 1991. A review of recent archaeological research on food-producing communities in southern Africa, *The Journal of African History,* 32(1), pp. 3-24.

Manyanga, M., 2006. *Resilient Landscapes: Socio-Enviromental Dynamics in the Shashe-Limpopo Basin, southern Zimbabwe c. AD 800 to the Present.* Uppsala: Department of Archaeology and Ancient History.

Mathema, N. C. G., 2013. *Zimbabwe Diverse, But One.* Bulawayo: Tepp Publishers.

Mazarire, G. C., 2009. Reflections on pre-colonial Zimbabwe, c.850-1880s. In: B. Raftopolous and A. S. Mlambo, eds. *Becoming Zimbabwe a History from Pre-colonial Period to 2008.* Harare: Weaver Press, pp. 1-38.

Mitchell, P., 2002. *The Archaeology of Southern Africa,* Cambridge: Cambridge University Press.

Mhlanga, B., 2013. Ethnicity or tribalism? The discursive construction of Zimbabwean national identity. *African Identities* 11(1), 47-60.

Mlambo, A. & Raftopolos, B., 2009. *Becoming Zimbabwe: A History from the Pre-Colonial Period to 2008,* Weaver Press: Harare.

Mlambo, A. S., 2014. *A History of Zimbabwe,* Cambridge: Cambridge University Press.

Msindo, E., 2012. *Ethnicity in Zimbabwe: Transformations in Kalanga and Ndebele Societies, 1860-1990.* New York: University of Rochester Press.

Mwandayi, C., 2011. *Death and After-Life Rituals in the Eyes of the Shona: Dialogue with Shona Customs in the Quest for Authentic Inculturation,* Bamberg: University of Bamberg Press.

Ncube, G. T., 2004. *A History of North Western Zimbabwe 1850-1960,* Kadoma: Mond Books.

Ndhlovu, F., 2009. *The Politics of Language and Nation Building in Zimbabwe,* Bern: Peter Lang AG.

Ndlovu-Gatsheni, S. J., 2009. *Do 'Zimbabweans' Exist? Trajectories of Nationalism, National Identity Formation and Crisis in a Postcolonial State,* Oxford: Peter Lang.

Nyathi, P., 2001. *Traditional Ceremonies of the AmaNdebele,* Gweru: Mambo Press.

Nyathi, P., 2006. *Zimbabwe's Cultural Heritage,* Bulawayo: African Books Collective.

Nyota, S., 2013. Exclusion of minority languages in Zimbabwe: the case of Shangani and Venda. *Dzimbahwe: Journal of Humanities and Social Sciences,* 1(1), pp. 204-228.

Owomoyela, O., 2002. *Culture and Customs of Zimbabwe,* London: Greenwood Publishing Group.

Pikirayi, I., 2001. *The Zimbabwe Culture: Origins and Decline of Southern Zambezian States,* New York: Altamira Press.

Pwiti, G., 1996. *Continuity and Change: An Archaeological Study of Farming Communities in northern Zimbabwe,* Uppsala: Uppsala University.

Ranger, T., 1985. *The Invention of Tribalism in Zimbabwe,* Gweru: Mambo Press.

Ranger, T., 1989. Missionaries, migrants and the Manyika: the invention of ethnicity in Zimbabwe. In: L. Vail, ed. *The Creation of Tribalism in Southern Africa,* Berkeley: University of California Press, pp. 118-146.

Swan, L., 1994. *Early Gold Mining on the Zimbabwean Plateau,* Uppsala: Societas Archaeologica Upsaliensis.

Ucko, P., 1994. Museums and sites: cultures of the past within education-Zimbabwe some then years on. In: P. G. Stone & B. L. Molyneaux, eds. *The Presented Past: Heritage, Museums and Education,* London: Routledge, pp. 237-282.

Vail, L., 1989. Introduction: ethnicity in southern African history. In: L. Vail, ed. *The Creation of Tribalism in Southern Africa,* Berkeley: University of California Press, pp. 1-18.

Walker, N. J., 1995. *Late Pleistocene and Holocene Hunter-Gatherers of the Matopos: An Archaeological Study of Change and Continuity in Zimbabwe (Studies in African Archaeology 10),* Uppsala: Societas Archaeologica Upsaliensis.

Wuriga, R., 2012. *Of Sacred Times, Rituals, and Customs: Oral Traditions of the Lemba Jews of Zimbabwe,* Washington, DC: Epic Centre Stories.

Chapter 2

Western hegemony and conquest of Africa: Imperial hypocrisy and the invasion of African cultures

Munyaradzi Mawere

Introduction

In Africa, colonialism is a shared experience given that almost the entire continent was at one time subdued by imperial countries of Europe. Colonialism, thus, has always had perennial bearing on the African people's lives and worldviews. This is also premised on the fact that colonialism differed 'from other episodes of domination in *world history in* that it involved a different mode of production (capitalism) and technology (industrialisation) on a virtually global scope' (Pieterse and Parekh 1995: 1, emphasis original). Besides, colonialism unlike previous forms of imperialism and domination such as racial slavery, targeted at dominating and at most eliminating other societies' religio-cultural norms and values, replacing these with Western/European particularities: it is a project whose main objective was to conquer 'the other' wholly including his [her] mind and spirit. This is what Ivy Goduka (2000) mean when she argues that with the advent of colonialism in Africa the African indigenous values, beliefs and practices that did not conform to European norms were considered odious and repugnant. The three factors highlighted above – capitalism, industrialisation and domination – make colonialism one of the most complex and profoundly far-reaching de-humanising processes that the world has ever experienced before on a large scale.

In Africa, the 'universal' features of Western imperialism were felt not only in religion and culture. Other spheres of life such as politics, production and commerce, science and technology were equally affected by the whims and caprices of the colonial ghost. This connotes that with colonialism; Africa was painted and tainted with a brush of Western particularity, but in the false name of civilisation. Such a move, no doubt, had incredibly adverse and extraordinary ramifications on the sons and daughters of Africa especially in terms of their social life, culture, and religion. The ramifications cannot be underestimated: neither can they be ignored given their lasting and enduring legacy on Africa. This chapter explores the impacts of Western colonialism on the African people's dignity, norms and values though more examples shall be drawn from Zimbabwe to which this book is primarily addressed.

Cultural imperialism in African societies and the dilution of African cultural values

Nowadays, the saying that 'repeat a lie and it will be number one truth' seems to be commonplace in Africa. Yet, it appears the saying was adopted from the European imperialists who used the technique to advance their foreign cultures and interests in Africa and elsewhere. They found it peremptory to 'soil' the image of Africa to justify their nefarious project, colonialism.

When the Europeans came to Africa, they masqueraded as guardians of civilisation and purveyors of justice and democracy. They [Europeans] were 'able to impose more of their culture to Africans, using a variety of means and institutions' (Falola 2003: 4) including education (in formal schools), religion (in synagogues/churches), medicine (hospitals built to replace traditional healers), science and technology (industries and factories built to replace indigenous knowledge systems and technologies). Least was it known by the indigenous African people that Europeans had an ominous agenda behind their altruistic slogans and mantras of peace and civilisation. The truth only revealed itself as time unfolded that the 'newcomers' who came with a Bible on the right hand had their minds plagued with sadistic traits of conquer and subjugation. No wonder 'with the advent of colonialism, African cultures and indigenous knowledges were despised and relegated as superstitious, primitive, irrational and unscientific' (Mawere 2014a: 23; Mawere

26

2012; Mawere 2011b; Mawere 2014b). This observation has been noted by a number of African scholars. Shizha (2013: 4), for example, argues that 'African culture has been invaded by Western belief systems, ways of knowing, and ways of experiencing the world thus reinforcing the colonisation of African indigenous knowledges'. This is what Frantz Fanon (1967: 217) reminded us more than four decades ago when he argued that 'the lack of culture of the Negroes, as proclaimed by colonialism ought logically to lead to the exaltation of cultural manifestations which are not simply national but continental, and extremely racial'. Colonialism thus hijacked and diverted the African cultures to a totally different direction that no one on the African soil had imagined before.

To pave way for colonialism in Africa and indeed the hijacking of the African cultures, Eurocentric scholars and some missionaries spread several myths about the backwardness of the African peoples' belief systems and ways of knowing, institutions and philosophies of life in general. Scholars such as David Hume, Hegel and Immanuel Kant (among others) are well known as forerunners of colonialism in Africa and for their dirty work on messing the face of Africa labelling it a 'dark continent' full of 'savages' – humans that were less rational or irrational so to speak. As Ntuli (1999: 188, emphasis original) argues, this parochial and narrow 'view of considering anything non-European as inferior *and useless, irrational and illogical* was based on the misconception that Western cultural knowledge orientations were used to determine the value of blacks' ideas, belief systems and religion'. In fact the Europeans used their cultural values as the yardstick to measure cultures of other societies resulting in their labelling of Africans as *savages* and *blacks* (as opposed to civilised and white), terms with strong racial innuendos and pejorative overtones. It is this kind of thinking that critical scholars like Collingwood (1958) challenged a long time ago echoing the prophetic words – '*Mapfupa angu achamuka*/My bones shall rise against those who kill me' – of Mbuya Nehanda of Zimbabwe, when he [Collingwood] prophetically warned his fellow colonialists:

27

Savages are no more exempt from human folly than civilised men, and are no doubt equally liable to the error of thinking that they, or the persons they regard as their superiors, can do what in fact cannot be done. But this error is not the essence of magic; it is a perversion of magic. And we should be careful how we attribute it to the people we call savages, who will one day rise up and testify against us (Collingwood, pp. 67).

Collingwood warned the overindulgent colonialists against the binaries they set between themselves and the other – what has come to be known as 'othering' and 'saming' (Lacan 1964; Mawere 2013). It is untoward that the binary oppositions such as those initiated by racist Eurocentric theorists continue even today in many parts of the world and have been exported even into some academic disciplines across the board. Appadurai (1986: 1) for example, observed and lamented that 'anthropology is [still] excessively dualistic'. Harris (1989: 12) confirms this observation when he warned that binary oppositions (as civilised and uncivilised societies) are still 'built into the very structure of anthropology as a discipline. In view of racial binary opposition between Europeans and Africans, I underline that the binary was set out to demonstrate the superiority of European race over the African race. This is what Mengara (2001: 2) calls 'the systematic and systemic manufacturing of a continent' – an African continent classified on the basis of 'superiority versus inferiority, civilised versus uncivilised, pre-logical versus logical, mythical versus scientific, among other epithets'. The settlers' systematic manufacturing of the continent, Africa, clearly reiterates that 'Europe's intervention in Africa was the beginning of the most nefarious images, the black labelling of Africans and their *philosophies*. An African invented for European purposes could no longer serve the interests of its own people' (Asante, 2001: xiv) as Europeans despised all African traditions, customs, philosophies and knowledge systems (Mawere 2011b).

Yet the European 'demon' of colonialism did not only end with caricaturing Africans and their cultural values. Many of the African people who were understood to be custodians of the African culture and anti-colonial architects were persecuted to ensure that not only the African cultural values were destroyed but also the institutions that made these resilient. In Mozambique, those who were resistant to the Portuguese conquerors and their alien ideas like Ngungunyani were persecuted. During apartheid regime that was officiated in 1948, South Africa lost a number of luminary gallant sons and daughters of the soil such as Robert Mangaliso Sobukwe, Stephen Bantu Biko, Albert Luthuli (only to mention but a few) and many others who unjustifiably languished for decades behind bars like Nelson Mandela and Walter Sisulu. In Zimbabwe, many resistant chiefs and spirit mediums were killed especially since the beginning of the first Chimurenga war in 1893. Nehanda Nyamita Nyakasikana (commonly known as Mbuya Nehanda), a Zimbabwe legend and spirit medium, for example, was executed on the 27th of April 1898 allegedly accused of influencing the Shona people to rise up and resist the reprehensible colonial rule. The other arch spirit medium, Sekuru Kaguvi was also executed by the settlers for the same reasons. In the eastern part of Zimbabwe, Chief Rekayi Tangwena oftenly clashed with the settlers for his strong support of the culture of his forefathers and interests of his own people. This means that for the European settlers in Zimbabwe (as elsewhere in Africa), it was necessary to eliminate the connoisseurs of the indigenous peoples' cultures in order to water down resistance against their newly introduced institutions and values. In other words, this, the settlers did to deter combative culture of nationalism and resistance among Africans. I therefore agree with Meki Nzewi's (2007:4, emphasis mine) argument that 'irreverent and irresponsible abandonment *of the African cultural values* as well as flippant change started when the human and cultural practices of the invaders from outside began to make insidious intrusions into the African's human and cultural psyche'.

Decolonisation and postcoloniality: Rethinking the impact of colonialism in Africa

While it is a fact of history that in the largest part of formerly colonised Africa and the rest of the world colonialism ended about three decades ago or so, the nuanced analysis of the nature and impact of colonialism on the [former] colonies is yet to be fully realised. The reason why Africa, for example, remains one of the poorest continents in the world when it is one of the continents that greatly enriched Europe both in human resource and raw materials has not yet been fully worked out. So is the reason why Africa remains languishing in abject poverty when to date the continent is one of the richest in mineral resources the world-over. This is not to undermine efforts by some scholars such as Walter Rodney who on realising the same gathered the extraordinary audacity and committed himself to come up with a meticulously researched and powerfully written text on the subject: *"How Europe underdeveloped Africa"*. I acknowledge that immediate after its publication in 1972, Rodney's book turned the European tables upside down and shook the walls of Europe from both inside and outside, an effect that is believed to have culminated into his untimely death. My argument here is that owing to the premature death of Rodney, the economic balance sheet on the gains and losses of Africa as a result of Western colonialism was left unfinished: it remains an "unfinished business" that other scholars especially those in fields of studies such as economic history, political science, business studies and other social sciences should have pursued and completed.

If one deepens his [her] analysis on the logic of colonialism and its lasting impacts on Africa and in particular Zimbabwe, the picture becomes even multidimensional, eclectic and multifariously complex such that the logic require penetrating rigorous scrutiny. Due to the diverse impacts of colonialism and for purposes of this chapter, more focus is devoted in rethinking the impact of colonialism on the Zimbabwean cultures (or Zimbabwean culture rather given that various ethnic cultures across the country share a lot in common).

30

First, because the colonial regime introduced dislodged African and in particular Zimbabwean peoples' values and institutions, replacing them with the European ones justifying this in civilizational terms. Second, because while the present volume rethinks and explores the past and present politics and future of African cultures, particular focus is devoted on Zimbabwe where most of the case studies are drawn from.

Coming back to the impacts of colonialism on the culture of the Zimbabwean people, it is evident that the continuity of the colonial rule was only guaranteed by the continued resilience and domineering of the introduced values and institutions. In fact colonialism lasted as long as the people of Zimbabwe operated, willingly or otherwise, within the ambit of the colonial institutions. This explains why before and during colonialism, Europeans and Eurocentric scholars did everything within their power to despise, arrest and even freeze the local (or indigenous) institutions, customs and values. In Zimbabwe, those who were recruited in missionary schools were, for example, taught to despise and reject their own culture and even their own parents as long as they [their parents] adhered to the traditional norms and values. This colonial education is evident in some of the first products of the missionary schools such as Patrick Chakaipa (1961) who in most of his literary works radically questions and attacks the culture and way of life of his own people – the Shona people. In fact 'one of the dominant motifs in Zimbabwean literature is how missionary education produced alienated individuals. It is charged that they sought to promote an elite class that would despise Shona culture and consider worthless/inferior all those who remained attached to tradition' (Mawere 2011: 7). In African literature, Ndatshana in Samkange's (1975) *The Mourned One* represents such a character. Ndatshana having been raised at the Mission Station by the Methodist missionaries, he finds himself at pains to adjust to the reality of village life in his real home. He had become married and so much into the ostentatious pampered life at Waddilove, with a full breakfast being a daily experience, to the extent that the coarse mealie-meal porridge of his mother's kitchen

31

could not settle in his stomach. The creation of characters like Ndatshana was a clear depiction of what was happening in reality in many parts of Africa. In the then Portuguese colonies like Mozambique, Cape Verde, Angola and Guinea Bissau, the Portuguese settlers, for example, granted a small percentage of indigenous Africans the status of *assimilados*, that is, privileged Africans on the basis that they had renounced their African cultures, acquired Portuguese names and mannerism such as speaking, dressing and writing, and above all had been Christianised. Elsewhere (in Belgian and French colonial territories), such indigenous Africans were known as *evolues* which literary meant the evolved ones (Temples 1959: 161). To Tempels, this group of indigenous Africans were like rootless trees, money obsessed, 'empty and unsatisfied souls', 'moral and intellectual tramps', 'a class of pseudo-Europeans without principles, character, purposes, or sense' (1959: 180, 184). Yet for Portuguese settlers, the labelling of some indigenous Africans as *assimilados* was in view of the fact that for the Portuguese (as with other European settlers elsewhere on the continent), 'to bear African names, eat indigenous food, and wear local attire were seen as powerful anti-colonial statements' (Falola 2003: 8). European settlers, thus, adopted all these strategies to ensure that their culture was imposed on their [African] subjects, a policy that is commonly known in Political Science as Indirect Rule. The settlers also knew that what sustain a group is history, culture and tradition, hence they worked so hard to distort and destroy the histories, cultures and traditions of the African people. Yet the depiction of characters like Ndatshana (and the existence of *assimilados*) should not be translated to mean that all first generation Zimbabwean and by extension African writers were uncritical of the colonial regime especially the education they received as some of them like Chinua Achebe (1958), Okot p'Bitek (1966), and Ngugi wa Thiongo (1964) wrote reacting to the colonialist's reprehensible activities and colonial education. Nevertheless, with the fast growing foreign European values in Zimbabwe during and after colonialism, the cultural fabric of the local people have not been spared as there exist many of the locals who gullibly and uncritically embrace whatever is from the West even if it is the worst: those who do not realise that the "European colonial regime 'was determined to denigrate, diminish *and vanquish* traditional culture' (Garlake 1982:4, emphasis mine). Others have been brainwashed to the extent that they are now "black skins in white masks" (to use Fanon's [1967] phrase). This is what Pan Africanists like Julius Nyerere (1968) and scholars like Ngugi wa Thiongo and Chinua Achebe, among others, protested against. Nyerere's (1968: 278), observation, for example, is critical in rethinking African identities:

> At present our pupils learn to despise even their own parents because they are old-fashioned and ignorant; there is nothing in our existing educational system which suggests to the pupil that he [she] can learn important things about farming from his [her] elders. The result is that he [she] absorbs beliefs about witchcraft before he [she] goes to school, but does not learn the properties of local grasses; he [she] absorbs the taboos from his family but does not learn the methods of making nutritious traditional foods. And from school he [she] acquires knowledge unrelated to agricultural life. He [she] gets the worst of both systems!

In this passage, Nyerere highlights the confusion, dilemma, and identity crisis that the African child faces both at home and school since the advent of colonialism on the continent. He laments the dearth of indigenous literacy skills that are now being turned away from. Wa Thiongo also advocates the decolonisation of the African mind to ensure that Africans shun away mimicry and respect their own values as a people. Writing of the narrowness and parochialness of colonial education that Africans received, Wa Thiongo (1986: 7), wrote:

> Colonial education [in Africa] was far from giving people the confidence in their ability and capacities to overcome obstacles or to become masters of the laws governing

external nature as human beings and tends to make them feel their inadequacies and their inability to do anything about the conditions of their lives.

As wa Thiongo rightfully observed, with colonial education many Africans became very much concerned and cared to learn the colonial master's values including language and mannerism, a thing that is still visible across the country and even the continent's cultures. In Mozambique, for example, I observed that as recent as 2010, pupils with local names were still forced to change them and adopt the Portuguese ones as soon as they start their primary school education. This is similar to what happened to many Zimbabweans during colonialism who were forced (directly or otherwise) to change or shorten their local indigenous names to facilitate the colonial administrative work. Today many people across the country hold name tags that are foreign to their ancestral roots and which do not reflect any meaning in everyday life. But what value does this accords to a Zimbabwean to whom names are known to carry important meanings or significance?

The so-called globalisation has even aggravated the plight of the African people's cultures. In the name of globalisation which if fairly practised entails the mutual sharing and benefitting, people have been coerced (directly or otherwise) to replace their own values, tastes and institutions with the foreign ones, particularly from the West and the Americas. This raises critical questions about globalisation: "What do we mean by globalisation if some cultures are made to despise all their values and embrace those from outside? Is Europe or America the global? Who defines the global and by what measure is this done?" All these questions could not only be raised in view of the present day globalisation process but colonialism which had as one of its objective to globalise the world. This entails that the impacts of colonialism did not end with the demise of colonial administration on the African soils. They can still be felt even today through the 'invisible' hands of Europe and America who are understood to be the architectures of globalisation. Through media and continued interaction between Africans and those from the West, many Africans who feel inferior to their foreign counterparts have been co-opted to adopt the Western mind-set and values. While sharing experiences (including ideas) per se is not negative what remains worrying and nerve-racking is the fact that many of the Africans I have asked on why they do certain things have simply answered: "But even those in Europe and America does this. Why not us?" The implication of this ostensibly simple answer is far-reaching: it means that whatever the Europeans or Americans do is perfectly right and should never be questioned. Questioning such things means that one is too backward and conservative. Such labels are common in Zimbabwe where some people commonly known as *masalads* or *masala* now think that speaking with a European accent or walking semi-naked is being fashionable though considered un-African from a cultural perspective and consciousness. Those who criticise their dress codes (for example their mini-skirts akin to waist belts) are considered culturally backward. Sometimes they are charged of violating women's human rights. Yet while the question of human rights is greatly considered here, that of cultural identity and consciousness is overlooked regardless of the fact that it is equally important. Many others now shun traditional foods in favour of the Western processed food stuffs not realising that most of the processed foods have adverse effects to their health. In fact there is ample evidence through research that traditional foods or the so-called organic foods are healthier than processed food stuffs. Yet this analysis should not be interpreted to advocate stasis of human culture, particularly the African culture. I understand that culture is dynamic and will always change in view of the societal challenges at hand, but the point is 'the abandonment of *cultural* values or older traditions may not necessarily be positive, unless there is a consensus on values to replace them. Without a consensus, a sense of alienation, *division or detachment* might *unpleasantly* accompany changes or adjustments to new realities' (Falola 2003: 17, emphasis mine).

It goes without mention that 'the success of European conquest was largely dependent on technological superiority *and not rational superiority*' (Falola 2003: 6, emphasis mine). It is this aspect that Europe and subsequently America use even today to impose their influence on the global sphere. What this means is that since technological products are at the same time objects of culture, Africa is by no means assuming a foreign culture. While this interpolation and technological transfer is not always wrong, there is, however, need to be careful on how the technology reaches Africa and with what implications. This calls for quality control, cultural censorship and desist from the 'culture' of gullibility (by the affected societies) which in fact has taken many Africans by storm to the extent that whatever comes from the West is always considered the best even if it means the worst from the vista of African culture.

Cultural decadence: So what?

From the discussion above, it is clear that culture in many African societies will soon be history or a stranger to its own people if we (as Africans) continue folding our hands doing nothing to control our situation and determine our destiny as a people. This calls for urgent action on the issue of culture in view of the tide of globalisation that is sweeping across the continent. There is need for decolonisation, now not only decolonisation of the mind as Ngugi wa Thiongo advocated. There is need to decolonise African cultures that for centuries now have been under the influence and duress of the colonial whim. Yet the problem of the decolonisation process that started after independence in many African countries remains unfocused. It has failed to realise that colonialism was a complex process which also require complex solutions to deal with those who engineered it and those it [negatively] affected. In many African countries, for example, emphasis was placed on political independence whilst neglecting other spheres. Besides, the decolonisation process has been led by the former colonialists through scholarship (or theories) and institutions. A case in point is the reconciliation process in South Africa that after the dethronement of apartheid regime in 1994 was influenced and largely steered by the

36

former apartheid technocrats. I argue that in issues that directly affect Africa and the [indigenous] African people, it is the African people themselves (and without external influence) who should be at the vanguard of the forum addressing the problems at hand. On this, I strongly agree with Meki Nzewi (2007: 4, emphasis mine) that 'contemporary Africans *themselves* must strive to rescue, resuscitate and advance our original intellectual legacy, or the onslaught of externally manipulated forces of mental and cultural dissociation now rampaging Africa will obliterate our original intellect and lore of life'. This is what Masolo (1995: 2) calls: "The call for a 'return to the native land' – one of the many revolutionary expressions of the then rising black militantism, nationalism and Africanism [...] to counter Westernism's arrogant and aggressive Eurocentric culture". With this in order, I remain with fervent hope in the words of Nzewi (2007:5) that 'after the bombardment of the invading tornados of fanciful knowledge, the indigenous lore of life will revive with innately refurbished shoots, and fulfil again the human mission of the musical arts in original Africa, and edify Africa's mental and human posterity'. I also remain enlivened by Molefi Kete Asante's belief that 'critical insight and keen sense of propriety *on Africa and by Afrocentric scholars will always give* us ample opportunity to declare the images of Africa will not remain forever *shattered and* locked in the negative chambers of the past' (Asante in Mengara 2001: xv, emphasis mine).

Conclusion

This chapter discussed the Western conquest of Africa, particularly the invasion and insincerities surrounding the colonial project and its legacies in Africa. It has been made clear that while interaction between societies is always a worthwhile endeavour, it has to be at best symmetrical, mutual, and symbiotic. This has never been the case between Europe and Africa since the beginning of their historical interaction. In fact Africa's relationship with Europe since the dawn of colonialism (and even racial slavery) to the present has been largely asymmetrical and unprofitable to the continent: the relationship has always been working in favour of Europe. Resource-wise, raw materials from the continent were looted (and continue to be looted even today) while culture-wise the African norms and values have been dominated and bequeathed to the dustbin of oblivion. In view of this observation, I have argued in this chapter that this is high time that Africa critically reflect on such a relationship and renegotiate its position for a better and bright futuristic possibility that reinstates the dignity and cultural identity of the African continent and peoples.

References

Appadurai, A. 1986. Introduction: Commodities and the politics of value, In Appadurai, A. (Ed.), *The social life of things*, Cambridge University Press, Cambridge.

Achebe, C. 1958. *Things fall apart*, Heinemann: United Kingdom.

Asante, K. M. 2001. *African American history: A journey of liberation*, Peoples Publishing Group, USA.

Asante, K. M. 2001. Preface, In Mengara, D. 2001. (Ed.), *Images of Africa: Stereotypes and realities*, Africa World Press, New Jersey.

Chakaipa, P. 1961. *Rudo Ibofu*, Mambo Press, Gweru.

Collingwood, R. G. 1958. *Principles of Art*, Galaxy Book, Oxford.

Falola, T. 2003. *The power of African culture*, University of Rochester Press, New York, USA.

Fanon, F. 1967. *Black skin, white masks* (translated by Charles, L. Markmann), Grove Press: New York, USA.

Garlake, P. 1982. *Great Zimbabwe described and explained*, Zimbabwe Publishing House: Harare, Zimbabwe.

Goduka, I 2000. Indigenous ways of knowing: Affirming a legacy, pp. 134-145, In E.M Chiwome, et. al (Eds). *Indigenous knowledge and technology in African and diasporan communities: Multi-disciplinary approaches*, Southern African Association for Culture and Development: Harare, Zimbabwe.

Harris, O. 1989. The earth and the state: The sources and meanings of money in northern Potosi, Bolivia, In Parry, J. and Bloch, M. (Ed.), *Money and the morality of exchange*, Cambridge University Press, Cambridge, pp. 232-269.

Lacan, J. 1964. *The four fundamental concepts of psychoanalysis*, Hogarth Press. London.

Masolo, D. A. 1995. *African philosophy in search of identity*, East African Educational Publishers, Nairobi: Kenya.

Mawere, M. 2011a. Possibilities for cultivating African indigenous knowledge systems (IKSs): Lessons from selected cases of witchcraft in Zimbabwe, *Journal of Gender, Peace and Development*, 1 (3): 091-100.

Mawere, M. 2011b. Epistemological and moral implications of characterisation in African literature: A critique of Patrick Chakaipa's 'Rudo Ibofu' (love is blind), *Journal of English and literature*, 2(1): 1-9.

Mawere, M. 2012. *The struggle of indigenous knowledge systems in an age of globalisation: A case for children's traditional games*, Langaa RPCIG, Bamenda: Cameroon.

Mawere, M. 2013. Rethinking epistemological divide between science and other knowledge forms in environmental studies: An anthropological view, *The International Journal of Humanities and Social Studies*, 1 (2): 1-6.

Mawere, M. 2014a. *Culture, indigenous knowledge and development in Africa: Reviving interconnections for sustainable development*, Langaa RPCIG, Bamenda: Cameroon.

Mawere, M. 2014b. *Environmental conservation through Ubuntu and other emerging perspectives*, Langaa RPCIG, Bamenda: Cameroon.

Mengara, D. M. 2001. (Ed). *Images of Africa: Stereotypes and realities*, Africa World Press: Trenton and Asmara.

Ngugi wa Thiongo, 1964. *Weep not child*, Heinemann, London.

Ntuli, P. 1999. The missing link between culture and education: Are we still chasing gods that are not our own? In: Makgoba, M. W. (Ed.). *African renaissance*, Mafube –Tafelberg: Cape Town, South Africa.

Nyerere, J. 1968. Education for self-reliance, pp. 278-290, In Nyerere, J. 1968. (Ed). *Freedom and socialism/Uhuruna Ujamaa: Essays on socialism*, Oxford University Press.

Nzewi, M. 2007. A contemporary study of musical arts: Informed by African indigenous knowledge systems, *Volume 4 Illuminations, Reflection and Explorations*, Ciima Series.

Okot p'Bitek, 1966.*Song of Lawino*, Heinemann, London.

Pieterse, J. N and Parekh, B. 1995.Shifting imaginaries: Decolonisation, internal decolonisation, postcoloniality, In Pieterse, J. N and Parekh, B. (Eds).*The decolonisation of imagination: Culture, knowledge and power*, Zed Books: London.

Rodney, W. 1982.*How Europe underdeveloped Africa*, Harvard University Press: Washington DC, USA.

Samkange, S. 1975. *The mourned one*, Heinemann Educational Publishers, London.

Shizha, E. 2013. Reclaiming our indigenous voices: The problem with postcolonial sub-Saharan African School curriculum, *Journal of Indigenous Social Development*, 2 (1): 1-18.

Temples, P. 1959. *Bantu philosophy*, Presence Africaine: Paris.

Wa Thiongo, N. 1986. *Decolonising the mind: The politics of language in African literature,* Heinemann: Portsmouth, UK.

Chapter 3

Legislation and management of heritage landscapes in Zimbabwe

Henry Chiwaura and Tapuwa Raymond Mubaya

Introduction

The problems haunting institutions mandated to look after heritage in Zimbabwe today arise from the way the discipline of heritage management was introduced in the country. The colonisation of Zimbabwe by European settlers had profound implications for the Zimbabwean legal systems and institutions. Zimbabwean traditional systems of looking after heritage were almost completely destroyed and replaced by European oriented systems which restricts rather than expand the idea of what heritage is and what should be protected. Zimbabwe inherited forms of protective legislation drafted by the colonial government. That being the case, the local communities developed resentment and responded by either vandalising the cultural heritage or by withholding social practices that bestowed value and respect to some of the heritage sites. The local communities in some instances reacted by simply becoming indifferent to the heritage that they used to give respect. The same state of affairs is still evident in the legislation in force in post-colonial Zimbabwe where colonial structures that were inherited at independence have not been changed to date despite various attempts by the National Museums and Monuments of Zimbabwe (NMMZ).

The attainment of independence by most African countries in general and Zimbabwe in particular saw several cultural and ethnic groups expressing interest in active management of cultural heritage (Pwiti 1996). Regrettably this interest has not been explored further because legislation pertaining to the management and protection of heritage in the country only recognises NMMZ as the sole custodian of heritage. Resultantly, local communities have developed an indifference towards the country's heritage. The negative attitude by local communities in Zimbabwe towards their cultural and natural heritage emanates from the alienating legislation, which has not undergone significant changes since the attainment of independence in 1980 to accommodate local aspirations (Muringaniza 1998).

The purpose of this chapter is manifold inter alia: to discuss the effectiveness and role of legislation in protecting heritage in Zimbabwe. Second, the chapter also discusses the relationship between state laws and traditional management systems pertaining to the protection, interpretation and presentation of cultural heritage. Third it, argues that sustainable management of heritage resources cannot be meaningfully achieved without the active involvement and participation of traditional custodians and communities who are also involved in the management of heritage.

A brief overview of heritage management in Zimbabwe

History of heritage management as a concept has been expounded by different scholars from diverse ideological backgrounds. Management of heritage can be viewed from the Western (formal/state based) and African (informal/traditional/community based) perspectives in Zimbabwe. From the former dimension, Cleere (1989:1) notes that "...heritage management is believed to have started with the Swedish Royal Proclamation of 1666 which considered all antiquity objects as the property of the Crown." He further asserts that "by the end of the century (19th) most European ancient monuments were covered by protective legislation of varying degrees of efficacy" (Cleere 1981:1). The use of legislation in the management of cultural heritage then spread to other parts of Europe and America. For instance, the United Kingdom's Ancient Monument Protection Act of 1882 and the United States of America's Antiquities Law of 1906.

In this regard, the heritage discourse and action were strongly expert-dominated as very small self-defining cadres of well-educated individuals, often from relatively privileged personal backgrounds, identified and selected the "best" of the nation's heritage for attention through interpretation, conservation and presentation, working sometimes through private channels, sometimes through legislation and state action (Palmer 2009). Initially, largely self-resourced, many of these "gentleman experts" started working for government departments and agencies but with little thought of democracy in their operational policies. The ordinary population was invited, if not positively instructed, to admire these experts' choices, while anyone from outside the charmed circle of expertise was looked on with deep suspicion (Palmer 2009). In short, the conception of heritage was narrow, heritage practice was exclusive and conservation was seen as an end in itself. During the 19th century in the world's industrial and modern development, there was no mention of heritage resource management in Africa since there was a western belief that development and management of all kinds commenced in Africa during the colonial era (Rodney 1972).

On the contrary, from the African dimension, heritage management dates back to the Pre-Arab and Pre-European times in the world's history. This is the period when various cultural materials were fashioned, preserved and conserved in temples or shrines (Ekechukwu 2003). Some were preserved in the palaces of kings and chiefs depending on their socio-political value to the community. For (Ekechukwu 2003), these cultural materials were kept in the custody of households, priests of shrines/deities and any of the kings' or chiefs' officers. The westerners took advantage of the absence of modern and systematic method of heritage management during this period to claim that there was no heritage management in Africa prior to their arrival. It is however fundamental to set the record straight that heritage management and cultural legislation have always existed in the African continent, even before the days of written laws. This can be evidenced by the fact that when Europeans arrived in Africa they found most of the heritage sites intact indicating that there was some form of management that was administered. However, it is wrong to perceive that it was with the 'taking over' of the continent that civilisation and heritage legislation were first implemented. The so-called 'new' legislation did not recognise the indigenous means of management and ignored the fact that heritage sites have existed long prior to the scramble for the continent (Ndlovu 2011).

The fact that Europeans enacted and introduced legislation now considered as formal management systems does not in any way point to the idea that there was no form of management insofar as the preservation of cultural heritage is concerned. The fact that they found many archaeological sites impressive and intact is a clear indication that the sites were being looked after in a sustainable manner, and that legislation and management to that effect existed. The situation that perhaps obtains is that coming from an ideological background that perceives culture and nature as separate entities, the Europeans failed to come to terms with the African managerial systems which were heavily rooted in aspects of intangible heritage. As a result of this misunderstanding, the Europeans viewed the indigenous people of Zimbabwe as potential threat to the heritage sites hence they were forcibly alienated from their heritage sites through the infamous Land Apportionment Act of 1931 and other similar Acts that followed thereafter. They were considered threats because they were freely interacting with the sites a thing that totally opposes the western philosophy of protecting heritage sites rather than using them. The European settlers removed the indigenous people from their heritage sites and eliminated African local management systems.

Heritage legislation: Conceptual analysis

Heritage is a fragile and non-renewable resource, such that there must be a strong legislation that protects it for posterity. International heritage law in the form of the World Heritage Convention is a landmark for the protection of the cultural and natural heritage of mankind. Since its approval in 1972, it has become one of the most effective and important mechanisms for the protection of sites and

44

monuments worldwide. This was after the realisation that the heritage of the various cultures was being destroyed.

Africa's heritage is being affected largely negatively by different factors. Political and social conflicts, massive development projects, governmental complacency, ignorance, corruption and lack of funding, substantial tourism growth, and other factors have all seriously impacted the continent's ability to maintain, conserve and protect the world's longest record of human cultural achievement. This concern has led to the enactment of legislation in various countries to protect heritage resources. Zimbabwe like most of the countries in Southern Africa has recognised the importance of identifying and preserving its unique and diverse heritage. Thus it has enacted legislation to govern and direct the management and protection of heritage.

Despite creating a regulatory framework and defining the roles of different agencies and departments legislation also formalises institutional arrangements (Ndlovu 2011). In the heritage sector, the main objective of such legislation is to protect heritage resource from destruction. All Southern African countries have passed protective heritage legislation to govern the protection and use of heritage resources and Zimbabwe is not an exception (Ndoro and Pwiti 2001). Heritage protection means taking care of natural and cultural heritage values of a place and these include legislation, policies and management frameworks (Getty Conservation Institute 2009). It is important to clarify what this study means by 'legislation'. In simple terms legislation is normally referred to as 'written law.' Legislation consists of laws made by Parliament or by people who are given power by Parliament to make laws. Acts are laws enacted by Parliament hence they are sometimes referred to as 'Acts of Parliament'. Protection shall be understood as the legal action initiated by one or more parties acting on behalf of the heritage, especially the administration, under the auspices of an institutional structure (Bermúdez and Adelina 2004). For Bolfy Cotton (2004), cultural inheritance constitutes a cultural heritage, as a set of material or immaterial assets which, having relevant significance due to their

45

historic or artistic value, must be protected by law in a precise manner and be the object of actions by the state, through suitable means.

The evolution of formal heritage management in Zimbabwe

Zimbabwe became a British colony in 1890 under Cecil Rhodes' British South Africa Company (BSACo) and was named Sothern Rhodesia. Apart from Rhodes' Cape-to-Cairo dream, the occupation of the country was motivated by economic greed based on reports of rich goldfields on the Zimbabwean plateau (Pwiti and Ndoro 1999). Soon after the occupation of Zimbabwe many of the settlers started searching for the second Eldorado, the first one was in South Africa. During this period, irreparable damage was made to the cultural heritage especially that of the Zimbabwe tradition sites. Great Zimbabwe and related sites appear to have suffered most, particularly at the hands of the Rhodesian Ancient Ruins Company Ltd (a private company registered under the BSACo mandated to mine or excavate treasures at these sites). However, it was soon realised that many important heritage sites were being destroyed and from this realisation the Legislative Council belatedly passed the Ancient Monuments Protection Ordinance in 1902. According to Garlake (1973), the British High Commissioner at the time advised that it should not become law because he considered the protected sites ill-defined and penalties too severe. Nevertheless it became the first formal law to govern heritage in colonial Zimbabwe.

The early inhabitants of Southern Africa known as the Bushmen and Relics Ordinance followed in 1912, passed in order to include the protection of rock paintings that fascinated the settlers. The 1936 Monuments and Relics Act established the Monuments Commission as the implementing body, replacing the 1902 and 1912 Ordinances. However, the first statutory body to protect heritage sites in Zimbabwe was the Rhodesian Historical Monuments Commission established in 1958. Soon after its establishment of the commission, it sought to formally and completely prohibit all previous 'unlawful' excavations. The next major development in the history of legislation in Zimbabwe was the passing of the National Museums and Monuments Act Chapter 313, in 1972. Following independence in 1980, the Act was adopted almost verbatim as the National Museums and Monuments of Zimbabwe Act Chapter 25.11, 1972.

Heritage legislation and administrative structures in Zimbabwe

The archaeological heritage in Zimbabwe is governed by the National Museums and Monuments of Zimbabwe Act of 1972 (chap. 313) and its associated By-laws (GN 253 of 1973, and GN 683 of 1976). The Act protects all areas and objects of archaeological, historical, architectural and paleontological value (NMMZ Act 1972). These statutory instruments were promulgated before the attainment of majority rule and they have not been substantially altered since independence.

The Act created a parastatal organisation National Museums and Monuments of Zimbabwe, under a Board of Trustees. The trustees administer all national museums and other properties, such as national monuments, in trust of the people of Zimbabwe. The parastatal falls within the Ministry of Home Affairs. The functions of the organisation are broadly custodian: it is expected to make provisions for the preservation of the heritage. Administration of the legislation governing the archaeological heritage is the responsibility of the Executive Director of NMMZ (Collet 1992). As stipulated in the preamble, the NMMZ Act was promulgated to:

Establish a Board of Trustees and administer museums and monuments in Zimbabwe, to provide for the establishment and administration of museums, to provide preservation for the ancient, historical and natural monuments, relics and other objects of historical or scientific value or interest (NMMZ Act 1972).

Important aspects of the NMMZ Act include:

a) The immediate reporting of any "discovery of ancient monument or relic" to the NMMZ. Knowledgeable contravention is deemed an offence with fines and/or imprisonment provided for.

b) The Act specifies that the alteration of any site of archaeological, cultural, historical and paleontological presence cannot be undertaken without the prior written consent of NMMZ. This includes the removal of any artefact from its original context. Contravention is an offense.

c) Only approved persons are entitled to undertake such work as directed by the Executive Director of the NMMZ.

d) Article 26 of the Act provides for the protection of all buildings in Zimbabwe that predate to 1st of January 1910. Notice of any intended alterations and demolitions of such "historical buildings" has to be submitted to the Executive Director NMMZ, indicating details of any proposed alteration for consideration approval. Failure to follow this procedure is an offense.

In an effort to explain the law to potential developers and Local Authorities, NMMZ issued a guideline document in 1998 entitled "Archaeological Impact Assessments: Guidelines for Planning Authorities and Developers". The document explains the law as well as specifying additional requirements that have subsequently appeared as various Statuary Instruments (Chikohomero 2012). Apart from NMMZ Act, there are other pieces of legislation that also support the management and conservation of Zimbabwe's cultural heritage. Below are some of them:

National Trust Act Chapter 25.12 of 1960

The National Trust Act 25.12 is one of the unobtrusive laws in the management of heritage places in Zimbabwe. The Trust holds seven properties throughout the country, six of them in Manicaland. The latter include Nyanga Historical Exhibition (the Rhodes Nyanga Museum) and World's View in Nyanga, Fort Gomo Kadzamu and La Rochelle Estate (Penhalonga) and Murahwa's Hill (Mutare). It therefore has an important stake in the conservation and management of the country's natural and archaeo-historical heritage. There is need for greater engagement between the NMMZ and the Trust in seeking solutions to the cultural landscape management problems being faced in the Eastern Highlands. Some of the problems encountered in the Eastern Highlands are to do with wild fires, illegal occupation of land, and destruction of heritage sites by plantation owners among others. There are opportunities for joint management of some of the archaeological sites like Murahwa's Hill and Fort Gomo Kadzamu (Mupira, 2008:307). Unlike NMMZ Act Chapter 25.11 National Trust Act prohibits mining on Trust property (Chiwaura 2011). The Act's preamble states:

> An Act to establish a trust for the purpose of accepting and holding property in trust for public purposes, of acquiring and thereafter preserving and protecting for the benefit of the people of Zimbabwe land, buildings, natural resources, fauna, flora and objects of any description which have a national, archaeological, historical or aesthetic interest, and of holding and maintaining lands and buildings as places of public recreation, entertainment, resort or instruction; and to provide for various other matters connected with and incidental to the foregoing.

The Urban Councils Act Chapter 29.15 of 1974

The Urban Councils Act Chapter 29.15 enacted in 1974 empowers City Councils to acquire land they deem fit. Although this Act does not relate directly to the NMMZ Act, such powers can be used in protecting land with cultural heritage. In terms of the Regional Town Planning Act Chapter 29.12 of 1976, buildings that are not national monuments may be subject to a Building Preservation Order if they are of special architectural or historic interest. Such an order restricts the demolition, alteration or extension of a building.

The Land Acquisition Act Chapter 20.10 of 1992

The 1992 Land Acquisition Act Cap 20.10, section 3 empowers the President to acquire compulsorily, land in the interest of public health, safety and morality. Further, any rural land may be acquired where the acquisition is reasonably necessary for the utilisation of that land for the purpose of land reorganisation, environmental conservation or utilisation of wildlife or other natural resources. This Act can be used to acquire land where cultural heritage sites are located for the purposes of buffer zone. Section 23 of NMMZ Act stipulates that where the Board of Trustees wishes to acquire a national monument or relic on a given piece of land on which the monument is situated, the Board shall reach a mutually agreed settlement with the landowner. If however this fails, the Board shall apply to the President for authority to compulsorily acquire the land for NMMZ using the Land Acquisition Act Cap 20.10. Land has been acquired for the purpose of protecting a national monument recently at Danamombe/Dhlodhlo and Ntabazikamambo/Manyanga in Gweru. The land initially belonged to settler famers who did not want NMMZ, Department of Parks and Wild Life and surrounding communities to benefit from the cultural and wildlife resources within the farms, hence the compulsory acquisition.

Environmental Management Act (Chapter 20.27) of 2002

The government enacted the Environmental Management Act (Chapter 20.27) of 2002, whose Part XI addresses environmental impact assessments (EIAs). Mining and quarrying are covered under the first schedule of the Act that prescribes projects for which EIAs are required. While it is an offence, in terms of Zimbabwe's EIA policy of 1997 to carry out mining without an EIA certificate, it does not look as though EMA is adequately capacitated to monitor all mining activities in the country both legal and illegal (The Sunday Mail, January 15-21, 2012). EMA is a hybrid organisation where the former Department of Natural Resources Management was in

January 2007 merged with the Water Pollution Control Unit of the Zimbabwe National Water Authority, the Air Pollution Control Unit, both of the Ministries.

Traditional Leaders Act Chapter 29:17

The Act provides for chiefs to promote and uphold cultural values among members of the community. Chiefs are also to ensure that communal land is allocated in accordance with part 111 of the Communal Land Act (20.04). A Chief's duty among others is to prevent any unauthorized settlement or use of any land. The Act enables chiefs to be custodians of traditional institutions. As such the Act assumes that chiefs are the custodians of the intangible heritage within communities. NMMZ must, therefore, encourage chiefs to look after intangible heritage in their jurisdictions. The chiefs also have the power to protect archaeological heritage that is threatened by development within their areas because they can refuse to allocate land that has archaeological heritage or close to it. More often than not mainly archaeological heritage that is deemed sacred to the locals is the one that is protected. Sometimes it becomes difficult for local leadership to stop development from interfering in archaeological resources. Chiefs Murinye and Mugabe in Masvingo objected to the setting up of a communication booster in Sviba Hills because the hill is an ancestral burial place for chiefs. At Domboshawa National Monument near Harare the Chief gave permission to a developer to build a leisure centre on the edge of *Ramabakurimwa* sacred forest? When NMMZ raised concern over the development the traditional leadership sided with the developer (Chiwaura 2012). The Domboshava case indicted that corruption and bread and butter issues can affect the way traditional leadership operates hence there is need to have checks and balances and also that what the community respects as important might be different from what NMMZ might want to protect. There is the problem of shifting values in communities.

51

The NMMZ Act CAP 25.11 1974

The NMMZ Act has remained static and is not changing with the changing world. There have been calls for amending the Act in the past and all efforts have not yielded any results. Failure by NMMZ to repeal the Act hinders on the disinclined government that views the process as not important at the moment. The main purpose for amending the Act is to bring it in line with developments that have and are taking place in the world in the preservation of cultural heritage and to reduce illegal trade in cultural objects. Since the promulgation of the Act, Zimbabwe has since become a signatory to the World Heritage Convention and has become a member of organisations such as International Council of Museums (ICOM) and the International Council on Monuments and Sites (ICOMOS) under which Zimbabwe has certain obligations. Some of the obligations under these bodies include, introducing acceptable international standards, to incorporate archaeological and environmental programmes which are now a prerequisite before developmental programmes are undertaken and to regulate against adverse effects of some of the Acts such as the Mines and Minerals Act that super cede the NMMZ Act in the event of mineral discovery and new technologies such as metal detectors on heritage sites. In this regard, the amendments seek to redefine certain terms and introduce new ones that are universally accepted in the field of archaeology, museology and heritage studies.

Chipunza (2002) pointed out that the present Zimbabwe legislation turns to favour monuments, which are no longer in daily use and are uncontested. This is however against the notion that heritage is always contested. Thus the legislation fails to recognize and consider this contemporary dimension. He went further arguing that the NMMZ Act was meant for uncontested heritage and not cultural heritage since there is no mention of culture in the Act. Apart from that, the declaration of a site into a national monument transfers ownership to state and takes away the heritage from communities. Thus the community loses in the process. He also pointed out that the Zimbabwean heritage legislation is weak because it is overridden by the Mining Act which is given more priority. Thus minerals are considered more useful than cultural places.

The other problem is that most of the policies and legislation segregated the traditional African culture. Owen Seda (2004:136) observes that, 'in colonial Rhodesia, cultural and social life had been marked by forced separation, prejudice and cultural polarisation.' Kaarsholm (1990:249) affirms this by saying: In the narrowly exclusive Rhodesian colonial cosmology, dramatic and other cultural modes of expression of black Africans were firmly situated outside the boundaries of art or culture and relegated to the dark hinterlands of anthropology.

Zimbabwe has ratified Conventions and has international obligations to meet. Very few people and institutions, let alone policy makers, institutions and individuals are aware of these obligations. NMMZ should be able to play leading role in raising awareness among law enforcement agencies and heritage institutions.

Community-based legal system

Many ancient monuments are located in rural areas where in the normal course of events, the local people are governed and adhere to customary law. Most, if not all people who live in rural areas are not aware of the provisions of the NMMZ Act, while even if they were to be made aware there will be conflict since many of the provisions of the formal Act would clash with their own beliefs and traditions. An example is the case of late stone Age rock art site in Domboshava near Harare in Zimbabwe. The locals regard the site as sacred and occasionally carried out rain making ceremonies within the rock shelter. Damaging the rock art in the process, as a result NMMZ prohibited the community using the site. The locals retaliated by defacing the rock art with paint (Taruvinga and Ndoro, 2003).

The NMMZ Act does not have provision for co-management of cultural heritage with the community based legal management system. Where communities intend to use archaeological sites for ceremonies

53

they are prohibited under the NMMZ Act. It is often argued that communities will destroy the sites and therefore there is need for supervision of activities. Communities around Great Zimbabwe World Heritage site are permitted to carryout rituals under the supervision of a scientifically state trained heritage manager. Heritage managers often engage communities when it's sympathetic to them. In particular when they are carrying out research or appeasing communities when something wrong happens. There are sites, because of their national significance, that are totally managed under the community based legal system. For example sites such as Njelele Shrine in Matobo Bulawayo, Mt Muozi in Nyanga, Nerumedzo Forest in Bikita and many others have remained under community based legal systems to this day. If that is the case, the state based law on the management of physical heritage need to be changed to re-orient the relationship between state and community based legal systems (Mumma 2005). He posits that the two systems must be brought into a relationship of complementarity and symbiosis rather than antagonism and competition.

Heritage legislation challenges in Zimbabwe

Munjeri (2002) argues that the Zimbabwean legislation legal instrument needs revision. He premises his argument on the basis that the legislation was made during the colonial times and has survived without any changes. In short the legislation is based on outdated colonial philosophy that did and has not adapted to African philosophy and thought as well as post-colonial changes. This is despite the fact that the cultural context had changed. He postulated that the major problem of the present legislation is that it misrepresents heritage by using narrow definitions which restrict us to terms like monuments, relics and sites. It is however fundamental to note that cultural heritage is much more than these static terms. Furthermore, part of the problem emanate from the fact that the community or the public in general is rarely consulted when legislation is being drafted or made. The definitions we use in our

54

legal instruments should come from a broad spectrum of society rather than from a few individuals or one sector of society.

In view of the above, the protective legislation related to cultural heritage will remain ineffective as long as it is not understood by the ordinary people and as long as it excludes them from the process of making it. This was so because a misunderstood legislation is difficult to implement. He also pointed out that a good legislation is however not a panacea to good protection of the heritage. The legislation must be supported by an equally good organisational structure. These structures of administration should be able to support the implementation of the legislation.

Negri (2002) highlighted that heritage legislation does not seem to reflect reality on the ground. Most legislation was created during the colonial period and has not been changed since. Thus most legislation concerning cultural properties does not reflect the post-colonial realities of Africa. Some attempts at cosmetic reforms can be noted in various countries; however these do not change the thrust of the laws. If heritage legislations are to be effective there is need to include environmental laws and also urban planning mechanism. In most African countries these issues are often fragmented and uncoordinated.

According to Eboreine (2005) most African countries' outdated laws have failed to meet the contemporary realities of integrated development, customary and community rights and value systems. Most African legislation tend to favour the concept of monumentalism to the neglect of other types of heritage such as cultural landscapes and routes, vernacular architecture or underwater heritage, and takes very little or no cognisance of associated intangible and spiritual values. There are two challenges that have negatively affected the implementation of cultural legislation the world over. These are the lack of community involvement and the difficulty of enforcing the law (Ndlovu 2012).

Nevertheless, it would be misleading to introduce an oversimplified view of African legal systems, which would give the impression that the laws of the former colonial states have been merely grafted onto the domestic legislation of African states. It would be more accurate to point out that the total renunciation of colonial law was not conceivable, especially considering the public structures and administrative bodies that the colonial powers had developed on African territories. The governments of the newly independent states were thus led to proclaim the principle of continuity in the legal domain.

There are general problems associated with the formal legislation in Zimbabwe. In most situations in Africa legislation without policy or policy without adequate legislation, i.e.: there is either no legislation or it is outdated and in need of replacement or revision. In many situations there is conflict with other bodies of legislation, e.g.: heritage and environmental legislation both cover the same areas or processes in Zimbabwe there has been conflict between NMMZ and the Department of Parks and Wildlife over the management of natural heritage. At one point the conflict over Victoria Falls had to be solved by the presidium. Our legislation concentrates on monumentalisation and neither caters for the types of situation found in our countries nor incorporates modern methods of conservation.

Formal law views heritage management in Zimbabwe through the telescopic eye of the western scientific world view. This is a result of colonial inheritance in legal systems. Heritage management in Zimbabwe is managed more by the state than communites. Heriatge legislation in Zimbabwe has failed to accomodate and promote indigenous knowledge sytems inherent in cultural heritage. This is evidenced by the appointment of NMMZ and Trustees as custodians of the heriatge while tradionally, chiefs and headmen were the custodians. Further, it totally excludes and ignores customary laws hence there is limited community participation in cultural heritage management in Zimbabwe. Despite the non existence of provisions that allows community participation NMMZ is introducing commnunity involvement policy to cater for the anomaly. Todate two chiefs sits in the local committee boards as a way of introducing community voice in heritage matters. Chief Chimombe and Mugabe of Buhera and Masvingo sit in Mutare Museum and Great Zimbabwe National World Heriatge site local commiiittee board respectively.

On a global level Zimbabwe plays a significant role in the implementation of international strategies on the protection and conservation of heritage resources. As a result, Zimbabwe is one of the signatories to the 1972 UNESCO Convention on Safeguarding Cultural and Natural Heritage. At local level Zimbabwe has got heritage legislation (the *National Museums and Monuments Act- which is administered by the Ministry of Home Affairs*) dating from 1972. The old piece of legislation protects buildings, objects and culturally or scientifically significant natural places. Intangible heritage such as sculptures, drama, traditional dance and instruments falls under the Ministry of Education, Sport, Arts and Culture. There are also associations such as the Oral Traditions Association of Zimbabwe (OTAZI), formed in 1988. It is closely linked with the Oral Traditions Association of Southern Africa (OTASA) and aims at promoting Zimbabwe's oral history and at improving the methodology of working with oral data.

Proposed amendments to the NMMZ Act CAP 25.11

The amendment of NMMZ Act has been advocated for by heritage practitioners, community groups and NMMZ organisation. The reasons for amendments include but not limited to the fact that the act excludes community participation in heritage matters, the act is also viewed as Eurocentric in approach as it is limited in terms of what it protects. In other words the act is silent on intangible heritage protection that is the basis of African heritage philosophy.

Recommendations

Broad policy generation upon which legislation and regulations can be based is necessary before the process of drafting new legislation begins. It should look at the type of structure that is needed to deal with the situations it identifies and areas it believes need concentrating upon. Re-evaluation of legislation in terms of the environment in which heritage finds itself nationally and internationally, for example, in terms of broad heritage policy, the national constitution and national developmental and planning priorities. Only after this can it be determined what type of action regarding legislation is required, i.e. a new Act, or amendment. Comparative research on legislation and legal mechanism used elsewhere and in other areas of governance should take place. Also, consultation and participation processes with stakeholders in the process of drafting or amending legislation are important and are strongly recommended. Stakeholders should include both proponents of heritage conservation at community and professional level and those opposed to it, for instance, developers and landowners. Areas of overlap and conflict with other bodies of legislation need to be identified and covered in new heritage conservation legislation. Thereafter, heritage conservationists need to keep abreast of developments in areas of potential conflict and engage other departments and ministries in their processes of revision of legislation to avoid the development of new conflicts. Publication of heritage legislation through pamphlets and other promotional materials is a good way disseminating legislative information to the majority of stakeholders and ordinary people. Legislation needs to provide for a variety of diverse methods of conservation that cater appropriately for different situations and types heritage, for example, conservation areas, inventories, landscapes, etc. Existing monuments and sites need to be re-evaluated and re-allocated to the appropriate new forms of protection.

Legislation cannot exist in a vacuum. Clear policy guidelines are required to ensure that the legislative amendments support the values, principles and vision for heritage and empower rather than impede implementation. However, the legal frameworks are often inadequate and/or outdated. There is a general recognition that legislation needs to be regularly updated to meet new challenges and improve the protection of cultural and natural heritage sites. This is reinforced, as there is no legal framework for involving communities in the identification or management process. The antiquities laws in

Zimbabwe must be replaced by others that take community sentiments into consideration.

The situation in the United States and Canada is somewhat different because here at least there are very strong laws that bind archaeologists to meaningful involvement of local communities. Native Graves Protection and Repatriation Act (NAGPRA) of 1990 is a very strong piece of legislation that gives Native Americans power to defend themselves against excesses, but archaeologists can appeal if they feel that their right to pursue knowledge is being undermined, as happened with Kennewick Man (Watkins 2003, 2005). Other countries like Angola, Namibia, Zimbabwe, Mozambique and Kenya have already or are now in the process of revising their legal frameworks. In addition, some countries, like Mali, Togo, and more recently Congo-Brazzaville, have also strengthened their institutional structures in relation with the changed legal framework.

Conclusion

The effectiveness of heritage legislation, whether colonial or post-colonial, has been severely questioned. Many archaeological sites have been vandalised (Strecker and Taboada, 1999), proving that cultural legislation on its own does not ensure the protection of heritage. Legislation has not only failed in South Africa, but in other countries as well (Clarke et al., 1976; Odak, 1991; Strecker and Taboada, 1999: 37).The cases of Kenya and South Africa illustrate that even if legislation exists on paper, its implementation can be ineffective, either due to staff shortages, lack of funding (Clarke et al., 1976; Rudner, 1989; Odak, 1991; Karega-Munene, 2009; Eboreime,2009), lack of community support, or other kinds of challenges. The failure of legislation to proactively protect cultural heritage has led to an argument that it is not stricter laws that are more effective, but rather the understanding and support of the general public (Mazel, 1988; Lippe, 1977: 22; Flood, 1979: 63).

Customary law should be recognised in cultural heritage management as the formal management system develops. It is important in this regard to recall Garlake's (1974) contribution when he recommended that traditional history and knowledge should be used to illuminate some of the more abstract problems associated with cultural heritage. For this reason the interest and cooperation of a much wider public than has to hither to been the case must be fostered and not discouraged by NMMZ. Customary law has the advantage that it embraces communities rather than alienates in its approach to management of heritage landscapes. It is a product of accumulation of indigenous knowledge systems over long period of time. It further involves people at grassroots levels where most of the heritage is situated. It is notable that because of the existence of traditional myths and legends as well as taboos, some heritage resources in Zimbabwe have managed to withstand destruction for a long time only to be destroyed when modernisation set in (Ndoro, 2002).the NMMZ Act is currently being reviewed. As this takes place, it is hoped that the resulting repeal will recognise traditional management systems. The two management systems though varied and rooted in different cultural ideologies should be adopted and used in a way that brings on board the positive attributes of each complimentarily given the changing societal composition as well as modernity and globalisation. The chapter further notes the need to establish ways to harmonise and synergise the two systems of management vis-a-vis the changing values of society. The chapter recommends that the outdated NMMZ Act be revisited and revised so that it is in sync with current dynamic developments in the cultural heritage sector both locally and internationally.

References

Bermúdez, A., Arbeloa, J.F.M, and Giralt, A. 2004. *Intervención en el Patrimonio Cultural*, Madrid: Editorial Síntesis.

Cottom, B. 2004. Julio Cesar Olivé Negrete. Obras escogidas. Serie Colección Científica. Mexico City: INAH.

Collet, 1992. *The Archaeological Heritage of Zimbabwe: A Master plan for resource Conservation and development*. Harare, National Museums and Monuments of Zimbabwe

Chikohomero, C.2012. *The Crystal*, April 2012, Issue No. 6.

Chipunza, K. T. 2005. 'Protection of Immovable Cultural Heritage in Zimbabwe: An Evaluation'. In: (ed). Ndoro, W. and G. Pwiti, G *Legal Frameworks for the Management of Immovable cultural heritage in Africa*. 42-45.Rome. ICCROM.

Chiwaura, H. 2011.*The Implications of Legal Pluralism in the Management of Archaeological Heritage*. Lambert Academic publishing.

Clarke, J. B., den Hoed, and Starreland.K.W.1976. *The Preservation and Recording of Rock Paintings*, Kearsney College.

Cleere, H.1989. Introduction: the Rationale of Archaeological Heritage Management, In: Cleere, H. (ed.) *Archaeological Heritage Management in the Modern World*. London: Cambridge University Press.

Davison, G. 1991. The Meanings of 'Heritage,' In: A Heritage Handbook (eds.) St Leonards NSW 1-13.

Eboreme, E.2005. Nigeria's customary laws and practices in the protection of cultural heritage with special reference to the Benin Kingdom, *ICCROM CONSERVATION STUDIES* 5. 9- 11.

Ekechukwu, L.C. 2003. Introduction to Cultural Resource Management, *An unpublished Reading Manual*, Department of Archaeology and Tourism, University of Nigeria, Nsukka.

David, H. 1997. *Heritage, Tourism and Society*. Great Britain: Pinter.

Flood, J. 1979. Cultural and Resource Management and Tourism: A National Perspective with special reference to Archaeological Sites. In: McKinlay J.R and Jones, K.L (eds). *Archaeological Resource*

Management in Australia and Ocenia. Wellington. New Zealand Historic Places Trust, pages 51-55.

Getty Conservation Institute, 2009. Conservation Management Planning: Putting Theory into Practice, The Case of Joya de Cerén, El Salvator.

Godden, L. 2002. Indigenous Heritage and the Environment, *Environmental and Planning Law Journal,* Vol. 19, no. 4, pp. 260.

The Difficult Types of Cultural Heritage at UNESCO Culture Portal, available at www.unesco.org/culture/heritage, accessed August 17, 2005.

Palmer. 2009. *Heritage and Beyond,* Council of Europe Publishing Editions.

Pwiti, G. 1996. Let Ancestors Rest in Peace, In: Tecutonico, J.M and Price, N.S (eds.) *Conservation and Management of Archaeological Sites,* Vol. 1 No. 3: 151-60.

Pwiti, G and Ndoro, W.1999. The Legacy of Colonialism: Perceptions of the Cultural Heritage in Southern Africa with Special Reference to Zimbabwe, *African Archaeological Review* Vol., 16 No.3, 1999.

Prott, L.V. and O'Keefe, P. J. 1984. *Law and the Cultural Heritage*: Volume 1. Discovery and Excavation (Professional Books Limited, London).

Kaarsholm, P. 1990. *Cultural Struggle and Development in Southern Africa,* Cambridge University Press.

Karega-Munene, 2009. Towards Recognition to the Right to a Cultural Past in the 21st century: An example from East Africa. In: Schmidt, P. (ed). *Postcolonial Archaeologies in Africa.* Santa Fe: School for Advanced Research Press, pages77-94.

Mazel, A.D.1998. Hunter-gatherers in the Thukela Basin during the last 1500 years, with special reference to Hunter-Gatherer Agriculturalist Relations. In: Bank, A, (ed.), *The proceedings of the Khoisan identities and Cultural Heritage Conference.* University of Western Cape, 12-16 July 1997, The Institute of Historical Research, pages, 94-101.

Muringaniza, J.S.1998. *Community participation in archaeological heritage management in Zimbabwe*: The case of Old Bulawayo. Unpublished MPhil thesis, University of Cambridge.

Mupira, P. 2008. *Managing the Archaeological landscape of the Eastern Highlands of Zimbabwe*, Unpublished D.Phil. Dissertation, University of Zimbabwe.

Mumma, A. 2005. The link between traditional and formal legal systems, In: Ndoro, W and Pwiti, G (eds.) *Legal Frameworks for the Management of Immovable cultural heritage in Africa*. Rome. ICCROM.

Munjeri, D. 2002. Smart partnerships: Cultural landscape issues in Africa. *In Cultural landscapes: The challenges of conservation, shared legacy*, Common Responsibility Associated Workshops, World Heritage Papers: 134–43.

Ndlovu. N. 2011, Legislation as an Instrument in South African Heritage Management: Is it Effective? In: *Conservation and Management of Archaeological Sites*. Vol. 13 No. 1, 31-57, Rock Art Research Institute, University of the Witwatersrand, South Africa.

Ndoro, W. Mumma, A. and Abungu, G. (eds.) 2008. *Cultural Heritage and the Law: Protecting Immovable Heritage in English Speaking Countries of Southern Africa*. ICCROM Conservation Studies 8. Rome: ICCROM.

Prott, L.V. and O'Keefe, P.J. 1989. *Law and the Cultural Heritage*: Volume 3. Movement Butterworths, London.

Rodney, W. 1972. *How Europe Underdeveloped Africa*. Washington, D. C.: Howard University Press.

Rudner, I.1989. *The Conservation of Rock Art in South Africa*, Cape Town: National Monuments Council.

Smith, Laurajane. 2006. *The Uses of Heritage*. London: Routledge.

Streker, M and Taboada, F. 1999. Rock Art Protection in Bolivia, *Rock Art Research*, 16 (1):36-40.

Odak, S, 199. *Status of Rock Art Legislation in Kenya*. In: S.A Pager, ed, Occasional SARARA Publication, No 1, Johannesburg, South African Rock Art Research Association, pp.235-40.

O'Keefe, P. J., and L. V. Prott. 1984. *Law and the Cultural Heritage*. Abingdon: Professional Books Ltd.

Lipe, D. W.1977. A conservation model for American archaeology. In Schiffer, M. B., and Gumerman, J. G. (eds.), *Conservation Archaeology: A Guide for Cultural Resource Management Studies, Academic Press,* New York, pages. 19-41.

Taruvinga, P and Ndoro, W. 2003. The vandalism of the Domboshava rock painting site, Zimbabwe. Some reflections on approaches to heritage management, *Conservation and Management of Archaeological Sites* 6(1):3-10.

Loulanski, T. 2006. Revising the Concept for Cultural Heritage: The Argument for a Functional Approach, *International Journal of Cultural Property,* 13:207–233.

Throsby, D. 1999. 'Cultural Capital'. *Journal of Cultural Economics* 23: 3–12.

Throsby, D. 2001. *Economics and Culture.* Cambridge: Cambridge University Press.

Vossler, G. 2000. Sense or Nonsense? Heritage Legislation In Perspective in Common Ground? In: Trapeznik, A. *Heritage and Public Places in New Zealand.* University of Otago Press, Dunedin.

Warren-Findley, J. 2001. *Human Heritage, Management in New Zealand in the Year 2000 and Beyond.* New Zealand Fellowship in Public Policy. Wellington.

Watkins, J.2003. Beyond the margins: American Indians, First Nations, and anthropology in North America. *American Antiquity* 68:273-85.

Chapter 4

Memory, Space and Contestations in Living Traditions: The case of Chitungwiza chaChaminuka Shrine in Zimbabwe.

Farai M. Chabata and Henry Chiwaura

Introduction

Until the ratification of UNESCO's Convention on the Safeguarding and Protection of Intangible Cultural Heritage in 2003, most discourse surrounding the definition of heritage tended to concentrate on material heritage such as buildings, monuments, natural and archaeological sites with no reference to intangible heritage which in most cases is intricately linked to the material heritage. However, in recent years, there has been an increased recognition that heritage takes a plurality of forms (Harrison 2013). The 2003 Convention on the Safeguarding and Protection of Intangible Cultural Heritage defines intangible cultural heritage as the practices, representations, expressions, as well as the knowledge and skills, which communities, groups and, in some cases, individuals recognize as part of their cultural heritage.

In the same vein, the influential, relatively-recent work of Lowenthal (1996), Darvill (2005) and others, integrate in various ways intangible traditions into discussion of heritage. As Thomas (1992: 213) notes, culture is inevitably tailored and embellished in the process of transmission. The Chitungwiza shrine is one such place famed not for its aesthetic or tangible outlook but its significant and outstanding intangible values which are predicated on its historic links with the legendary spirit of Chaminuka. The name Chaminuka is associated with the most famous Shona 'lion spirit' or *mhondoro* but the identity of the historical Chaminuka personage is uncertain and believed to go back to several hundred years (Gelfand 1959; Rasmussen 1979: 51). Bourdillon (1974: 33) refers to lion spirits like

Chaminuka as cults which were more significant than any other cults. In addition to being part of an early Shona settlement, Chitungwiza chaChaminuka was the residence of Pasipamire, who was a Chaminuka spirit medium, considered by many as the most senior rainpetitioner and the great fortune teller of the Rwizi people. This gave both Pasipamire and the place itself what Bourdillon (1974) has called 'a permanent high status in their communities' with important territorial connections. It is a sacred site of cultural and historical value that is associated with both the legendary spirit of Chaminuka and its last 'undisputed' medium, Pasipamire of the Rwizi people. The name Rwizi is said to have been a traditional clan name with probable links with the sacred river or stream which flows through the shrine or site. Like many similar sacred places such as Shavarunzi or Gomba in the upper Mazowe valley of Zimbabwe, Chitungwiza is an epicentre of a highly contested cultural and religious landscape both in terms of the outstanding values and custodianship of the site. It also signifies the fatality of colonial administrative boundaries with issues of cultural and religious heritage.

The people who claim the closest links reside in Mhondoro approximately 120 kilometres from the site, whereas Chitungwiza administratively falls under the jurisdiction of Chief Seke way outside the community that has a claim for Chitungwiza. Contestation for ownership of the shrine is shrouded by the realization that if you own the shrine you can own the prime farm land where the site is located. The group that wins ownership will be in a position to own farm land. The other reason for conflict is the idea that owning the shrine legitimises authority, be it for religious or political power. Cultural activists and independent African church followers visit the shrine to pray and appease their gods and sometimes conflicts as to who has the right to use the shrine arise. NMMZ has been called upon by the community to solve the differences by taking over control of the site, a position that NMMZ is not willing to do since the site is still in use and hence a lot of problems might arise. Custodial claims and counter claims are the order of the day at the shrine.

Location and description of the site

The site is located about 35 kilometres south of Harare on Boronia Farm in a commercial farming zone in Seke District which is situated on map 1830B2 and 1831A1. Records in the Archaeological Survey at the Zimbabwe Museum of Human Sciences in Harare refer to the site as Mutsike Ruins, named after the nearby stream. The site comprises, among other things, the controversial Pasipamire's soil grave and two graves that have alternately been associated with Chaminuka's aides, and/or Pasipamire's two wives. The site has dry stone enclosures reminiscent of the refugee tradition. The refuge tradition is a period of upheaval in Zimbabwe that was a response to the Mfecane episode in Southern Africa. Communities in Zimbabwe responded by constructing defensive rough dry stone walls, locating settlements on hill tops as well as placing grain bins in hidden places. At national level, comparable sites include Nharira Hills, Njelele and Shavarunzi or Gomba in the Upper Mazowe Valley. Maringove and Chigara shrines in Zvimba and Chivhu district respectively are similar shrines that are also being considered by National Museums and Monuments of Zimbabwe (NMMZ) for listing as national monuments on the National Register List. A National Register List is a database of known confirmed heritage sites that is in custody of the department of NMMZ. Like many shrines of its nature, it has also inspired contemporary Christian beliefs and practices among some African Independent Churches. Followers of these churches are part of the diversity of people who pay homage to this religious-cum-political shrine. The purpose of the visit to the shrine is the attraction offered by the sacredness of traditional shrines to African initiated churches. The NMMZ Board of Trustees approved to recommend to the Minister of Home Affairs, the listing of the Chaminuka Shrine as a national monument to enhance its protection and preservation. To this end, the proclamation process is ongoing.

Historical background

The phenomenal growth in the popularity of the spirit of Chaminuka particularly towards the end of the nineteenth century and thereafter has not made the job of establishing hard facts of this super-*mhondoro* any easier. Conflicting, confusing and even fictitious accounts of the exploits of the legendary Chaminuka have been captured and recorded in both oral and written sources. Beach (1980) made two significant points about Chaminuka. First, he pointed out that Chaminuka, like Kaguvi, was comparatively a super-*mhondoro* who became famous by the end of the nineteenth century. According to Ranger (1982: 349), the famous hunter Selous recounted in his travel and adventure in south east Africa, published in 1883 that he had heard in August 1878 from white elephant hunters of a 'very powerful "Umlimo" or god', who lived at Chitungwiza, near present day Beatrice. Ranger (1982), further points out that this was Pasipamire, a medium of Chaminuka who was regarded as the owner of the land such that hunters sought his permission to kill elephants and also gave him goods such as ivory and cloth. In his earlier work, Beach (1979: 399) even claimed that Gumboreshumba (the Kaguvi mhondoro spirit medium) was possibly related to Pasipamire, the medium of the Chaminuka *mhondoro* spirit who was killed in 1883. Beach refers to Chaminuka as a cult, maintaining that the evidence of the origins of Chaminuka is by no means satisfactory precisely because it has achieved such fame in the present. Beach's, Bourdillon's and Ranger (1974) view of Chaminuka as a cult cannot go unchallenged as this is a euro-centric view of African Traditional Religion. African Traditional Religion is at equal footing with all other religions of the world. There are more similarities between African traditional Religion and Old Judaism. Consequently, we have not come across any work expressing Old Judaism or Christianity as a cult. The issue though is beyond the scope of this chapter. Suffice to mention that it is pejorative to use the term "cult". Why is it that, for example, the Roman Catholic Church or any Protestant denomination are not regarded as "cults". One has to qualify what

68

s/he means by the term if s/he insist using it. In some way, every *svikiro* was independent centre point or consultant though indeed they could hold common *biras* under Mutapas.

According to the members of the Rwizi family, they were forcibly moved in 1924 to the Mhondoro area by the white settlers. Lan (1985: 6) has described Chaminuka as a *mhondoro* or royal ancestor of the Zezuru peoples of Central Zimbabwe and as the only hero of the nationalist resistance who rival Nehanda and came to be regarded as her brother. Native Commissioner, Posselt (1926) also pointed out that Chaminuka was the foremost and great *mhondoro* in the area surrounding this Chaminuka shrine.

Significant values of the Chaminuka Shrine

The significant values of Chitungwiza shrine are largely but not exclusively intangible. The tangible heritage is prevalent at the shrine the community places more value on the intangibility of the site. Intangible heritage is defined in this chapter as a term used to describe aesthetic, spiritual, symbolic or other social values that people may associate with a site, as well as rituals, music, language, know-how, oral traditions and the cultural spaces in which these 'living heritage' traditions are played out (Deacon 2009:310). Heritage becomes heritage only when society ascribes value to it. It is important to note that values are produced through cultural-social processes, learning and maturing of awareness within a given community. Intangible cultural heritage is therefore culturally diverse and very difficult to give it universal appeal. In the case of Chitungwiza Shrine religious, social, cultural, spiritual and of late scientific values have been attached by the communities as well as the academia. Myths, taboos and Chaminuka legend are some of the snippets of heritage prominent at the shrine.

As we write a an indigenous medicine practitioner has put up dwellings at the site claiming that she is possessed by the Chaminuka spirit. Spirit mediums continue to be influential in Zimbabwe, not only at the level of cultural nationalist rhetoric, but in the rural areas hence the continued use and association of Chaminuka shrine by various groups with different interest (Ranger 1985).

Proclamation efforts to date

Documentation at the Zimbabwe Museum of Human Sciences shows that the first proposal to declare the site a national monument was made by the Ministry of Education, Sport and Culture through the Ministry of Home Affairs in 1983. This followed a meeting which was held between the Ministry of Education, sport and Culture and a Zimbabwe National Traditional Healers' Association (ZINATHA) Committee on Bira reZimbabwe. The meeting also suggested, among other things, the proclamation of Shavarunzi (the Mbuya Nehanda stronghold in the Upper Mazowe Valley) as a national monument. Attempts to have both Shavarunzi and Chitungwiza declared national monuments were unsuccessful throughout the 1980s and 1990s. Shavarunzi was only gazetted as a national monument in 2006 and Chitungwiza is yet to be inscribed on the national monuments register. With both the National Museums and Monuments Act Chapter 25/11 and the NMMZ lacking a clearly defined guidelines for the nomination such heritage, it has generally not been such an easy process to get places 'monumentality' is not necessarily in the physical space or structure but in living tradition or intangible cultural heritage. One such significant place is Gomba or Upper Mazowe valley, the stronghold of the legendary Nehanda spirit, which lies northeast of Harare on the highway to Bindura town, was only declared a national monument in 2007. Mataga (2003) is of the view that the post-colonial government failed to seriously pursue gazetting of intangible heritage because most of the curator's mind-set was pro scientific management and the legislation alienated communities. The proclamation resuscitation effort only came after the UNESCO 2003 Convention was promulgated. The other reason for the concerted effort to proclaim intangible heritage in Zimbabwe after year 2000 was to do with a government that was changing its mind set to what Ranger terms patriotic history. For the first time after independence the number of African and liberation war heritage increased on the nomination list. Some of the sites for example the Nharira Hills, Shavarunzi / Gomba and Manicaland Provincial Heroes Acre's gazetting was 'fast tracked'.

A number of meetings have been held between NMMZ and many relevant stakeholders including the Provincial Governor and Resident Minister of Mashonaland East province Mr. A. Chigwedere, the traditional custodians, farm owner and officials from the Ministry of Lands and Resettlement. NMMZ is also in the process of demarcating both the spatial extent and the management framework of the site. An updated and revised nomination dossier for Chitungwiza chaChaminuka has been recently prepared for consideration by NMMZ Board of Trustees and the parent ministry of Home Affairs. Perhaps NMMZ needs to broaden its scope of documenting and archiving these heritages and appropriateness of proclaiming religious shrines as national monuments. Proclamations do not only enhance legal protection of shrines but may inadvertently open them up for desecration through tourism development activities. In principle, nationalising or proclaiming a site is making a tradition dominant. In indigenous culture, a place becomes dominant when there is an active medium. With death and or dearth of mediums and emergence of new ones, centres of consultation change.

The Chaminuka Legend and the enshrinement of the site

The Chaminuka legend is characterised by claims of his mysterious disappearances and defiance of death and demise in the 1880s. Even today descendants of the Rwizi clan maintain that a genuine medium of Chaminuka should be able to perform these mysteries. Chaminuka is believed to have played a very important role in guiding Shona resistance to Ndebele raids, as well as in inspiring the resistance against both colonial encroachment and colonial rule. In this role Lan (1985) argues that Chaminuka is in competition only with Nehanda. Beach (1980), however, puts him at par with Kaguvi.

71

Unlike its identification as a senior lion spirit in colonial administrative reports and some historical accounts, the Chaminuka spirit is characterised and given some attributes of a mermaid spirit in oral traditions, folklore and literary works. Some of the famous predictions credited to Chaminuka are that he predicted the coming of white settlers whose knees cannot be seen (the wearing of trousers). He predicted that settlers will enter the country and that these people will come over strips of iron and the things that bring them will be like caterpillars and will have eyes and that they will pass through mountains (the railway). He also further predicted that a big city will be built at Dzivarasekwa (the pool of laughter) in Harare. Many people will come and stay there (Salisbury) and that people to whom you will seek advice (the missionaries at Chishawasha) will settle there. He is also said to have predicted the establishment of a mission (Waddilove) in the Marandellas (now Marondera) area and a school at Domboshawa and near Great Zimbabwe a place where people will be treated for sickness (Morgenster Mission Hospital). Pasipamire is said to have used a leaf that was stained by an insect as similar to what people would be shown at Chishawasha (writing). He also predicted that there are many riches below the earth and the people without knees will bring the riches to the surface (Woollacott 1975).

Pasipamire is also attributed with being able, through Chaminuka, to foretell if there will be bumper harvest or drought as well as the coming of enemies and turning water in rivers into a bright red colour and plunging a spear into solid rock and calmly seating on it. Historically, the identity of Chaminuka is uncertain. A great deal has since been written about Chaminuka and there is much confusion between the activities of this most famous spirit medium and the spirit itself. As usual, fact and fiction, history and legend, are irrevocably blended together in what is undoubtedly one of the fascinating stories of heritage. As a spirit, Chaminuka communicated with the *Varozwi* speaking from out of trees, rocks, grass or the air as it pleased him. According to Gelfand and Abraham, the Chaminuka spirit acted as an intermediary to *Mwari* (God) with all other ancestral spirits operating at a lower level in the spiritual hierarchy.

Graves at the site

The most contentious and highly emotive issue around the custodianship of the shrine seems to revolve around the exhumation of the remains of Pasipamire, the spirit medium of Chaminuka from Ntabazinduna for reburial at the Chaminuka shrine at Chitungwiza. This issue has divided the claimant family groups such as Nyakudya, Rwizi and Pasipamire families for a long time. The process was carried out with the blessings of the ZANU PF party and some relevant authorities such as the police and the Chiefs Council involving such families as Nyakudya and Rwizi.

One of the most significant features at the site is the controversial symbolic Pasipamire's soil grave (Moyo 1983). It has been treated as highly sacred by some pilgrims to the site and some of the groups claiming to be the traditional custodians of the site. Many people have come from various parts of the country to pay their respects and offerings to the Mhondoro Chaminuka. The grave is built of stones and measures approximately 320cm x 180cm x 50cm with three different varieties of trees growing on/through it. The authenticity and appropriateness of its existence on site has been disputed by some of the members of the Rwizi clan who regard themselves as the direct descendants of Pasipamire. Although the authenticity of the grave is in doubt, the grave remains symbolic to those who pay pilgrimage to the site. There are other graves associated with Chaminuka's aides and Pasipamire's two wives. Woollacott (1975) refers to these as altars. In 1983, a Mr Mutandwa who resided at the farm and reported to have deserted homestead claiming to be possessed by the *mhondoro* of Chaminuka, referred to the graves as burials of Pasipamire's four wives.

Similar case of symbolism is found elsewhere in the world. In Japan for example in the town of Ise is a shrine called Grand Shrine of Ise. The shrine is constructed of wood and thatch and it dates back to as early as 690 AD. A decree was issued by the Empress of Japan that the shrine should be renewed every twenty years in a custom known as shikien zotai (Munjeri 2004:14). This means constructing the whole building afresh with new materials. Therefore what the shrine lacks in terms of originality, it retains in total originality in setting. The Ise shrine like Chaminuka shrine is a unique example of a living tradition where values must not be defined by criteria of materiality. However, one could also argue that the graves at Chitungwiza whether real or fictitious may have been sited to spiritualise a contested historical claim. For there are groups and individuals from Chiweshe such as Petros Muunganirwa who claim that Chitungwiza chaChaminuka is a place of traditional worship and ceremonies and not a dormitory or residential place.

Site modification and politics of association

Inflows of various people or pilgrims visiting the site for ritual purposes have been reported over the years as well as the successive occupation of the site by claimant groups of 'traditional' custodians. The site abounds with overwhelming paraphernalia left by such groups and perhaps by pilgrims to the site as well. Various groups of Independent African Churches the different sects of the so called *Mapositori* as well as African traditional religion followers visit the landscape for different reasons. Followers of Independent African Churches are 'notorious' for wanting to pray at places regarded as sacred by African traditional practitioners. Perhaps the reason for choosing sacred sites is not unusual because the Independent African Churches seem to derive their religious philosophies from both Christian and African Traditional Religious thought. Consequently, cases of confrontation abound to occur in such instances. African churches that pay homage to shrines such as Chitungwiza seem to confirm the notion that some African churches represent a critical bridge of faith between Christianity and African traditional religion. Are African Christian prophet's traditional spirit mediums using Christian language? If not, why is it that *svikiros* (spirit-mediums) become prophets or prophetess on joining the Zionist and apostolic churches and vice versa. One of the reasons for choosing sacred sites is because the Independent African Churches derive their religious philosophies from both Christian and African Traditional Religion. As a result, cases of confrontation abound to occur in such instances.

Contested landscapes

It is vital to know that the management of sacred landscapes is mired in ownership wrangles and Chitungwiza chaChaminuka is no exception. Elements of commercialization, commoditisation and authority are some of the issues that stimulate and perpetuate ownership wrangles. Custodianship of the Chaminuka spirit and of the places used by the mediums most notably Chitungwiza, have generated heated and complex contestations of memory and space. Descendants of Pasipamire whose major group seems to be the Rwizi clan in Mhondoro have been clamouring for the presiding role of all traditional ceremonies that may be conducted at the site. Although those who claim that the Rozvi descendants should oversee the Chaminuka spirit which possessed Pasipamire do not seem to obviously oppose the fact that Pasipamire's descendants have the traditional right to preside over Chitungwiza, they too wish to manipulate the intangible cultural heritage of the site to legitimise their power as evidenced by people who settled in and around the site claiming to have been brought there by Chris Pasipamire. Both the memory and space associated with the Chaminuka shrine are highly contested in terms of custodianship and legitimation of narratives.

There are various issues surrounding the custodianship of the site among traditional claimants including Chris Pasipamire, members of the Rwizi clan and farm owner (Mr. Shito). Chris Pasipamire contends that those of Rozvi descent like him are the ones responsible for the custodianship of the spirit of Chaminuka but not its mediums. Yet, those of the Rwizi people question the legitimacy of Chris Pasipamire's claims and involvement in the Chitungwiza chaChaminuka site. The first known medium of Chaminuka is Kachinda (The Patriot 14-20 December 2012). Historical accounts seem to reveal the fact that Chaminuka's medium of Pasipamire is the one who made the spirit of Chaminuka as famous as we know it today. The question that begs an answer in this regard is whether or not it is possible to separate the medium of Pasipamire with the spirit of Chaminuka in the preservation and management of Chitungwiza chaChaminuka. If the medium of Pasipamire is regarded as insignificant in the declaration of Chitungwiza, then one would wonder if the need to preserve any traditional or historical space associated with territorial spirits like Chaminuka or Nehanda would remain tenable. The important thing about heritage is that it is about relationships with the past. Heritage is what the present values in the past, and the value of the past lies in its contribution to contemporary senses of worth and identity (Sabloff 2005). Lowental (1996), a prominent academic commentator on heritage, has argued that heritage is neither history nor archaeology, because it has no need to respect accuracy of fact and can simply deal in fantasy and invented tradition that distort history.

Chris Pasipamire's claim to be custodian of the shrine came about when his car broke down near Chitungwiza. He narrated in an interview with the authors that when the car broke down Chaminuka spirit led him to the site and was told that from that encounter he was supposed to be the custodian. The breaking down of the car was incidental due to the spirit after getting to the site and returning back all was well. Heritage can be anything. The contestation of custodianship of spirit, mediums and space at Chitungwiza chaChaminuka shrine emanates from claims such as Chris'. When centres are marked as national, they should not blind people to the current relevant manifestations of the spirituality. People may focus on deifying the past losing sight of the relevant creative activity of the spirit in the present. Deifications of the past have had serious problems and developmental fallacies.

Memorialisation of Chaminuka

American writer Richard Bach once said, '*Here is the test to find whether your mission on earth is finished: if you are alive, it isn't...*'

Looking at the life of Chaminuka who was killed by the Ndebele in 1883 (Ranger 1982: 349) under their King Lobengula, it can be discerned that he was so influential that he had become a larger than life figure in his community and beyond. Many believed that he was immortal. Although Pasipamire the medium of Chaminuka was indeed mortal, the spirit lived on through the Second Chimurenga and lives on today. The death of arguably the most famous or prolific of the Chaminuka spirit ushered a period of intense contestations over both the Chitunmgwiza chaChaminuka and the very spirit itself. Some people who claim Rozvi descent like Chris Pasipamire further claim that appeasement and custodianship of the Chaminuka spirit is their sacrosanct and exclusive privilege. Chaminuka played an important role in shaping Zimbabwe's traditional religious image and he has an immortal mark on African Traditional Religion landscape in the past, present and the future. His deeds are still inspiring Zimbabweans today. Perhaps in recognition and in perpetuation of the myth or belief that Nehanda and Chaminuka were brother and sister, two of the early ZANU operational zones in the north-east were named Nehanda and Chaminuka Sectors. In the Chaminuka Sector the spirit medium of Chaminuka (whose real name was Resipina Gwerevende) worked and inspired combatants in the Chesa and Gwetera areas but was later captured at Gomo in 1973 and detained in prison until independence (Tungamirai 1995:42).

In Mozambique at Chimoio, ZANLA headquarters had one of the camp bases named after Chaminuka. The Chaminuka camp was the headquarters for all forms of security, intelligence and counter intelligence. In the poem Soko Risina Musoro published in 1958 by Herbert Chitepo, president of ZANU until his assassination in 1975, an old warrior bemoans the destruction of the land and invokes the spirit of the heroes of the old like Chaminuka and Nehanda in the poetic rhetoric. The nationalist movement named one of the spaces given to them by Tanzania government Chaminuka square. Buildings, institutions and roads have been named in apparent honour of the legendary Chaminuka. These include a building in Harare which houses some government as well as a vocational training school specialising in building and agriculture in Mt Darwin and a stadium ten kilometres from Nyamhunga in the Kariba town. In songs and myth, Chaminuka just like Nehanda came to represent the protracted struggle of Africans in Zimbabwe against colonial and other forms of oppression. Mutsvairo (1983) immortalised Chaminuka's life history in a historical novel. In many ways the legacy of Chaminuka, whether real or constructed or even imagined, has been documented quite extensively. Chaminuka's life is instructive to Zimbabweans and his role in African and Zimbabwean history is best appreciated in relation to his stature as a religious martyr (The Patriot 14-20 December 2012) hence the memorialisation in most of Zimbabwean's facet of life.

Conclusion

Memory is not merely selective, creative and even imaginative, it is also as much a process as it is a product. In essence memory is packaged and downloaded by various factors. Space gives memory physical reference and tangibility but not without controversy. It is barely surprising, therefore, that Chitungwiza chaChaminuka is a cultural landscape that is pregnant with contestations emanating from a myriad of claims and counterclaims that seek to legitimise identity, political opinions, spiritual positions, economic self-worth as well as land rights. Long after Pasipamire's death, the cultural landscape continues to give Zimbabwean society memory and the space to remember about his legendary exploits and presumably the significance of Shona spiritual heritage. Different stakeholders have different narratives on both Pasipamire the medium and Chaminuka the spirit as well as over the management and control of Chitungwiza Shrine. Living traditions unlike monuments constantly change and what remains at Chitungwiza chaChaminuka is the theatre, that is, the space, cultural material and paraphernalia that are found within the landscape as the tangible testimony of Pasipamire's history, exploits and legacy. Living traditions become heritage whether they are fact, fiction or derived from history because heritage tends to be created, recreated, consumed, even imagined and dumped by the society. Chaminuka has been immortalised in Zimbabwean heritage landscape through songs, legends, books and naming of buildings, institutions and places, not least among them, the famed Chitungwiza chaChaminuka.

References

Beach, D.N.1980. *The Shona of Zimbabwe 900-1850*. Mambo Press, Gweru

Beach, D.N. 1979. 'Chimurenga': the Shona Risings of 1896-97, In: *Journal of African History*, 20, 3, 395-420.

Bourdillon, M.F.C. 1974. Spirit Mediums in Shona Belief and Practice, In: *NADA*, XI, 1, 1974, 30-37.

Darvill, T. 2005. 'Sorted for ease and whiz'? Approaching value and importance in archaeological resource management', in C. Mathers, T. Darvill and B. J. Little (eds.), *Heritage of Value, Archaeology of Renown: Reshaping Archaeological Assessment and Significance*, Gainesville, FL: University Press of Florida.

Deacon, H. 2009. 'Intangible Heritage in Conservation Management Planning: The Case of Robben Island', *International Journal of Heritage Studies*, 10:3, 309 — 319.

Harrison, R. 2013. *Heritage Critical Approaches*, Routledge, London.

Gelfand, M. 1959. The Mhondoro-Chaminuka, In: *NADA*, 36, 6-10.

Lan, D. 1985. *Guns and Rain: Guerrillas and Spirit Mediums in Zimbabwe*, Zimbabwe Publishing House, Harare.

Lowenthal, D. 1996. *The Heritage Crusade and Spoils of History*, Penguin Books, London.

Sablooff, J. 2005. 'Public Archaeology/Memory/Conservation/Heritage', In: ed(s)

Renfrew, B. and Bahn, P., *Archaeology, The key Concepts*, Routledge, New York.

Mataga, J. 2003. Managing Intangible heritage of monuments and sites in Zimbabwe: A case study of National Museums and Monuments of Zimbabwe (NMMZ), (Unpublished MA Thesis, History Department, University of Zimbabwe).

Moyo, J. 1983. Unpublished Report on Chitungwiza Old Site (Chaminuka's Stronghold) submitted to the Monuments Department, Zimbabwe Museum of Human Sciences on 27/05/83.

Munjeri, D. 2004. Tangible and Intangible Heritage: from difference to converge, MUSEUM (Vol. 56. no.1-2), pg 221-222.

Mutsvairo, S. 1983. *Chaminuka: Prophet of Zimbabwe,* Harper Collins Publishers, Harare.

National Museums and Monuments of Zimbabwe Act, Chapter 25.11

Posselt, F.W.T. 1926. Chaminuka Wizard, In: *NADA*, 4, 35-37.

Ranger, T.O. 1974. Traditional Cults in the history of Central Africa, In: *Journal of African History*, xv, 4.

Ranger, T.O. 1982. The Death of Chaminuka: Spirit mediums, Nationalism and the Guerrilla War in Zimbabwe. In: *African Affairs*, Vol. 81, No. 324, 349-369.

Ranger, T.O. 1985. *Peasant Consciousness and Guerrilla War in Zimbabwe*, Zimbabwe Publishing House, Harare.

Rasmussen, R.K. 1979. *Historical Dictionary of Rhodesia/Zimbabwe*, The Scarecrow Press, New Jersey.

Thomas, N. 1992. The Inversion of Tradition. In: *American Ethnologist*, vol. 19, No. 2, 213-232.

Tungamirai, J. 1995. 'Recruitment to ZANLA: Building up a War Machine'. In: (ed.), N. Bhebhe and T. Ranger, *Solders in Zimbabwe's Liberation War*, Vol. 1: 36-37.

The Patriot 14- 20 December 2012, Chaminuka: A religious martyr of peace page, 15.

Woollacott, R.C. 1975. Pasipamire – spirit medium of Chaminuka, the 'wizard of Chitungwiza', In: *NADA*, xi, 2, 154-167.

Chapter 5

The Shona Folktale: An Enduring Legacy[1]

Jacob Mapara

Introduction

Shona folktale is a major component of Shona folklore and the Bantu people as a whole. It belongs to the realm of oral art forms that make up a chief constituent of the cultural heritage that has been bequeathed to Africa and the world from its progenitors. It has been handed down as a means for education and entertainment. Its educational value was also observed and acknowledged by the curriculum planners in Zimbabwean schools and colleges. This is so because folktales are also a major component of the education curriculum right from primary school up to university. Their inclusion may be a result of the realisation on the part of curriculum that folktales like other oral art forms carry vital cultural information and values. They highlight a society's major concerns. In the light of this the chapter argues that contrary to what is taught to some students studying Shona at Advanced Level and those studying oral literature in colleges and universities in the country, the folktale is not a dying art but has shown resilience. It argues that such a conclusion is rather hurried. The Shona folktale has not died but is in fact thriving. The chapter observes that the environment within which the folktale is told has changed to match the changing times that include Western influence and modern Zimbabwean politics. The folktale, like other oral art forms has defied this approach and through the artistic creativity of its reciters has continued to live through various modes and media. Those aspiring for high office at times resort to

---

[1] This chapter with the same title was originally presented at the Southern African Folklore Society (SAFOS) Conference, University of Venda, Thoyoyandou, South Africa, 28-30 September 2011.

folktales in an effort to try to gain support or tell folktales to draw attention to political foibles by some leaders. It is also in the light of the above realisation that the chapter further asserts that the story teller (*sarungano*) has evolved from being an old village woman (*Mbuya Muzavazi*) to radio and television presenters, film script writers, pre-school teachers, politicians as well as musicians and preachers. The examples that are going to be discussed in this chapter draw attention to this evolution that has taken place.

Theory of the folktale

In this chapter, much use will be made of the theories of the Russian structuralist Vladmir Propp (1958), Dundes (1964), Olrik in Dundes (1965) and Scheub (1975) in analysing the structure of folktales and its function. Although these theories are largely Eurocentric, since they focus on Indo-European folktales, they have been chosen because they have also been applied successfully in the analysis of folktales' structure not only in Europe but also in Africa, especially sub-Saharan Africa. One person who applies the Proppian approach, in combination to that of Dundes is George Fortune (1974) who confirmed that the approaches of Propp and Scheub can be utilised to analyse the Shona folktale as Moephuli and Scheub in their study of Sotho and Xhosa folktales respectively.

In his highly influential work, *Morphology of the folktale* (1958) the Russian structuralist and folklorist Vladmir Propp analyses the folktale according to its component parts or morphology. Dundes, his disciple observes that by morphology of the tale, Propp meant "...the description of the folktale according to its component parts and the relationship of these components to each other and to the whole." (Dundes, 1964: 93) Propp divides the folktale's component parts into two categories. These are given as variables and invariables. Variables are the dramatis personae or characters and items in a tale that make up the substance of each folktale. The invariables (which he calls functions) are the unchanging actions in a tale for instance the role of trickster or the success of good over evil as is the case in folktales such as "Rungano rwomukomana nherera" (The boy who was an orphan [Mufuka and Tshekeche 1985/2010: 88-96]). This role can be played by a hare or a lizard in a tale or even an underprivileged who is also despised person as happens with the case of the orphan who is in the above folktale. Propp further states:

> The names of the dramatis personae change (as well as the attributes of each) but neither actions nor functions change. From this we can draw the inference that a tale often attributes identical actions to various personages. This makes possible the study of the tale according to the function of its dramatis personae (1958: 20).

This idea that the names of the characters do change is however, contrary to what is found in the Shona folktale. What changes could be a character's fortune, but the name remains as is the case in the folktale "Chinyamapezi" (The Warty One [Fortune 1985/2010: 66-70]). The basic structural unit of Propp's theory of the folktale is the function. In a study of a hundred Russian folktales, Propp identified thirty-one major functions. He however noted that not all of these functions appear in one tale. Some of the functions are absentation, interdiction – "some command which must not be infringed, or some condition which must not be neglected" (Fortune 1985/2010: v). There are also the consequences that come after the violation. The concept of variables has important consequences for the constitution of the folktale. It boils down to the fact that the number of functions in a tale is limited and that the progression of functions in any tale does not change. Also, these functions remain constant regardless of who performs them. Finally, this means that all folktales have one and the same structure. Fortune, as already observed above has successfully applied some of these functions or characteristics of the folktale that have been propounded by Propp to the Shona one.

Nyaungwa who also relies on this theory sums up Propp's theory thus:

In a nutshell, exponents of this approach, describe the structure or final organisation of the folk-tale following the chronological order of the linear sequence of its elements. This analysis is termed the syntagmatic structural analysis. This term is borrowed from the notion of syntax in linguistics (2008: 12).

Propp's theory is very important because it has even influenced Dundes, an American folklorist. His theory is an extension of Propp's. He has been described by Oosthuizen (1977: 20) as the foremost disciple of Propp. Dundes' theory is largely inspired by Propp although he has also spiced it up with modifications of Kenneth Pike's (1954).

Dundes is the first person who noted that Propp's theory could also be applied to non-Indo-European folktales as well. He further noted that while Propp had made significant contributions to the understanding and analysis of the folktale Propp had ignored the context in which tales were told and had failed to isolate and specify the contents of his functions. Dundes' hypothesis has three main aspects. First, he says that a folktale must be studied in its social and cultural context. He calls the unit of content, the etic unit and that of structure, the emic unit. These two terms etic and emic unit were coined from the word phonetic and phonemic. An etic unit is a unit of content while an emic unit is a structural unit in a folktale. Dundes called the emic unit the motifeme, which is an equivalent feature to Propp's function. Dundes' motifeme is made up of three modes that are namely the feature, the distribution and the manifestation mode. The feature mode describes the action of the folktale characters, the manifestation mode defines the essentials which fulfil the action and the distribution mode is concerned with the place of the feature mode within the storyline.

In his analysis of the folktale, Dundes notes that motifemes come together to form motifeme sequences e.g. lack-trickery-lack liquidated. Even though Propp also observes that motifemes tend to cluster but notes functions only as pairs e.g. 'lack' coupled with "lack liquidated' Dundes goes on to further note that the following functions: interdiction, violation, trickery, complicity, lack, lack-liquidated, difficult task and solution. He, nevertheless changes some of Propp's, jargon. Dundes observes a function pair as a nucleus motifeme sequence. He further says that motifemic depth is determined by the number of motifemes intervening between the initial situation and the last motifeme. When certain sequences recur in a tale, for example in cyclic tales, then we have sequential depth.

While what Propp and Dundes' theories are significant to the study of the folktale, Msimang (1986: 13) notes that Marivate was "... among the first to establish that African tales have a fairly simple plot compared to European ones if motifemic depth is considered i.e. each tale consists of a small number of motifemes." In his study of Tsonga folktales, Marivate (1973) comes to the conclusion that notwithstanding the lack of motifemic depth the folktales have an incredible complex plot. This is largely due to a combination of the simple motifeme sequences to form a number of moves. It is these moves that result in the folktale's sequential depth. This is clearly the case in cyclic folktales. This feature of sequential depth which was first observed by Dundes is so characteristic of most if not all African folktales. This goes to explain why several academics have applied the Proppian model as modified by Dundes.

Makgamatha (1991: 22) makes an interesting observation relating to Harold Scheub. He notes that Scheub does not concern himself "... only with the structure and function of folktales, but mainly with the performer and the performance occasion, regarding the folktale as a dramatic oral art." This observation is quite insightful and informative because through it, it can be noted that Scheub emphasizes the vibrant and lively creativity in addition to the living quality of this form of art. Scheub (1975) notes the basic structural unit of the folktale as the core-image. It is this core-image that fleshes out the tale's structure. Scheub goes on to further make a note of the fact that the centre of the core-image is the core-cliché, which is itself a chant or song. During the performance of the folktale the core-image is expanded to create tensions of conflict and resolution. It is during the performance that the repetition of the core-cliché plays a significant role in moving the plot forward and in the process heightening tension and suspense in the story. According to Nyaungwa (2008: 14), "Even though the core-image has constant distinctive details, it appears more of a semantic than a structural unit." Oosthuizen (1977:109) who is quoted in Nyaungwa (2008: 14) feels the same. In disagreement she goes on to further state, "We cannot agree with Scheub that the core-image is primarily a structural unit. It is essentially a semantic unit, a unit of content, although there is admittedly a structural relevance in the fact that its distinctive details are constant" (cited in Nyaungwa 2008: 14). Notwithstanding the criticism that has been brought against Scheub's theory is very useful to the study of the Bantu folktale, more so the Shona one. It Scheub's analysis of character portrayal and theme that very is perceptive. He has managed to successfully distinguish between complex characters that are realistic and stock characters that are mostly allegoric and represent certain virtues or vices. His argument that the setting of the folktale is the real world while that of cannibals and ogres is fantastic is however questionable given the fact that the folktales' events take place in a very far away land which cannot to be located for obvious reasons.

Like the other theories that have been discussed it can be observed that Scheub's theory of the core-image is more semantic than structural. As a result, it can be observed that this theory can be applied alongside Propp's theory (which is more structural than semantic) in analysing the structure of folktales. It is in the light of this that the core images (the unit of content), although having a structural relevance, have to be chosen in relation to the pattern of function sequences in a move.

For example in the folktale, "Vakomana vaisanduka kuita shumba" (The Lion changelings [Fortune 1985/2010: 71-81]) the core image and core-cliché is the song of the boy to propel his winnowing basket so that they escape the lions and his flying low to pin wings of the night jar on one of his sisters who had always not believed him (Fortune 1985/2010: 76). In the folktale "Mukadzi nemurume" (A wife and her husband) (Fortune 1985/2010: 1-6). This folktale also influenced Tsitsi Dangarembga's film *Kare kare zvako,* (A long time ago/Once upon a time) the core – image and core-cliche are the visit to the buck and the husband's milking it after sing the song *"Sve sve bembwe, pembereka"* (Fortune 1985/2010: 2) (Sve sve buck, come out). This would be followed by a visit to a place where he would get mealie-meal and prepare his food. These core-images and core clichés are so catchy that one is reminded of the folktales once they hear them. This folktale is similar to another one called "Gore renzara" (A year of famine) (Fortune 1983: 9-11).

Another scholar who has focused on the folktale is the structuralist Axel Olrik. He is the exponent of the oral formulaic approach. While other scholars look at the performance, Olrik looks to the narrator and his performance for the key to the composition and structure of the folktale. Olrik in Dundes (1965: 129-141) posits that there are common rules for the composition and creation of the folktale. These rules he calls the epic laws. As far as he observes these laws are universal. Some of Olrik's epic laws included the law of opening and closing, the law of contrast, the law of two to a scene, concentration on a leading character, the law of repetition, the law of three, the law of single strandedness, the law of patterning, the logic of the sage, the use of tableaux scenes and the unity of plot. Canonici (1993: 17) gives opinion on Olrik and states that Olrik maintains that, "An oral narrative, as most narratives has a beginning, a body and an ending." This, as can be seen equates folktales to written prose narratives. The result is that the implication of Olrik's theory sets limits that govern the composition of folktales. A tale will consequently have a beginning, a body (made up of rising action, a climax and falling action) and a definite end. Even though this is largely the structure of Shona folktales, it does not always apply to all of them as there are some folktales that are told through song only or are largely songs (see Fortune *Ngano* Volume 4).

Like in the other theories that have been discussed in this study, this one can also be applied to the study of the Shona folktale and by extension to other Bantu and sub-Saharan folktales. In the analysis of

Shona folktale's structure it can be observed for example, that Olrik's law of opening and closing is applicable. When a folktale is told or recited, it always almost begins with a leisurely introduction which is also called the initial situation. This is where the main characters are introduced. Even at this stage, the type of relationship that exists between characters, like uncle and nephew in the case of baboon and hare is given. The folktale further unfolds by proceeding to the rise in action and beyond the climax. From there it proceeds to a point of stability and it does not end abruptly. Another rule that is applicable is the law of contrast. In this law, there is the contrasting of characters that have an encounter with each other in a tale or are related but have different traits. The examples that can be given are those of hero and villain, good and evil, the law of concentration on the leading character, the law of unity of plot and the law of repetition (manifested by repeated episodes). Some elements of these laws appear in the Shona folktale.

The folktale as verbal art

Africans are not different from any other people in the world. They have traditionally, loved good stories and storytellers and continue to do so, as have most past and present peoples around the world who are rooted in oral cultures and traditions. There are ancient writing traditions that do exist on the African continent, but most Africans today, as in the past, are primarily oral peoples, not because they are caught in a time warp, but because they like it that way since it is a cultural aspect that is so deep rooted, and resultantly some of their art forms are oral rather than literary. In contrast to written "literature," African "orature" (to use Ngugi wa Thiong'o's phrase) is orally composed and transmitted, and often created to be verbally and communally performed as an integral part of dance and music. It gives other performers to continuously create and recreate depending on their situation. As already noted above in this paragraph, it is not an indication that Africa has remained trapped in a time warp where other societies have moved on to the written word. It has remained a vibrant artistic element because in Africa storytelling is an active exchange in which the audience participates with responses, songs and at times dance. It is therefore clear that the oral arts of Africa are not just rich and varied as some scholars have observed(Agatuccihttp://web.cocc.edu/cagatucci/classes/hum211/a frstory.htm) but have their genesis in the beginnings of African cultures and continue to be part and parcel of the African cultural complexion and as such they remain living traditions that continue to evolve and flourish today.

It is important to also note that the folktale as verbal art is as well highlighted by the activities of the story-teller (*sarungano*). This is so because the success or failure of each story depends on how the *sarungano* articulates his or her verbal artistry. The *sarungano* does not just throw words, but carefully weaves a story that is informed by the immediate environment in which s/he finds her/himself in. Besides knowing where and when to throw in proverbs and other related figures of speech or bring in a song, the story-teller should also be in a position to 'read' the audience. S/he should know the composition of her/his audience. The following questions are some that are pertinent to a successful story-teller: Who is the audience? Are they youngsters only? Are they a mixed bag of both adults and youngsters? What is the situation like? Is it a funeral, church service or another type of gathering? These questions and other related ones will give guidance on how one is to employ language for the successful execution of a well-crafted folktale. Kumbirai (1983: *ii*) confirms this when he states that in the performance of a folktale, the story-teller transmits the story to the audience through his verbal art since the story's attractiveness does not only lie in its theme but also in the story-teller's linguistic resources.

Although there are some scholars who may see African folktales as not having complex plots, Kahari (1990: 110) disputes this. He asserts that *ngano* (folktale) plots are either simplex or complex. He says that a folktale has a complex plot if it includes peripeteia or reversal and recognition. If these elements are not included, then the plot is simplex (Kahari 1990: 110). This assertion is a pointer to the creativity that goes into this verbal art form. The plot of the same folktale can be simplex or complex depending on the situation. When a folktale is retold, the *sarungano*, may depending on the type of audience embellish his tale with more events and characters as well as twists and turns to make it more entertaining. In an introduction to the collection *Ngano* Volume IV, Kumbirai notes the following concerning the plot of the Shona folktale:

> The plot generally comprises a number of incidents which involves the characters, a series of linked episodes which are carefully woven around the characters. Each episode is usually an entity in itself, with its own climax followed by the beginning of the next. It is an open ended series, and the story-teller can go on adding episodes and adventure according to inclination (1983: *i*).

These words of Kumbirai echo the words of Kahari who makes reference to two types of plots in the Shona folktale – the simplex and complex ones.

Oral literature in a changing world

The world is always in a constant state of change. Because of travel and technology, the issue of cultures coming into contact and feeding into one another has become a reality. This is possibly best summed up by the Ndau proverb, *Varara veshe havanyimani matako* (Those who have shared a bed cannot deny one another their buttocks). The point of the proverb is that those who have come into contact will always impact on one another. From a cultural perspective this is clear in the sense that there are elements that are western that have been adopted by the Shona and other blacks. The same is also true of the west adopting certain ways of doing things that were originally not western, although the west always makes claim over many creations and inventions.

It is clear from the foregoing paragraph that contacts between different peoples always influence the way they carry out their activities after the contact. It will never be business as usual after each contact. This realisation rings true when we analyse the impact of technology and other western forms of cultural practices on the Shona folktale in particular and the African one in general. The impact has been positive more than negative. It has ensured that certain oral art forms such as the folktale do not die. This is further confirmed by Mapanje and White who observe:

> So far from dying under the impact of western ways, oral literature remains a vigorous art, rooted in rural communities but flourishing too in the towns. It is adapting to modern circumstances just as it adapted to and reflected change in the past (1983: 1).

Even though in their book these two scholars are writing on oral poetry, their words also ring true when applied to the folktale. Another scholar who confirms the nature of the changing environment within which oral literature is found is Vambe. He observes that advances in technology that include the introduction of writing, television; radio and film have contributed to the validation of the existence of orality in new forms. He further asserts that orality as spoken word thus exists alongside and within the structures of new technological innovations such as the novel (2001: *vii*). The researcher would like to extend this even to the short story in any language. Two examples here would suffice. They are taken from the short story anthology written by Memory Chirere (*Tudikidiki* 2007). These two are, "Pempani Pempani" (pp. 17-22) and "Chichena, chirefu, chinonhuwira" (pp. 46-50).

While Vambe is writing an introduction to the book that he edited, what he notes is also relevant in highlighting the reality of the fact that oral literature in all its various forms is not dying but is adapting to the changing and technological world. He states:

The present book also extends the meaning of orality to refer to the forms of oral genres such as myths, legends, folktales, dance, drama, speech and dialogue especially when they are realized through the electronic media such as film, television, radio or even written modes such as the novel. These, we would call secondary orality, following the lead provided by Walter, J. Ong's distinction of the orality of the spoken word (primary orality) and that which has been technologized (secondary orality) (2001: *vii*).

As has already stated, these worse are a clear pointer to the reality of the fact that oral literature is not going to suffer a fate similar to that of the dinosaur because it is constantly adjusting to its changing circumstances. This reality comes out unambiguously in some of the situations that are going to be discussed below. These include the political situation, humour through the internet, in the film industry, in songs that are recorded today as well as in religious sermons where preachers are found taping into this rich intangible cultural heritage in an effort to drive home their sermons.

Political examples of the enduring legacy

One area that has ensured that the Shona folktale continues to occupy space in people's economic and social space is the political one. Some politicians in Zimbabwe have relied on various oral literature forms to push their political agenda. One example is the use of the Shona proverb, *Zuva haribudi rimwe risati ranyura* (A new sun does not rise before the old one sets). This proverb has been used by ZANU (PF) supporters to justify why Robert Mugabe should remain in power. It is such exploitation of oral literary forms that we also see being extended to the Shona folktale. Two high profile politicians who used this form are Eddison Zvogbo and Simon Muzenda.

The late Edison Zvobgo, a Zimbabwean politician, and formerly Professor of law at Howard University is said to have told a story that most people in their wisdom or lack of it have stated relates to the current president of Zimbabwe Robert Mugabe who they perceive as unwilling to retire from active politics and hand over the political baton to a successor. In an effort to bring to the fore this reality, he tells the story of four men who are participating in a relay race. May be being the lawyer that he was, he avoided a potential lawsuit or political backlash by using this mode. Here goes the story but in this case it is a reconstruction of what was given to the researcher by an informant:

There were four men who were participating in a relay. They arranged one another according to who was going to come first, then second, the third and finally the last one. The first one then went to the starting line. This first one in the race who was given the baton made a good head start over the other competitors. However, instead of handing it over the baton to the next team mate, the first sprinter overtook his teammate, the one who was to take over from him and went out of the sports track. After doing this he ran into the Ngomahuru Mountains. Up to this time the first sprinter is still up the mountain.

The image of a mad person and the mountain Ngomahuru that are used are not mere fictive creations. They were deliberately chosen because those who know Masvingo Province, from which Zvogbo hailed, will remember that Ngomahuru is not just a mountain. It is also the name of a mental health institution. So Zvogbo, through this folktale is saying that anyone who does not adhere to the agreed political principles is as a good as a mental health patient who is being looked after at this sanatorium.

Even if it is debatable, the above story uses examples of a person who is insane to refer to as people see it, the current President of the Republic of Zimbabwe who is said to have refused to hand over power to a younger leader in his ZANU PF party. According to the website http://www.newzimbabwe.com/pages/quit41.16004.html Mugabe, "reiterated there was no vacancy for the country's

93

presidency, warning ambitious government colleagues to stop jostling to succeed him." This same position that Robert Mugabe took is also captured in another regional paper that is published outside Zimbabwe, the *Namibian* (http://www.namibian.com.na/index.php?id=28&tx_ttnews%5Btt_news%5D=34237&no_cache=1). It is clear that Zvobgo has used the folktale to draw attention to his political ambitions. In the same story he is pointing out Mugabe's unwillingness to step down. He has deliberately used the image of a mad man. Legally and culturally no one can point a finger at him and accuse him of being disrespectful of the president because he does not in any way refer to him by name. The name only comes out when people try to puzzle it out and guess who may be referred to in the folktale.

Another politician who has used the Shona folktale to gain political mileage is the late Vice President, Simon Muzenda. In a folktale that Muzenda told to party supporters at a political rally, he recited the story of a faithful family dog that guarded the family and its property for a very long time. One day the owner of the dog came back from the fields and found the dog covered in blood and thought that her son had been eaten by the dog that she had left to keep guard over. She then grabbed an axed and felled the dog. After killing the dog she went into her hut to look at the remains of her son. When she got into the kitchen she found her son lying on an animal hide mat and besides him were the remains of a venomous cobra. The bloodied dog that the woman had killed had in fact protected her son and the woman who had doubted its loyalty had killed it. (*The Sunday Mail* Supplement 18 September 2005 p. M5). Muzenda who was campaigning so that his party would get maximum support in presidential elections that were to be held that used the folktale to lambast the Zimbabwean electorate that appeared to him to have abandoned or were beginning to abandon the faithful and 'loyal' ZANU PF and embraced the Movement for Democratic Change (MDC). In this context ZANU PF is the faithful dog while MDC is the venomous cobra. Through this folktale Muzenda is also telling the electorate that even if his party appeared 'bloodied' it is because of fighting the MDC that it labelled a puppet party.

Folktales were also used during the war of liberation. An example of a folktale that was used to mobilise the masses against the Rhodesian settler whites was an adaptation of Jomo Kenyatta's story of the hunter and the elephant. In this story, the elephant got to the hunter's hut and asked for space to cover his body and protect it from the rains. The hunter told the elephant that he was too big. The two of them could not fit in the hut. The elephant then asked the hunter for space to put his head. The hunter grudgingly accepted and allowed the elephant to put in his head. As the rains poured down incessantly, the elephant pushed in a little bit. When the hunter reminded him that he was squeezing him out the elephant pleaded and said that it was only a small movement. With the passage of time the hunter was finally pushed out of his hut. This folktale was rendered into Shona and was used to show that the whites were bad guests because they ended kicking most blacks off their land. They had come into the country asking for land to build their churches as well as to mine, but in the end they kicked blacks off their land and even killed some of them, claiming that this was their land. This last example shows how the folktale has adapted to the changing political and cultural landscape. While in the traditional set up the folktales were told by old people, most women generally referred to as *Mbuya Muzavazi* (Grandmother Muzavazi [One who talks a lot) because of their wit and verbal creativity, these ones were being told by an armed guerrilla who was a political commissar. This use of folktales in issues such as politics and other related ones is best summed up by Isidore   Okpewho (http://www.forumjournal.org/site/issue/09/isidore-okpewho) who states:

> Beyond fables dealing with animals and their relationships, then, there are African tales about serious experiences in human life; the origins of a people's religious,

cultural, or cosmological traditions; or wars between peoples led by men of unusual qualities and powers.

Folktales and the cyberspace

It is interesting to note that the folktale has also gone cyber. It has adapted to this environment just as much as most youths have also embraced this new means of communication. Through the internet and on social media such as Facebook and other related ones, folktales are being circulated among friends. The following is an example of a modern folktale that is being told in the above mentioned set-ups:

> *Tsuro akapinda mushop ndokuti, "Mune macarrots?"*
> *Zvikanzi nemutengesi, "Hamuna."*
> *Mangwana acho tsuro akauyazve, "Mune macarrots?"*
> *Zvikanzi, "Hamuna."*
> *Next day akadzoka futi, "Mune macarrots?"*
> *Zvikanzi nemutengesi nehasha, "Hamuna mhani! "Ukadzoka futi ndotora*
> *zvipikiri ndokurovera nzeve kumadziro."*
> *Mangwana acho tsuro ndokuti, "Mune zvipikiri?"*
> *Zvikanzi, "Kwete!"*
> *Tsuro akati, "Ko macarrots?"*

Translation of the folktale

The following is a translation of the above folktale that has done rounds between friends on the internet:

Hare got into a shop and asked, "Do you have any carrots?" The shopkeeper responded, "We have none." The following day Hare visited the shop again and asked, "Do you have any carrots?" to which the shopkeeper responded in the negative. On the third day Hare came and asked the same question he had asked in the past two days. Then the shopkeeper responded harshly, "We do not have them. If you come back I will take nails and pin your ears to the walls." The following day Hare came and asked, "Do you have any nails?" and the shopkeeper said, "We do not have any".

Then Hare asked, "Do you have any carrots?"

The above folktale does not appear to have any moral lesson yet it highlights the folly and stiff-neckedness of some people. It is a modern folktale that teaches the importance of giving full information to clients. If the shop keeper had given information earlier on and the dates when they were likely to get carrots, s/he would not have felt bothered by Hare. It also teaches other people in service industries to avoid situations that will cause them to be perceived in a ridiculous way.

The tale also has entertainment value. In fact this folktale is being circulated among friends on the internet. This is happening because the people who are forwarding it realise its entertainment value. It is also a brain teaser. This is one clear indication that the folktale is not a dying art, but is an art that is enduring. This reality of the Shona folktale as well as other African oral art forms is well articulated in the words of Okpewho (http://www.forumjournal.org/site/issue/09/isidore-okpewho) who observes that "the survival of the African oral narrative tradition is equally guaranteed by its appropriation into traditions of modern creativity on both sides of the Atlantic."

The folktale and the film industry

The film industry has always relied on folktales. Even though the creators and critics of the film *The Lion King* argue that it was influenced by the biblical stories of Joseph and Moses, as well as William Shakespeare's *Hamlet* as McElveen states when he observes, "The work that Disney's TLK parallels is none other than Hamlet: Prince of Denmark, and the film shadows this work so closely, that parallels between the main characters themselves are wildly apparent" (http://www.lionking.org/text/Hamlet-TM.html), the influence of the African folktale on the film is very much evident. A look at the major characters of this film shows that the creators relied on the African folktales to create them. For example, the Lion is a major character in the folktales of Eastern, Central and Southern Africa. Among the Shona whether they are in Mozambique or Zimbabwe, they are referred to as *mambo wesango* (King of the Jungle). This is exactly what film goers will observe in the film *The Lion King* and its sequel *The Lion King II: Simba's Pride*. This is contrary to what is found in Europe. In Europe, the major characters in folktales, which they refer to as fairy tales are the Fox, Dwarfs, Mermaids etc.

Another character which is African is Mufasa, the baboon. This one is a major character, especially among the Shona where there are folktales such as "Tsuro naGudo" (Hare and Baboon). This is the same with Simba himself, a lion. In fact, among the Shona, the term *Shumba* is used while the term *Simba* is used among the Swahili to mean a lion. Another aspect that brings to the fore the influence of African folktales is that of the despised, downtrodden as well as outcasts overcoming obstacles as happens with Simba who manages to discover himself and reclaims Pridelands from his uncle Scar. Besides the issue of characterisation, the film also refers to the belief in ancestral spirits, which is a major religious aspect of African traditional religions. Besides the American films sponsored by giants such as Walt Disney, the Zimbabwean film industry has also borrowed from the folktale.

One script writer who has tapped in the folktale is Tsitsi Dangarembga in the film *Kare kare zvako* (A long time ago). The website http://spot.pcc.edu/~mdembrow/KARE.htm makes this clear. It states, "In her fiction, her screenplays, and her films, Zimbabwe's Tsitisi Dangaremgba frequently shows us men who are selfish bullies, taking advantage of tradition to force their will improperly upon dependent women and children. By exercising their traditional prerogatives, they destroy, or nearly destroy, that most central of traditional institutions, the family. Inevitably, though, the women and children in these stories find a way to rise up and assert themselves, often using the institutions of modernity to their advantage, and keep the family alive."

The same website states: "Blending stark, depressing realism with moments of whimsy and fantasy (including songs and dancing termites!), Dangarembga offers us an unusual, provocative mix of the traditional (Shona tales traditionally reveal didactic lessons and have sung choruses) and the post-modern." These words are another example that is a pointer to the fact that the Shona folktale is not dying.

The above case of Tsitsi Dangarembga shows that while the fireside story telling act is on the decline, the use of film and its effects as well as the inclusion of songs has helped to ensure that the folktale is sustained. In her doctoral thesis, Lizelle Bisschoff also confirms the use of a folktale in the creation of the film *Kare kare zvako*. She states that the film is based on a Shona folktale (2009: 172-3). It also has to be noted that in an interview with Lize Ehlers, Dangarembga herself confirms that she developed her film *Kare kare zvako* (A long time ago) weaving her plot around a folktale. Although she refers to the folktale as primordial, what is important is that she acknowledges use of the folktale in the making of this award winning film. She states:

> ... and I realised that basically all successful national cinemas tell the half a dozen or so great human stories that exist in the world from their particular point of view, thus providing their own particular development of the narrative of that common story and their own particular visual spectacle which is all important in film. On the other hand, the stories must be told in a way that is not so culturally bound as to make them incomprehensible to a wider audience. That is where I found that primordial forms of narratives such as myths provided the content I was looking for. So KARE KARE was an experiment: a primordial Zimbabwean story that deals with universal themes told in a

99

way that can incorporate elements of Zimbabwean cultural spectacle. I actually heard the story from my grandmother when I was very young and never forgot it, so I thought it might make a memorable film also if I developed it in the right manner (http://www.africavenir.org/index.php?id=32&tx_ttnews[tt_news]=1638&cHash=c96c4e990dcc7925f87fcdb4f8f84395).

Dangarembga also confesses to having been told the story by grandmother. This confession goes a long way in confirming that the Shona folktale has not died neither is it dying. What it is doing and continues to do is to adjust to the changing cultural space that has been affected by colonialism, neo-colonialism and lately globalisation. In some films such as *Neria* there are folktales that are told within the story. In this film, the major folktale aspect that continues to linger is the song, "Jari mukaranga."

When the above examples are looked at, instead of having the story teller imitating termites as in the film *Kare kare zvako*, the actual termites can be seen. This is different from the old set up when folktales always depended on the linguistic and extra-linguistic dexterity of the story teller. In such films, there is the use of colour effects. Another film that Tsitsi Dangarembga did that was heavily influenced by a folktale is *Peretera Maneta*. It has a theme similar to the one found in folktales such as "Pimbirimano" (The One Born out of the Knee) and Chinyamapezi (The Warty One). In these folktales, just like in Maneta, the main characters rise against all odds to get the best that their world was offering. In the case of the film *Peretera Maneta,* Maneta an albino is the one who exposes a teacher who was sexually abusing her. In this time and age when the rights of the vulnerable such as children and worse still albinos are being championed, Maneta is a real heroine.

Animation and digitisation of folktales

The world has become a global village. For nations to remain relevant in this village, there is need for countries of the South to work hard so that they also place something on the global table. This practice is not new especially to the Shona since it is well known in Shona culture that one cannot fraternize with other men at the *dare* (traditional meeting place for men in a homestead or a cluster of homes belonging to one clan), so for the countries of the South to avoid being irrelevant they have to work creatively. Some areas of creativity that they need to work on involve those that relate to the adoption and use of animation technologies. These technologies will go a long way in keeping the Shona folktale very much alive and relevant. Chimhundu points out that the issue of animation will go a long way in ensuring that such created works will have a wide audience in the region because most countries for example in Southern Africa share similar cultures and practices. In the case of folktales he notes that some of these people's folktales are the same, with the only difference being the languages in which they are narrated. Chimhundu further posits that the use of sub-titles in other languages will ensure that these folktales that would have been animated would reach a bigger audience not only in the region but also that in the Diaspora (Discussion on 16 April 2014, at Chinhoyi University of Technology).

The digitization of folktales entails the conversion of analogue information into digital information. This process is a technical procedure that is used to produces a reliable copy of any content existing in analogical form (for example a printed book) in a machine readable form. In the case of folktales, there are some that are archived at the University of Zimbabwe that are on tape. These need to be digitized so that they are not lost for use by future generations. It is therefore clear that digitization is important because it can provide a means of preserving the content of the materials by creating an accessible duplicate of the object in order to put less strain on already brittle originals that may have been in most cases under many hands and some have been broken and have been repaired using cello tape.

Schools as new platforms

Schools also play a major role in the sustenance of the folktale. In pre-schools and primary schools, the telling of folktales by both teachers and students is a major part of the curriculum. This, the researcher confirmed this when he visited the Catholic Preschool of St. Peter and St. Paul in Masvingo on 5 July 2011. He also observed a similar trend when he visited Victoria High School on the same date. At Advanced level, some creative and innovative teachers also ask their students to recite folktales. Even though they may be in a classroom situation, most of them enjoy the stories. What the schools help to draw attention to is the actuality that while the set up in which the folktale was largely told is changing, such as seasons and time of day, the reality of the matter is that this artistic genre is still very much alive.

It is important to note that from the look of things, schools are likely to continue to be the major bedrock for the perpetuation of the story-telling act because it seems most students and even some adults just love folktales. This is despite that fact that at times some people perceive those who like them as backward. In fact, the very reference to certain acts as "Ndezvana Tsuro naGudo izvo" (Those are the actions of Hare and Baboon) is in itself an indicator that even the one who would be saying those words is confirming that the folktale is still very much alive.

Folktales in music

One area where the Shona folktale has continued to show its endurance is in the music industry, although this is also evident in other types of music as Paul Clarke observes. He says, "Apart from its rhythms, another aspect of Afrobeat that Soul Jazz Orchestra has co-opted is the use of the music as a vehicle for storytelling in the

tradition   of   the   African   griots
(http://www.metro.co.uk/metrolife/233300-soul-jazz-orchestra-
fuse-70s-funk-and-afrobeat). There is amble evidence that proves
that folktales have as well been used in some music compositions,
especially in Shona music. One of Zimbabwe's star musicians,
Thomas Mapfumo has sung folktales among his songs. An example
is the song 'Nyarara mukadzi wangu' (Hush my wife) off the *12 from
5: Collection* Volume I compact disc album. In the folktale Mapfumo
tells of the success of good over evil when as woman who kept a big
snake in her granary was exposed after her daughter-in-law whom she
had got for the 'son' (the snake sang a song she had been forbade
from singing. The result is that when she had been left alone working
on the grinding stone she started enjoying her work. She then started
singing the forbidden song. The consequences of this are that her
'husband' (the snake) responded as a chorus. In the ensuing
developments that snake broke out in order to eat the woman. The
daughter-in-law then ran away but towards where there was a work-
party (*nhimbe*) and when she got there she fell down. Those working
in the fields then killed the snake and the mother-in-law as she
attempted to run away.

Another example of a musician who has done this is the late
Joseph Mutero of Zvishavane Sounds who together with this band
recorded 'Mutongi Gava' (Judge Jackal). In this story a man rescued a
leopard that had fallen into a trap (*chizarira*). Instead of going its way
after the rescue operation, it wanted to eat its rescuer. In an effort to
save his life the man appealed to passers-by. All of them except
Jackal decided that the leopard had to eat him. They possibly did this
because they wanted to save themselves. When finally the Jackal
came by, the man appealed to him to hear his case. Jackal asked the
man to go to the place where he was before he rescued leopard. He
also asked leopard to go where he was before being rescued. Leopard
went back to the trap and went. Jackal asked the leopard to explain
what the trap door was like. Innocently, leopard stated that it was
locked. Jackal asked, "This way?" Leopard replied in the positive and
Jackal locked it. He then asked the man what he was doing, to which

the man responded, "Ndange ndichiendawo zvangu kwandaga ndichienda" (I was going wherever I was going). Jackal then said to the man, "Chiendaka eyi!" (You now go). The man then left and leopard because of his being ungrateful was again left in the trap.

Another folktale that was turned into a song is one that was sung by Biggie Marasha (alias Biggie Tembo) and the Bhundu Boys. This musical group had in the 1980s a hit song that is called "Simbimbino". This song was so popular that a day would not pass by without it being played on all of the nation's four radio stations. It became even more popular among some urbanites, especially who in those years had televisions when it was played on the Thursday evening programme "Mvengemvenge" after the Bhundu Boys had become popular on their tour of the United Kingdom.

One interesting aspect about music and the musicians' contribution to the continued survival of the Shona folktale is that during live performances, the songs involve audience participation, through dancing and singing along. This is reminiscent of the pre-colonial to early colonial performances, where the act of telling folktales was not a one-sided affair but one that involved both the story-teller and the audience

The folktale as gospel parables

Other practitioners who have helped to ensure that the folktale continues to live are preachers of various denominations. This issue of preachers using folktales to preach can be confirmed by this story that was told by a Roman Catholic priest, Reverend Richard Pundo at Don Bosco Church in Masvingo, Zimbabwe on 23 October 2010. According to the priest:

> *Mumwe murume ainge asina kujaira kuenda kuchechi akambofungawo kukuenda. Asvikako, akasendeka bhasikoro rake pamadziro echechi. Pakapera chichi akawana bhasikoro rake rabiwa. Akati, "Ah! Kuuya kuchechi kunobatsirei kana vanhu vanonamata vachiba. Zviri nani ndizvigarire zvangu kubhawa kwandisingabirwi*

bhasikoro kwandajaira"/A certain man who was not used to attending church sermons decided one day to do so. He rode his bicycle and rested it on the walls of the church. After the session he went to the place he had left his bicycle and found it gone. He then declared, "Ah! If coming to church means that I will be associating with thieves who pretend to be righteous, it is better that I quit. I would rather go back to the bar where I am accustomed and where my bicycle is never stolen".

This was being used to echo what Jesus had taught in the Sermon on the Mount in the Gospel of Matthew (5: 13-16). In these two parables Jesus said to the multitude:

YOU are the salt of the earth; but if the salt loses its strength, how will its saltiness be restored? It is no longer usable for anything but to be thrown outside to be trampled on by men. YOU are the light of the world. A city cannot be hid when situated upon a mountain. People light a lamp and set it, not under the measuring basket, but upon the lampstand, and its shines upon all those in the house. Likewise let YOUR light shine before men that they may see your fine works and give glory to your FATHER who is in the heavens.

Through his illustration, the priest managed to make his message clear. The congregants learnt that they had to live and lead exemplary lives so that those who are outside the church will learn positive things from them.

This issue of using folktales to buttress religious sermons is equally confirmed by the Kenyan Ezekiel B. Alembi who observed the prevalence of the use of folktales in religious communication. He notes that in African traditions, like among the Jews, there is the use of a number of communication forms. Some of these include riddles, proverbs, songs, dance and stories. It is also important to note that

Alembi goes on to state that "these forms do not just exist for the sake of it. They have an important role to play in transmitting information" (http://www.folklore.ee/folklore/vol13/kenya.htm). He rightly points out as has been observed above with reference to the Zimbabwean situation, that, "In delivering a sermon, a church minister can combine the reading of the scripture and the explanation with a narrative" (http://www.folklore.ee/folklore/vol13/kenya.htm).

Conclusion

This chapter has raised indicators that prove that contrary to the generally held belief that the Shona folktale is a dying art, research has shown that this is very much a vibrant art. It is an art that is in fact adjusting to its changing environment. It is not a fossilised type of art but one that is adaptable. This has been proved by looking at various art genres as well as life situations where the folktale continues to show its resilience. Some of these areas include films, songs as well as church sermons. Educational centres have also played this significant role that has played a significant role in ensuring that the folktale continues to see the light of day and that the youngsters as well as some adults continue to enjoy this important feature of the nation's intangible cultural heritage. It is, therefore, the submission of this chapter that what is true of the Shona folktale is also equally true of other Bantu folktales.

References

Books, Theses and Dissertations
Bisschoff, L. 2009. Women in African Cinema: An aesthetic and thematic analysis of filmmaking by women in francophone West Africa and Lusophone and Anglophone Southern Africa, Unpublished doctoral thesis. University of Stirling.

Canonici, N. N. 1993. *The Zulu Folktale Tradition.* Durban: University of Natal Press.

Chirere, M. 2007. *Tudikidiki.* Harare: Priority Projects.

Dundes, A. 1964. *The Morphology of North American Indian Folktales* Helsinki: Folklore Fellows Communications.

Fortune, G. 1982/2010. *Ngano.* Volume 2. Harare: Mercury Press/Prestige Books.

Fortune, G. 1983. *Ngano.* Volume 3. Harare: Mercury Press.

Fortune, G. 1983. *Ngano.* Volume 4. Harare: Mercury Press.

Kahari, G. P. 1990. *The Rise of the Shona Novel.* Gweru: Mambo Press.

Kumbirai, J.C. 1983. "Introduction", in Fortune, G. (Ed) *Ngano. Volume 4.* Harare: Mercury Press, pp i-iii.

Makgamatha, P.M. 1991. *Characteristics of the Northern Sotho Folktales: Their Form and Structure.* Johannesburg: Perskor Publishers.

Mapanje, J. and White, L. 1983. *Oral Poetry from Africa: An Anthology.* Essex: Longman Group.

Marivate, C.T.D. 1973. *Tsonga Folktales: Form, Content Delivery.* Unpublished MA Dissertation Pretoria: UNISA.

Moephuli, I.M. 1972. *A structural analysis of Southern Sotho* Folktales, BA: Pretoria: UNISA.

Msimang, C. T. 1986. *Folktale influence on the Zulu novel.* Pretoria: Acacia (via Afrika).

Mufuka, R.T.C and Tshekeche, C.R. 1984/2010. *Ngano* Volume I. Harare: Harare: Mercury Press/Prestige Books.

Nyaungwa, O. 2009. Folktale Influence on the Shona Novel. Unpublished MA Dissertation: Pretoria: Department of African Languages, UNISA.

Olrik, A. 1965. "Epic Laws of Folk Narrative." In Dundes, A. (Ed) *The Study of Folklore.* Englewood Cliffs, NJ: Prentice Hall. Pp 129-141.

Oosthuizen, M. 1977. *A study of structure of Zulu folktales with special reference to the Stuart collection.* Unpublished M.A Dissertation. Pretoria: UNISA.

Pike, K. L. 1954. *Language in relation to a unified theory of the structures of human behaviour Part 1.* California: Glendale.

Propp, V. 1958. *The morphology of the folktale.* Austin: University of Texas Press.

Scheub, H 1975. *The Xhosa Nstomi.* London: Oxford University Press.

Vambe, M.T. 2001. "Introduction: Orality and Cultural Identities in Zimbabwe." In Vambe, M.T. (Ed). *Orality and Cultural Identities in Zimbabwe.* Gweru: Mambo Press. Pp vi-xii.

Discography

Mutero, J. and Zvishavane Sounds. 1988. "Mutongi Gava" off the album *Mutongi Gava* ML1032. Harare: Zimbabwe Music Corporation.

Mapfumo, T. and The Blacks Unlimited. 2000. "Nyarara Mukadzi Wangu", off the CD *12 from 5,* ZCD 186. Harare: Gramma Records.

Tembo, B (alias Marasha) and The Bhundu Boys. 2001. "Simbimbino", off the cassette *Early Hits, 1982-1986,* L4RUG1007. Harare: Gramma Records.

Internet

Agatucci, C. African Storytelling, An Introduction . http://web.cocc.edu/cagatucci/classes/hum211/afrstory.htm Accessed on 12 January 2012.

Alembi, E. Telling Tales: The Use of Oral Narratives in Religious Sermons in Kenya http://www.folklore.ee/folklore/vol13/kenya.htm Accessed on 12 January 2012

Ehlers, L. Interview: Tsitsi Dangarembga's Films & Thoughts http://www.africavenir.org/index.php?id=32&tx_ttnews[tt_news]=1638&cHash=c96c4e990dcc7925f87fcdb4f8f84395 Accessed on 19 January 2012.

McElveen, T. *Hamlet* and *The Lion King:* Shakespearean Influences on Modern Entertainment. http://www.lionking.org/text/Hamlet-TM.html Accessed on 19 January 2012.

Okpewho, I. The World of African Storytelling. http://www.forumjournal.org/site/issue/09/isidore-okpewho Accessed on 15 January 2012.

Chapter 6

Connoisseurs of traditional medicine: The use and efficacy of traditional medicine in pregnant women's health care

Jane Sigauke, Henry Chiwaura, and Munyaradzi Mawere

Introduction

Before the advent of Western science in Africa (as elsewhere), indigenous people used spiritual and herbal healing to cure ailments. In fact, the use of traditional medicine and in particular plants as drugs is known to have been prevalent for millennia now. In South Africa, for example, the use of medicinal plants by the indigenous people of South Africa dates back to the early settlement when the native Hottentots used many plant species to treat different diseases which included the use of willow species for the treatment of rheumatic fever in the Cape of Good Hope (Stone 1764; Maclagan 1876; Lewu and Afolayan 2009). In Lesotho, it is also reported that in 1897, Charles Stevens, an Englishman, was cured of tuberculosis by a Basuto traditional healer using a decoction prepared from the root of *Pelargonium sidoides* DC (see Thompson 2004). To that effect, at least 121 chemical substances are known and allegedly still extracted from plants that are useful as drugs throughout the world (Farnsworth and Soejarto 2011). Many indigenous communities of the world in Australia, Americas, Asia and Africa continue using traditional methods of treating diseases – traditional medicines. In South Africa, for example, 80 % of the South African population is said to depend on traditional medicine (Mawere 2011). The World Health Organisation (WHO) also estimates that up to 80% of the population in Africa makes use of traditional medicine (see Traditional Medicine Strategy [WHO], 2002-2005: 1). In Sub-Saharan Africa, the ratio of traditional healers to the population is approximately 1:500, while medical doctors have a 1:40 000 ratio to the rest of the population (see Abdool Karim, Ziqubu-Page, and Arendse 1994). In fact, in many African countries including Zimbabwe, Ghana, South Africa and Mozambique, traditional healers are now involved in the national system of care collaborating with western medicines in curing diseases (see also Romeo-Daza 2002). This is in spite of the fact that with the impact of western scientism and its 'sister force', globalisation, many other traditional medicines have been modified or processed to pass the logic of expert science and become modern: some traditional medicines have been modernised so to speak. It is, however, clear that in Africa (as in many indigenous communities elsewhere), the use of traditional medicine have persisted and will remain persistent owing to the fact that traditional medicine and religion are deeply connected to each other given that in traditional medical systems, disease and misfortune are regarded as having socio-religious foundations (Kazembe 2007:57). Interesting to note is that while some traditional medicines are universal in terms of their application and use, others are more specific and only used to treat different conditions related to gender. Besides, due to the influence of religious beliefs (as in the case of Christianity) and influence of westernisation, more often than not, some users of traditional medicine do it clandestinely under the cover of darkness for fear of being labelled pagan if they participate in church or not sophisticated by the modernising community (see also Kazembe 2007; personal communications 2014). Yet even colonial governments systematically tried to undermine and discredit traditional medicine but did not succeed. Traditional medicines' survival against colonial administration onslaught meant that people realised its efficacy and saw significant value in it.

This study, carried out in Chipinge District of Zimbabwe, was prompted by realisation for the need to document different types of traditional medicine used by pregnant women as the traditional medicine is part of these women's culture and by extension culture of many societies in Zimbabwe and beyond. It focuses on the use and efficacy of traditional medicine in Zimbabwe.

Micro and macro perspectives of traditional medicine

The World Health Organisation is promoting the use of traditional medicines to treat some diseases in the world as the medicine is cheap and appeals to people. This clarion call comes on the realisation that while most of the traditional medicines are strongly linked to culture of the people who use it, unlike modern medicine that is divorced from people, some other traditional medicines have proven to be cross-cultural, hence what we call "cross-cultural healings". In southern Africa (South Africa, Swaziland, Lesotho, Zimbabwe and Mozambique), for example, many people are resorting to the use of Chinese traditional medicines in the face of HIV/Aids scourge and also to deal with many other ailments that modern medicines have, over the years, failed to cure or at least is inaccessible to the users. Other scholars (Van Wyk and Gericke 2000; McGaw et al., 2005) attribute this to cultural diversity in modern day societies. Yet more others (Teshome-Bahiru 2005; LeBeau 1995) attribute this to urbanisation which has brought about new challenges and indeed increased the trade of traditional medicines. Basing on her research in the *Katutura* town of Namibia, LeBeau (1995), for instance, argued that there are new problems in urban centres that traditional healers have to confront, which were not found in the rural areas. We reiterate that it is in view of realisations such as these that organisations like WHO promote the deployment of traditional medicines in the treatment of HIV and Aids and related diseases. Most of the herbs grown are from indigenous vegetation species. By herbs, we mean medicine made from plants: "they refer to plant seeds, berries, roots, leaves, barks or flowers used for medicinal purposes" (Mawere 2011: 3). For WHO (2000), traditional medicine is the total knowledge, skills and practices based on theories, beliefs and experiences indigenous to different cultures whether explicable or not used in the presentation, diagnosis, improvement or treatment of physical and mental illness. The Declaration of Alma-Ata (1978) considers it as an essential health care, based on practical, scientifically sound and socially acceptable to individuals and families in the community and through their full participation and as a cost of that community and other countries can afford in order to self-reliance and self-determination. Traditional medicine was also defined by Mawere (2011: 3) as "the total sum of all knowledge and practices used by traditional healers in diagnosis, prevention and elimination of physical, mental or societal imbalance". Thus for Mawere, traditional medicine are diverse health practises, approaches, knowledge and beliefs incorporating plant, animal and or mineral based medicines, spiritual therapies, manual techniques and excises applied singularly or in combination to maintain well-being as well as treat, diagnose or prevent illness. It can be deduced from the preceding discussion that the use of traditional medicine includes the use of plant species and other natural materials normally found within the communities of the "prosumers" (to use Buscher's 2013 term), that is, both the users and consumers of the medicine.

One other crucial tenet of traditional medicine is that it has not been proven by the canons of expert science, regardless of their widely accepted efficacy in curing and helping stabilise people's health. Historically, women in indigenous cultures have used herbal medicine during pregnancy in order to cure pregnancy related diseases or assist with safe delivery, and for well-being (Wiley 2004). Yet, the use and efficacy of traditional medicine in maternal health has not been widely studied or even unmasked in Zimbabwe and by extension Africa (see also Fakeye et al 2009). In Zimbabwe, women use different types of traditional medicine for different reasons that may include abortion purposes, contraception, to cure irregular or painful menstruation (Vanderkooi 2006; personal communication by one of the researchers, 2014), for vagina cleansing, vagina tightening, to cure pregnant related diseases and other purposes. For pregnant women, traditional medicine has been successfully used to cure pregnant related diseases, for the upkeep of pregnant women and for the preparation of the birth canal.

Background to the use of traditional medicine in Zimbabwe

Studies of illness behaviour in many African societies (and elsewhere) have shown that traditional medicines are used in tandem with the so-called biomedical medicine to address problems that are chronic and not easily remediable by available biomedicines (see Colson 1971; Mawere 2011). Pretorious (1991: 11) makes this clear when she notes "while policy makers with the aid of international bodies such as the World Health Organisation (WHO) only recently have begun contemplating the co-ordination and integration of traditional and modem medicine, the public have been utilising both without any problems for a very long time". Elujoba et al (2001) confirm this when they argue that traditional medicine is a major African socio- cultural heritage that has been in existence for several hundreds of years. This means that traditional medicine has always played a pivotal role in providing salient diagnosis and remedy that is culturally linked to biomedicine. Health problems solved by the deployment of traditional medicine vary, and include maternal care. Yet contrary to this reality, the role played by traditional medicine especially in maternal care has been hardly recognised in biomedicine.

This research focuses on the use of traditional medicine by pregnant women in Chipinge, Zimbabwe in view of the realisation that traditional medicine has always been critical and continues to play an important role in African health care in general and Zimbabwe in particular. Traditional medicine forms part and parcel of the primary health care in most of southern African countries.

In the past (and even today in many rural communities) in Zimbabwe for example, it was considered rather a taboo for a woman to give birth without taking the medicine as doing so would lead to complications that would either kill the baby, mother or both the mother and the child (personal communication 2014). Moreover, taking the medicine was viewed as a move that would reduce labour pains and hours that would be spent by a pregnant mother in labour and also would aid in the protection of the pregnant mother and the child against evil spirits. In support of this, Vanderkooi (2006:1) notes that, "in pregnancy, herbs are normally used orally on a regular basis as a tonic to clean the womb, to attain an easy and quick delivery and in order to protect the child from evil and for the health of the child".

Apart from the above reasons other factors underlying the use of traditional medicine have been identified as pressure from family members, dissatisfaction with modern drugs, reluctance of clinic staff to give the drugs and lack of privacy within the clinic environment (Vanderkooi 2006). This connotes that while in some instances people who use traditional medicine (or herbs) are forced by circumstances, in others traditional medicine is taken out of choice.

Given the shift from the use of the traditional medicine to modern medicine administered by health practitioners, we found it prudent to document the different types of traditional medicine used by pregnant women for the future generation to benefit from the wealth of their culture. The herbs (and/or traditional medicine) that are normally used by pregnant women in the Chipinge, Manicaland Province of Zimbabwe, include leaves of musavamhanda plant *(Sansevieria Pearsonii)*, ruredzo plant *(Dicerozanyum zanguebarium)*, elephant faeces, mupfuta tree *(Ricinus communis)*, mufenje *(Diospyros mespiliformi)*, mushani *(Lippia javanica)*, chifumuro *(Dicomaanomala)* and many other tree species. The medicines are traditionally administered by elderly people in the family. As shall be discussed in detail later in this chapter, these include, but not limited to, mother-in-law to daughter-in-law, a mother administering to her daughter and a grandmother treating her granddaughter. Herbs used by pregnant women largely fall under the preventive category that is medicine given to women to guard against illness before conceiving (Chavunduka 1994:76; Mupfumira 2012; Pallivalappila et al 2013). This therefore means that traditional medicines are used to prevent pregnant related diseases and to deal with other such conditions.

The enduring legacy of traditional medicine

Despite strenuous efforts by colonial governments, during colonial period, to despise and ban the use of traditional medicine in Africa, the deployment of traditional medicine has persevered through time. Even efforts by some biomedicine protagonists after the demise of colonial administration to de-campaign and discredit traditional medicine on the grounds that it is unscientific and "dirty" have proven fruitless. This is exemplified by the high percentage of the African population that still rely and depend on traditional medicine for their health care. WHO (2008), for example, revealed that in Africa up to 80% of the population relies on traditional medicine for their primary health care needs. According to the same source (WHO 2008), even the world-over, out of the total of 4, 22,000 flowering plants reported [from the world] more than 50,000 are used for medicinal purposes. In India more than 43% of the total flowering plants are reported to be of medicinal importance (Alves and Rosa 2007). Furthermore, from the survey conducted by Kaingu et al (2011) in Nigeria with 1200 pregnant women, it was revealed that 12% of them used traditional herbs, and in South Africa out of 229 women interviewed 55% had used herbal medicine during pregnancy and have testified that they are effective in reducing pregnant related complications. In Uganda and Ethiopia, it is also estimated that 80 % of the population use traditional medicine (see Mussema 2006; Birhan, Giday and Teklehaymanot 2011). At world scale, 65 – 80% of the world population uses traditional medicine as their primary form of health care (see WHO 2003; Forster et al 2006; Hashem et al 2012).

The abovementioned statistical data clearly demonstrate that despite the resistance by western science or biomedicine to recognise other knowledge forms and medicines from other cultures, traditional medicine remains the most consumed medicine the world-over. Reasons for this are many. As Maroyi (2013) rightfully argued traditional medicines are widely used because they are available naturally and abundantly, and also they are the most affordable and easily accessible source of treatment in the primary health care system in indigenous communities and the developing world. Apart from affordability and local availability, the medicines are used because they are more acceptable from the cultural, social and spiritual perspective. This is one other reason why majority of the traditional herbal medicines used in Africa are provided by practitioners who live within the communities, have been trusted over time, and are often willing to assist the patients with their knowledge, skills and sometimes at minimal costs to the patience (Tamuno, Omole and Fadare 2002). To sum up all the reasons elaborated so far in this chapter, Elujoba et al (2012:3) note that, "the other reason why traditional medicine continue to be important to the society is because they are close to the people and also the administers of these traditional medicine live with the people and they provide the health care services in the same communication unlike the western type of health institutions that are out of reach of most people in terms of distance and costs especially at a village setting".

More so, traditional medicine continues to be used by the people because even not scientifically proven it has demonstrated its efficacy to cure diseases. Elujoba, et al (2012) captures this aptly when they say that African people have used traditional medicine to combat disease affecting the health of their families since the beginning of the existence of humanity on the continent. It was the only form of medicine used for prevention, diagnosis and treatment of social, mental and physical illness. Although it is considered a backward and unscientific practice, traditional medicine in Africa was always used before and during the colonial era and has continued to thrive even after colonialism and its associated forces such as globalisation not only because it is practically effective but also because it is culturally acceptable by the African population. Basing on his studies in South Africa, Mawere (2011) notes that it had been estimated that in South Africa, between 60% and 80% of the population currently rely on the traditional medicinal sector as their first contact for advice and treatment of health concerns. In fact, the use of traditional medicine in both developed and developing countries is on the increase. This is confirmed by a report by WHO (2000) which notes that:

> Trends in the use of traditional medicine are on the increase in many developed and developing countries. In Australia in 1998 about 60% of the population used complementary medicine and 17000 herbal products. In 1992 20million patients in Germany used homeopathy, acupuncture as well as chiropractic and herbal medicine as the most popular forms of complementary medicine. In Malaysia it is estimated that about as 500million is spent every year on traditional medicine compared to only about 300million on modern medicine. In Sri Lanka 50-60% of the population rely on traditional medicine and traditional attendants. In Benin and Sudan 70% of the population rely on traditional medicine while in Uganda traditional medicine make up 30% of the population. In Ghana, Mali, Nigeria and Zambia 60% of the children with fever were treated with herbal medicine at home in 1998.

Thus from the trends above it is clear that traditional medicine is important in the primary health care of people.

In Africa, the use of traditional medicine is also largely a result of the ubiquity of plant species with medicinal properties (Van Wyk and Gericke 2000; McGaw et al., 2005). In Zimbabwe, for example, Maroyi (2013) notes that out of more than 5000 plant species growing in Zimbabwe about 10% of them have medicinal properties and are used as traditional medicine to cure different diseases. The diseases cured include diarrhoea, liver disorders, amoebic dysentery, constipation, cough, eczema, ulcers, hypertension, diabetes, malaria, mental health, HIV and AIDS and many more examples (see also WHO 2000; Forster et al 2006; Hemminki et al 1991; Orief et al 2012). This really shows how traditional medicine is widely available in dealing with different ailments and health related conditions.

It goes without mention that in as much as traditional medicines are important in curing different types of diseases, they [traditional medicines] have been also used by pregnant mothers to cure pregnant related diseases and for the upkeep of their health. One of the eight millennium Development goals (MDGs) adopted by Zimbabwe is "to improve maternal health", besides eradicating poverty and hunger; achieve universal primary education; promote gender equality and empower women; reduce child mortality; combat HIV and AIDS, malaria and other diseases; ensure environmental sustainability; and develop a global partnership for development (see Zimbabwe MDG Progress Report 2012). Maternal health is considered as one of the MDG on the realisation that pregnancy remains one of the major health risks for women in many parts of the world (see Hashem et al 2012). In fact, as noted by Mutambara et al (2011), women suffer from a wide range of birth complications and a pregnancy that has progressed without any apparent hitch that can still be experienced during child birth.

In the African context and in particular Zimbabwe, traditional medicine in pregnancy and labour continues to play, as it did in the past, an important role in the health systems. This is partly a result of the Zimbabweans' close attachment to their culture and also the socio-economic problems that the country is suffering since the beginning of the millennium. In pregnancy, herbs are normally used orally on a regular basis as a tonic to clean the womb, to attain an easy and quick delivery and in order to protect the child from evil and to have a health child. Other factors underlying the use of traditional medicine have been identified as social pressure, dissatisfaction with the modern medicine, reluctance of clinic staff to give drugs and lack of privacy within the clinical environment (Vanderkooi 2006; personal communication 2014).

Research questions and methodological issues

This study was carried out in Chipinge urban District in February 2014. Chipinge urban District heretofore referred to as Chipinge urban was identified for research for the major reason that the district is generally believed to be home of large numbers of traditional practitioners in Zimbabwe, and hence it was assumed that they might have an influence on expecting mothers' health.

A total number of 20 women from across Chipinge urban were approached and kindly asked to participate in the research. From the total number of women selected randomly to participate in this study, half (50 %) of them admitted that they have used traditional medicines either in their previous or present pregnancy. As such, the sampled women were divided into two groups. The first group (Group 1) comprised of women who claimed to have used traditional medicine and the second group (Group 2) comprised those who claimed to have never used traditional medicine in their pregnancies. The first group to be interviewed were the first ten women who admitted having used traditional medicine during their present or previous pregnancies. This group were interviewed in order get answers on the names of traditional medicines that they use during pregnancy and how the medicines were administered as well as their healing effect.

From the first group, 5 women of young to middle age, that is, of between the ages of 25 to 40 were interviewed. This age group was chosen because most of the women in the group are still sexually active or still give giving birth. The group was very useful in revealing types of traditional medicine still in use and the impact of the medicines on the health of a pregnant woman. Those from 40 years of age and above were interviewed because some of them were believed to have used (or still using) and administered traditional medicines either on their daughters or daughters-in-laws. 5 elderly women aged 60 and above were also interviewed for the same reason and also in order to have some examples of the traditional medicine that they used during pregnant that might be no longer used by the present generation. The elderly were also believed to be custodians of culture such that they were expected to herald information on whether there is continuity and change in the way traditional medicine for expecting mothers is used.

The second group comprised those who confessed to have never used traditional medicine during their previous or present pregnancies. This group was interviewed in order to solicit answers on why they were not using traditional medicine, whether they once used or administered traditional medicines before, and if yes why they have stopped using traditional medicines. In other words, this group was interviewed to solicit answers on the changes experienced over the years in pregnancy and delivery system in Chipinge as in many other societies in Zimbabwe and beyond. See table 1 below which shows participant demographics for this study:

Age Group	Number	Reason for choosing the sample population
25-40	5	Women chosen are still giving birth and confessed using traditional herbs
40+	10	The women once used traditional medicine but have since stopped
60+	5	This group of women were believed to have at least used or administered traditional medicines. They were the key informants on the types of traditional medicines and how they were used in the past.

Table 1: Participant demographics

Research findings and discussion

This study has shown both the use and disuse of traditional medicines by pregnant women in Zimbabwe. For instance, some women claimed to have used, never used or once used (but have since stopped) traditional medicines. The variations in the use (or disuse) of traditional medicines were explained in terms of religion (or changing belief systems), availability (unavailability) of modern medicine, trust (or lack of trust) in health care personnel in modern hospitals, accessibility (or non-accessibility) of modern medicines, and compatibility (or incompatibility) of traditional medicines with one's culture.

Whatever the case, it has been revealed in this study that traditional medicine has always been used by indigenous communities across the world and forms the basis of peoples' heritage. It has revealed, for instance, that traditional medicines have always been used for different purposes that include curing diseases, boosting immune systems, diagnose conditions and diseases linked to culture, and for maternal health care. We have shown that traditional medicines though haven't passed the canons of western science, in many cases clinical tests have proven traditional medicine to be effective, besides its enduring efficacy among traditional communities of the world. In view of the research area for this study, Chipinge District of Zimbabwe, it was noted that the medicine is used to reduce labour pains, labour complications, and pains after labour, back problems, dilate birth canals, addition of iron and guard against evil spirits that haunt pregnant mothers. From the results obtained it was revealed that most women who use these medicines have them administered by their mothers, their mothers-in-law or grandmothers. The women who acknowledged using traditional medicine confessed that it is of great significant in easing complications that are associated with child birth, hence we argue for the full recognition of traditional medicine in health care and to be used as a complement of modern medicine. This would help immensely in easing the tapestry of health problems especially in developing countries were biomedicine is very expensive and far beyond the reach of the poor.

Group 1

The five participants from group 1 which comprises those women who claimed to have used traditional medicine explained types of traditional medicine they use during pregnancy and their effects to the health of the pregnant woman and the unborn baby. Some of the reasons given by women who use traditional medicine are that it is affordable and locally available. Besides, traditional medicine was considered as part of their cultural practices that have always been effective and in use for centuries now. For these reasons, the women had faith in the medicine. One of the respondents, for instance, remarked "traditional medicine is very effective. Our grandmothers used it without any problem. Our mothers also used it successfully. Now, it's us which means that traditional medicine is effective". One other important point highlighted during research is that those who administer traditional medicine are familiar (and in fact a family member in most cases) to the women to which the medicine is being administered, hence confidentiality cannot be compromised in these cases. It was further revealed by this group that lack of adequate drugs in clinics, mistrust of nurses also leads to the women using traditional medicine within familiar environs. The names of the medicine, its administration form, duration and time of use in pregnancy was recorded as it was explained by the respondents. From the interview, the researchers were furnished with the following names of traditional medicines used in pregnancy: mupepe tree (*Commiphora marlothii*), mupfuta tree (*Ricinus communis*), mufenje tree *(Diospyros mespiliformi)*, mushani tree (*Lippia javanica*), chifumuro (*Dicomaanomala*), dhinda/derere grass (*Corchorus tridens*), muembe (*Annona senegalensis*), demamhandwe/devereamvumi (*Adenia cissampeloides*), mupupu/mufufu (*Securidaca longepedunculata*), mavhuenhuta (mole rat soil) and ruredzo grass (*Dicerozanyum zanguebarium*).

Below is a table (table 2) that shows the name of the medicine, how it is administered, time of administration, duration, and the medicinal effect of each medicine cited above.

Botanical/ Scientific Name	Shona Name	Administration method	Time of administration	Duration of administration	Therapeutic/Healing effect
Ricinus communis	*Mupfuta*	The leaves are boiled and inserted in the birth canal	From the seventh month	Up until day of delivery	It dilates birth canal.
Commiphora marlothii	*Mupepe*	The barks are put in cold water and taken in when now slippery	From the seventh month of the pregnanc-y	Up until the day of delivery	It dilates the birth canal.
Diospyros mespiliformi	Mufenje	The roots are put in cold water and the water is drank	During the early months of pregnanc-y	Until the day of delivery	It reduces labour pains.
Lippia javanica	*Mushani*	The roots are boiled in water and the water is drank	Continuo-usly from the day of conceptio-n	No time limit	It cures whooping cough on the unborn baby.

Dicomaanoma l-a	*Chifumu-ro*	Roots are tied on a cloth and the cloth is wore everyday	Continuo usly from the day of conceptio -n	Up to the day of delivery	It guards against evil spirits that can cause miscarria -ges.
Dicerozanyum zanguebarium	*Ruredzo*	The leaves are inserted into the vagina	During the eighth month of pregnancy	Regularly until birth	It dilates birth canal and expulsio- n of placenta.
Corchorus tridens	*Derere/ Dhinda*	The whole plant is inserted in water then the water is drank or wash the hands in the water and insert the hand in the vagina	Starting from the fifth month of pregnancy	Continuo usly until birth	It dilates birth canal.
Annona senegalensis	*Muembe*	The roots are chewed	Regularly from the time of conceptio	Regularly until birth	It reduces labour pains.

			n		
Adenia cissampeloides	*Demamh andw-e/ Deveramv -umi*	The bark is put in water then drink the water	Regularly from the time of conceptio-n	Regularly until birth	Adds iron in the pregnant mother's body.
Mole rat soil	*Mavhuen-huta*	The soil is put in water and is drank	Regularly from the time of conceptio-n	Regularly until birth	Adds iron in the pregnant mother's body and reduce labour hours.
Securidaca longepeduncul at-a	*Mupupu/ Mufufu*	The roots are put in water for a day and the water will form foams which will be used when bathing	Regularly from the time of conceptio-n	Regularly until birth	It guards against evil spirits that can cause miscarriages.
Sansevieria deserta	Mushaya mha-nda	Rhizomes are added to non-alcoholic beverages taken by the pregnant woman	During the seventh month of pregnanc-y	Up until time of birth	To prepare birth canal and prevent delivery. complication-s

Table 2: Traditional Medicine administered

Group 2

Three of the women who claimed to have never used traditional medicine during pregnancy noted that they do not believe in taking traditional herbs since they did not trust the people who administer the medicine to them. Witchcraft practices were noted as one of the major reasons for this mistrust. Low level of education among some of those who administer the medicines was another reason for mistrust given during research. This raised worries in other women who were afraid of the after effects of the traditional medicine especially that there is no specific dosage from the traditional administers (of the medicine) who sometimes also lack of hygiene in their practices. However, from the interviews done, most women noted that they fear to be witched by the administers for different reasons which ranged from having grudges and not being in good relationship with their mother-in-law or grand mothers who are in the position to administer these medicines. Thus, they prefer going to hospital where there are maternal health carers not familiar to them.

Ten other women claimed to have never (or stopped) using herbs because of their religious convictions. These women noted that it was not acceptable in their religions to use traditional medicine which is administered by traditional healers or any other person as they said they trusted in God thus have to pray and not to mix with herbs. When asked for a change in the pain experienced by those taking herbs and those not taking herbs, the respondents believed that if you trust in God all the pain is eased in the same way it can while taking herbs. However, 2 of these women (who have now stopped using traditional medicine because of religion) confessed that they experienced a change in pregnant related pain when they used traditional medicine but because of religion they have no option except stop using traditional medicine. The women noted that during their first two pregnancies in which traditional medicine was used no complications were noticed. But the last pregnancy when traditional medicine was not administered on them complications set in that included induced baby delivery.

Recommendations and conclusion

This chapter has demonstrated the continued wide use and efficacy of traditional medicine in Zimbabwe and other societies the world over despite the fact that it [traditional medicine] once suffered pejorative labelling and caricature from colonialism and western science. The continued use of traditional medicine has been witnessed by the respondents interviewed by the researchers who in fact admitted the use of traditional medicine for maternal care by many women in the community where this research was carried out. From this observation, we have argued in this chapter that traditional medicine remain important in curing different types of diseases and conditions including helping pregnant women in rural and urban communities alike.

Given that traditional medicine remain an integral part of many people in Zimbabwe (and even beyond), we recommend that the Zimbabwean government should promote and support the use of traditional medicine as complementary medicine in health care. This could be done by fostering the recognition of multiple ways of knowing, disease diagnosis and cure and registering both traditional healers and prophets as qualified health care givers. Different religious sects and the community at large should be educated on the efficacy of traditional medicines as they have proven to be effective in helping in the reduction of pregnant related complications (and many other such problems) as evidenced by the results of the present study. In other words, although it should be underlined that inadequate reproductive health skills among health organisation providers, long distance to health facilities and other cultural beliefs are some of the contributing factors that have made people to continuously use the traditional medicine, the fact that people trust that even in the presence of modern ways of treatment they can turn to traditional ones means that traditional medicine are equally as modern medicine.

We, therefore, conclude that different types of herbs used during pregnancy need to be documented so that future generations will benefit by using traditional medicine. Failure to document them especially in the face of westernisation and globalisation will always impact negatively on the future generation who in no doubt would be deprived of enjoying the fruits and richness of their cultural heritage. Thus while the Zimbabwe government has so far taken stride towards that direction through the formation of a traditional healers association that issues out practising licences to registered traditional practitioners, a lot more still needs to be done in terms of documenting traditional medicines used to boost human immune system, cure different diseases, and solve health-related conditions such as pregnancy complications.

References

Abdool Karim, S. S., Ziqubu-Page, T. T., and Arendse, R. 1994. Bridging the Gap: Potential for a health care partnership between African traditional healers and biomedical personnel in South Africa, *(supplement) SAMJ* 1994; 84 s1-s16.

Aleves, R.R and Rosa, L. 2007. Biodiversity, traditional medicine and public health: Where do they meet? Journal of Ethnobiology – Ethonomedicine 13 (14): 15-26 Available at http://www.ethonobiomed.com/content/3/1/14. (Accessed: 01.03.14).

Birhan, W., Giday, M., and Teklehaymanot, T. 2011. The contribution of traditional healers' clinics to public health care system in Addis Ababa, Ethiopia: A cross-sectional study, Journal of Ethnobiology and Ethnomedicine 2011, 7:39. Available at: http://www.ethnobiomed.com/content/7/1/39. Accessed 27/04/2014).

Buscher, B. 2013. Prosuming conservation, *A Paper Presented to the Department of Sociology*, University of Cape Town, South Africa (presented 25/02/2013).

Chavunduka, G. L. 1994. *Traditional Medicine in Modern Zimbabwe*, University of Zimbabwe Publications, Harare.

Colson, A. 1971. The differential use of medical resources in developing countries, *Journal of Health and Social Behaviour* 12, 226.

Declaration of Alma-Ata. International Conference on Primary Health Care. 1978. Alma-Ata, USSR, 6-12- Available:

www.who.inte/publications/almaata-declaration-enpdf. Accessed on 17-02-2014.

Fakeye, T. et al. 2009. Attitude and use of herbal medicines among pregnant women in Nigeria, *BMC Complementary and Alternative Medicine*, 9: 53.

Elujoba, A.A, Odeleye, O. M and Ogunyemi, C. M. 2012. *Traditional Medicine Development for Medicinal and dental Primary Health Care and Delivery system in Africa*, Department of Pharmacognosy, Faculty of Pharmacy, University of Ife Ife Nigeria.

Farnsworth, N. R. and Djaja, D. Soejarto. 2011. *Global importance of medicinal plants*, College of Pharmacy, University of Illinois at Chicago.

Forster, D., Denning, A., Wills, G., Bolger, M., and McCarthy, E. Herbal medicine use during pregnancy in a group of Australian women, *BMC Pregnancy Childbirth* 2006; 6: 21 - 30.

Hashem, D. F., Abdollahi, F. M., Shojaei, A., Kianbakht, S., Zafarghandi, N., Goushegir, A. 2012. Use and attitude on herbal medicine in a group of pregnant women in Tehran, *Journal of Medicinal Plants*, 11 (41): 22 33.

Hemminki, E., Mantyranta, T., Malin, M., and Koponen, P. 1991. A survey on the use of alternative drugs during pregnancy, *Scand. J. Soc. Med.* 19: 199 - 204.

Kaingu, K. C, Oduma A. J and Kanui T. 2011. Practices of Traditional Birth Attendants in Machakos District, Kenya, *Journal of Ethno pharmacology Elsevier Vol10 (106) 5-8*Ireland. Nairobi.

Kazembe, T. 2007. Traditional Medicine in Zimbabwe, *In The Rose+CroixJournal*, Vol.4: 55-72 Available:www.rosecroixjournal.org.

LeBeau, D. 1995. Seeking health: Models of health care and the hierarchy of resort in utilisation patterns of traditional and modern medicine in multi-ethnic Katura, Namibia, *PhD proposal presented to Rhodes University*, Grahams Town: South Africa.

Lewu, F. B. And Afolayan, A. J. 2009. Ethnomedicine in South Africa: The role of weedy species, *African Journal of Biotechnology* 8 (6): 929-934.

131

Maclagan, T. 1876. The willow as a remedy for acute rheumatism, *Lancet* 1: 910.

Maloyi, A. 2013. Traditional use of Medicinal plants in South Central Zimbabwe, Review and Perceptive. *A journal of ethno biology and ethno medicine Vol9 (31):1-18*. Available: http//www.ethnobiomed.com/content/9/1/31. (Accessed on 17 -02-14).

Mawere, M. 2011. Ethnical quandaries in Spiritual healing and herbal medicine: A critical analysis of the morality of traditional medicine advertising in Southern African urban societies, *The Pan African Medical Journal*, 10(6):1-6. Available at: www.ncbi.nlm.nih.gov/pmc/articles/pmc3282931. (Accessed on 17-04-14).

McGaw, L. J., "Ager, A., Grace, O., Fennell C., and van Staden, J. 2005. Medicinal plants. In: van Niekerk, A. (Ed.), *Ethics in Agriculture—An African Perspective*, Springer, Dordrecht, The Netherlands, pp. 67-83.

Mupfumira, R. 2012. An assessment of African traditional medicines in pregnancy and on birth control outcomes: Pharmacists' perceptions of complementary medicines in pregnancy, *Master of Pharmacy Thesis*, Rhodes University, Grahamstown: South Africa.

Mussema, Y. 2006. A historical overview of traditional medicine practices and policy in Ethiopia, *Ethiopia Journal of Health Development* 20 (2):127-134.

Mutambara, J., Maunganidze, L., and Muchichwa, P. 2013. Towards promoting maternity health: the psychological Impact of obstetric Fistula on women in Zimbabwe, *International journal of Asian Social Science 3(1) :229-239*. Available http://www.accessweb.com/jounal-detail-php (Accessed on 17-02-14).

National policy on traditional medicine and regulation of herbal medicines, Report of World Health Organisation global survey, 2005. Geneva – Primary Health Care, Available at www.int/report/geneva Accessed: 17.02.14.

Odeoga, H.O, Okwu, D.E and Mbaebie, B.O. 2005. Phytochemical constituents of some Nigerian Medicinal Plants. *African Journal of Biotechnology Vol. 4(7)*: 1-9.

Orief, Y, Farshayi, N and Ibrahim, M 2012. Biodiversity, traditional medicine and public health: where do they meet? *Journal of EAthnobiology-Ethomedicinevol 5(3) 1-9.*

Pallivalappila, A., Stewart, D., Shetty, A., Pande, B., and Mclay, A. 2013. Complementary and Alternative Medicines use during pregnancy: A systematic review of pregnant women and healthcare professional views and experiences, *Evidence-Based Complementary and Alternative Medicine*, pp. 1-10. Available at: http://dx.doi.org/10.1155/2013/205639.   (Accessed 23/04/2013).

Pretorius, E. 1991. Traditional and modern medicine working in tandem, *Curationis* 14 (4): 10-13.

Stone, E. 1764. An account of the success of the bark of the willow in the cure of agues, *Philosophical Transactions* 53: 195-200.

Tamuno, I, Omole-Ohonsi, A and Fardare, N. 2009. Use of Herbal Medicine among Pregnant Women attending a Tertiary Hospital in Northern Nigeria, *The Journal of Gynaecology and Obstetrics* 12 (2): 1-5.

Teshome-Baahiru, W. 2005. Impacts of urbanisation on the traditional medicine of Ethiopia, *Anthropologist* 8 (1): 43-52.

Thompson, J. 2004. African folk remedy chases colds away faster, *Health Sci. Inst* 8: 7-8.

Traditional Medicine Strategy 2002-2005, World Health Organisation, Geneva, WHO/EDM/TRM/2002.1.

Vanderkooi, R. 2006. Traditional medicine in late pregnancy and labour: perceptions of Kgaba remedies amongst the Tswana in South Africa, *African Journal of Traditional, Complementary and Alternative Medicines. African Ethno medicines Network. Vol. 3(1):1-22.*

Van Wyk, B. E. and Gericke, N. 2000. *People's Plants: A Guide to Useful Plants of Southern Africa*, Briza Publications, Pretoria.

Wiley, J. 2004. Natural theory and Community Ecology, *A European Journal 10(2): 4947-5159* Neville Compton.

World Health Organisation. 2000. Regional Office in Africa. Promoting the role of Traditional Medicine in the Health System, *A strategy for the African Region: Fifthieth session,* Ouagadougou, Burkina Faso.

World Health Organisation, 2003. *Fact sheet N134: Traditional medicine.* Available online at:[http://www.who.int/mediacentre/factsheets/fs134/en]. (Accessed on 26/04/2014).

Zimbabwe Millennium Development Goals Progress Report, 2012. Harare: Zimbabwe. Available online at: www.zw.one.un.org/millenium-development-goals.

Chapter 7

Traditional dance as intangible heritage: In defence of the perpetuation of traditional dance and music in Zimbabwe

Tapuwa R Mubaya and Shadreck Dzingayi

Introduction

Throughout history and in many cultures of the world, social needs have been reflected in traditional dance forms. Africa is renowned for its rich musical traditions, through its dances, vocal styles and instrumentations (Maonera 2007; Mataga 2008). The traditional dance and music have always been instrumental in addressing issues affecting and bedevilling society. It has always been the case that in countries with strong oral traditions such as Zimbabwe, dance and music play an integral role in the lives of the people (Maonera 2007; Mataga 2008). In Zimbabwe for instance, traditional dances and performances such as Jerusarema are still important living traditions practiced in many contexts and still revered by local communities. Dance and music have evolved to become indicators of a nation's tradition, identity and uniqueness. As such, dances may be performed for a variety of purposes among them is enjoyment, educating, and entertainment. These dances may also be performed at religious ceremonies, rituals, festivals and for commemoration and celebrations (Badejo and Banerji 2002; Mataga 2008). Traditional dance therefore occupies a central role in economic, political and socio-cultural systems in African traditional society (Mataga 2008).

Dance and music fall under the broad category of performing arts. In Zimbabwe music and dance has since time immemorial been playing a pivotal role in inculcating traditional norms and societal values to the members of the community. This role survives to the present day manifested in several performances that have stood the test of time and alien influences (Mataga 2008). Scholars who carried out research on Zimbabwean traditional music and dance came to the conclusion that traditional music and dance was an integral aspect of their everyday life (Merriam 1982; Berliner 1993; Hassam 2012). In light of the above, traditional music and dance is an inherent component the different Zimbabwean ethnic group cultures which largely meshed into their personal lives, social organisation, economic life, religion, as well as their political life and history. Against this background, Zimbabweans have differing traditional music and dance that they practice and hold in high esteem. The various types of music and dance emanated from the divergent ethnic cultural groups that constitute the modern day state of Zimbabwe. As a unique form of cultural expression, these dances are an essential facet of heritage and should therefore be preserved for posterity.

Currently, due to a multitude of factors, different forms of dance and music have been negatively affected by the strong tide of globalisation which has strongly swept through the country particularly in the 21st century. As a result, they are mostly performed in rural areas, farms and townships mostly by school children and some selected groups which have formed their own dancing groups as the majority of the people have abandoned them in preference of Christianity an appendage of colonialism and globalisation. It is also disheartening to note that traditional music and dance have not been spared by rural to urban migration.

From the foregoing, the chapter argues for the conservation of the already existing forms of traditional music and dance which have survived the test of time and the influence of post-colonial cultural imperialism. If properly maintained, documented and packaged as cultural products traditional music and dance can be used to enhance and promote cultural tourism in Zimbabwe. The chapter presents a general outline of some of the traditional dances found in different parts of Zimbabwe. It is important to note that one of the Zimbabwean dances Mbende/Jerusarema has been listed on UNESCO's representative tentative list of Masterpieces of oral and intangible heritage of humanity making it one of Africa's few cultural expressions to be accorded such recognition (Mataga 2008). This dance has been passed down through many generations and remains one of the most important traditional performances in contemporary Zimbabwe. As a result of its importance, the dance is no longer restricted to the community in Murehwa but has been adopted by the Shona and non-Shona groups, urban-based dance clubs and traditional performing groups for tourists, political gatherings and other social events (Mataga 2008).

A closer look at Zimbabwean ethnic dances

Zimbabwe is one of the countries in Southern Africa rich with various forms of traditional music and dance. Dance and music constitute an important aspect of African identity in general and Zimbabwean ethnic cultures in particular. Songs and dances in the past despite being vehicles of communication between the living and the dead played a fundamental role in the religious life of the people. Zimbabwe is a multicultural society which is inhabited by numerous ethnic groups. The Shona people who are made up of the Manyika, Karanga, Korekore, Zezuru, Ndau and Kalanga linguistic groups are a dominant ethnic group in Zimbabwe (Asante 2000: 20). The Ndebeles are another ethnic grouping that occupies the greater part of western Zimbabwe. Other ethnic groups found in Zimbabwe include the Venda, Tsonga, Shangani, BaTonga, Nambya, etc. These diverse ethnic groups have unique and unparalleled traditional dances and music which were performed at different functions, occasions and ceremonies. The different traditional dances have unique cultural historical and spiritual contexts. Like any other people in the contemporary world, Zimbabweans have been variedly affected by the wave of globalisation that has to some extent changed their traditional cultural life.

Zimbabwe is exclusively rich in traditional dances which include *Mbakumba, Jerusarema, Muchongoyo, Mhande, Chidzimba, Dinhe, Chinyambera, Xinyambela, Xibelani, Amabhiza, Mbakumba, Isitchikhitcha* among many others (Rutsate 2007). These dances demonstrate not only religious beliefs but also reserved emotions such as anger, love, bravery, sadness and kindness. In this sense, dance is likened to a television show or a movie which can easily attract and manipulate an audience. When a person watches a good movie it leaves lasting impressions on his/her mind (Hassam 2012). Similarly, the methodological stories and images created by dance appeal greatly to the people to the extent that people can construe the message conveyed and accordingly learn from them. It is important to note that among the indigenous peoples of Zimbabwe, dance is the most developed of all the performing arts. Before the colonial period dance was an integral part of the socio-religious life of ethnic communities. The introduction of Christianity and the advent of colonialism consequently changed the lifestyle of the indigenous peoples to the extent that the colonial authorities and the Christian church considered many ritual and ceremonial dances to be magical, witchcraft and heathen dances and ultimately sought to suppress them (Tabex Encyclopaedia Zimbabwe 1987.

Below is a brief description of some of the traditional dances found in Zimbabwe. The dances are basically arranged in terms of their ethnic origin, name of dance, function and a brief description of the dance.

Group of People	Name of dance	Function	Narration
Shona people around Murehwa and Uzumba-Maramba-Pfungwe	*Mbende / Jerusarema*	Celebrates sexuality	Originally a puberty and fertility rite dance practiced by the Zezuru Shona people living in Eastern Zimbabwe, especially in the Murewa and Uzumba-Maramba-Pfungwe districts.(Asante 2000). The dance is characterised with the acrobatic and sensual movements by women and men, driven by a polyrhythmic master drummer. It is a very important "outside the house" dance tradition, once associated with weddings,

			celebrations, funerals, recreational and as a war dance. Allows young men and women to practice sexual movements, present themselves to the opposite sex, witness the opposite sex's movement to decrease fears of sexuality and prevent anxiety about sex (Rutsate 2007; Chauke 2013; UNESCO 2005; Impey and Nussbaum 1996).
Shona	*Chidzimba*	Motivates and orients people to the acts in hunting.	The *Chidzimba* dance communicates what had happened in the hunting expedition, for example, men would act out

			how they managed to capture antelope through the dance. (Impey and Nussbaum 1996; Machingura 2002; 2011; Rutsate 2007).
Korekore	*Dinhe/Dand anda*	Religious rites and ceremonies.	This dance originated from the Korekore people. It was originally preformed at religious rites and ceremonies but has now become associated with joyful occasions (Rutsate 2007). The dance uses different songs to accompany it, and the mood of the song indicates which spirits is being conjured. Apart from that the dance also

			enables men and women to acknowledge continuity of life, and prevents stress and tensions (Impey and Nussbaum 1996; Asante 2000).
Shona; Karanga people	*Mhande*	Community healing/Appeasement .	This is a social and entertainment dance common in parts of the Midlands; especially in Shurugwi and Mvuma areas (Rutsate 2007; 2010; 2011). The dance helps communities cope with anxieties associated with drought, sickness, and misfortunes. The dance is practiced by

			both males and females. When dancing the dancers avoid lifting their feet, instead they imitate the flow of water. Dancers use walking sticks *(tsvimbo)*, leg rattles *(magagada)*, traditional feathered hat *(ngundu)*, animal skins *(mhapa neshashiko)*; wooden plates, *(matende, mikombe)*. During the dance men whistle while women ululate (Rutsate 2010; National Arts Council of Zimbabwe 2013).
Kalanga and Ndebele	*Hoso/Amab hiza*	Performed when misfortunes arise.	This is one of the most popular dances of the Kalanga people in South

			Matebeleland (Rutsate 2007). Helps communities cope with anxieties associated with drought, sickness, and misfortunes. The dancer carries a rattle *(hosho)* in one hand and a flywhisk in the other and dances as possessed by a spirit of a galloping horse. The dancer would be trying to emulate the movements of a horse. The male dancers will use horse tail *(itshoba)* that they will throw about and dance in step while the women clap and sing while some play the

			drums. The drums harmonise to create the beat (Nyathi 2012).
Bikita-Duma people	*Chinyambera*	Hunting dance	Now a social dance, this was originally a ritual dance of the Duma people of Bikita. It was performed by hunters to prepare them for the hunt and to celebrate their return (Rutsate 2007). The dance gives strength to hunters by seeking on why they have failed (Impey and Nussbaum 1996). Although the function of the dance has changed, the traditional costumes are still used.

Tsonga and Xichangana tribes	*Xibelani/Shibelani*	To express pride of the culture.	It is customary for *Tsonga* girls to learn the xibelani dance, and it is a way for them to express pride in their cultural heritage (National Arts Council of Zimbabwe 2013).
Tsonga/Xichangana people	*Xinyambela*	A sacred courtship dance.	It is performed on specific occasions like graduation of the *Komba* (for girls from 14 years) and *Ngomen*i (from young men upwards). The females will demonstrate how they choose a man to marry and they both dance the woman shaking the waist advancing towards the

			man (National Arts Council of Zimbabwe 2013).
Ndebele	*Isitchikhitcha*	Praises celebrations and promotes fitness.	This dance is found among the Ndebele people. It was originally associated with spirit possessions and ritual ceremonies. Nowadays *Isitchikitcha* is performed at social gatherings; weddings or first fruits ceremonies accompanied by clapping, ululation, and whistling. (Nyathi 2012; Dance Africa 2013; National Arts Council of Zimbabwe 2013, Rutsate 2007).
Ndau; Ndebele; Shangani	*Muchongoyo*	Promotes solidarity, physical	Muchongo yo is found

		fitness.	among the Ndau people of Chipinge area. This dance is typical of the Nguni war dances. The dance demonstrates fighting techniques and was performed by warriors in preparation for war and afterward to celebrate victory. The Muchongoyo dance is also used as a military training exercise, and is characteristicall y performed with a stick and a shield. The Muchongoyo dance is also a social and recreational dance, and does not have a religious feature; instead

			it highlights the events of the society. The signature movement is stamping, and dramatic gestures as well as a mimetic element are essential. The dress is neo-traditional, accommodating the changing times, but still resembling the traditional costume. Males historically perform this dance; however females participate by creating the music. (The National Achieves of Zimbabwe 2010; Rutsate 2007).
Shona/Karang-a people	*Mbakumba*	Entertainment, celebratory and recreational	Originally this dance was performed by the Karanga

			people, a Shona ethnic group to celebrate good harvests. It is a special social dance performed mostly after a good or bumper harvest and it is associated with beer drinking parties *(ndari)*. Since the dance is a social dance performed mostly at beer parties, it does not have a particular dress code (Asante 2000); Rutsate 2007; Zimbabwe Music Festival 2007).
Shona	*Mbira*	Ritual dance; appeasement.	This dance is performed mainly at religious ceremonies and is danced to the mbira, one of the most

			symbolic musical instruments of the Shona people. The dancers sometimes become possessed by the spirits of their ancestors (2011 Zimfest.org). The dance is said to have originated from the Korekore people, a Shona ethnic group and is characterised by spiritual possessions (Rutsate 2007). In the liberation war it became a means of communication between the fighting cadres and the spiritual heroes of the First Chimurenga resistance

			(Sheehan 1993) The dance it is used to express the people and their traditional religious beliefs in the act of luring spirits to come out through spirit mediums and communicate with the people using the mbira as the primary instrument (Asante 2000).
Korekore	*Shangara*	Entertainment	This is a social dance which is usually preformed at beer parties, weddings and other joyful occasions by the people of central Mashonaland. (Turino 2000). In Shangara the dancing feet become a musical voice, producing a

			rhythmic melody. (Mujuru 1997; Rutsate 2007).
Shona-Buhera	*Jaka*	Entertainment	This is an entertainment dance which appears to have originated from the Ndebele people (Rutsate 2007).
Ndebele	*Isangoma*	Religious dance	This dance is found among the Ndebele people. It is a religious dance associated with spirit/ spiritual possession ceremonies (Rutsate 2007).
Karanga	*Majukwa*	Religious dance	This is a religious dance common among the Karanga people (Rutsate 2007).

Music in Zimbabwe

Traditional music formed an integral part of the daily life of the people of Zimbabwe. The aim of most traditional musicians' was to express life in all its facets through the medium of sound (Tabex Encyclopaedia Zimbabwe 1987). Two main categories of music in traditional society can be distinguished namely religious/ritual and secular music. Traditional religion and ritual were significant features of pre-colonial society and embraced the realm of spirits who were considered to have an influence in the lives of the living (for good or bad) depending on their conduct and efforts to appease and gratify the spirits (Tabex Encyclopaedia Zimbabwe 1987). The purpose of religious music was to direct the dynamism of the performance towards the culmination of a ritual ceremony. On the other hand secular music was classified into three main classes, namely, recreational, functional and ceremonial. Under these headings could be found music for many occasions including drinking parties, lamentations and battle preparations. This type of music was also performed to accompany work as well as to induce happiness (Tabex Encyclopaedia Zimbabwe 1987).

In addition, the music of Zimbabwe reveals people's spiritual beliefs, their modes of expression, patterns of communication and forms of entertainment. For example, traditional Shona songs were a medium of instruction through which young boys and girls were taught the values and expectations of adulthood. All social relationships were sealed, bonded and regulated through songs. Through songs, a daughter-in-law would express her bitterness against a horrible mother-in-law, a bitter wife against a greedy husband, and the whole community would protest against an unjust chief, hence there is a tradition of Shona protest songs (Makwenda 2005). There were songs to praise, urge, ridicule and reprimand. Most communication strategies in the pre-literate and oral African societies were musical in one way or another (Asante 2002).

Types of Zimbabwean Music

Mbira Music

Zimbabwe is one of the countries contributing to "world music" primarily through the mbira, wrongly called the thumb piano by the Western researcher (Berliner 1993 and Turino 1998). Music comes in varying forms, shapes, function, and types and is found in many of the parts of the country. Michael Williams (1997) in his study of mbira came to the conclusion that the instrument is of national importance as it is features on many institutions court of arms. Mbira (the name of both the instrument and the music) is mystical music which pervades all aspects of Shona culture, both sacred and secular (Berliner 1993). Its most important function is as a medium of communication between the dead and the living. Mbira music was mostly played at *bira* ceremonies. At these ceremonies, spirits of family ancestors (*vadzimu*), spirits of deceased chiefs (*mhondoro*) and the most powerful guardian spirits of the Shona (*makombwe)*, give guidance on family and community matters and exert power over weather and health (Andrew 1963).

In Zimbabwe, the mbira music is still played in rural areas at various traditional gatherings, and in the townships as part of Shona traditions and social parties (*madandaro).* According to Hugh (1969), Zimbabwe has a variety of mbira which has distinct places of origins (Turino 1998; Williams 1997). These are mbira *dzeNjari, mbira Yavadzimu/Nhare, mbira Matepe,* mbira *DzaVaNdau and the Karimba/Nyunganyunga* (Berliner 1993).

Jiti Music

Turino (1998) argues that *jiti* was called *Serenda,* before South African influence. Initially jiti songs were composed and sung by the liberation army (late 1960-1980) for political education. Many *jiti* songs are common in many parts of Zimbabwe (among the Shona people). Makwenda asserts that, *Jiti* is played by anyone and at any place for entertainment (urban and rural). It is interesting to note that composers of most *jiti* songs are unknown. This type of music is also played by professional musicians. Nowadays the music is played for recreational purposes and the songs are generally accompanied by drums (Makwenda 2005; Zindi 2003; Pongweni 1982; Yuji 2009).

Chimurenga Music

A new genre of political protest music emerged after the Shona and Ndebele uprisings of 1893 and 1896 (Eyre 2001). According to

155

oral tradition the name Chimurenga was coined after a great Shona traditional warrior and legendary hero, Sororenzou Murenga who was renowned for his fighting prowess (Vambe 2011). Great fighters after him were believed to be possessed by his spirit. They were believed to be fighting Chimurenga, which translated means "fighting the Murenga style." Hence the Zimbabwean liberation struggle of the late 1960s came and the genre of music that emerged from this spirit of struggle naturally acquired this nametag (Kwaramba 1997; Gonye 2013). This music was articulated from guerrilla bases in Tanzania, Mozambique and Zambia, and from some local artists inside Zimbabwe. After independence, Chimurenga music has criticised corruption, bad governance by the new leaders and delays in redistributing land to the African masses as Eyre (2001) puts it. Thomas Mapfumo coined the phrase "Chimurenga music" to his type of music to describe his revolutionary music which evolved during Zimbabwe's struggle to gain independence in the early 1970s and recorded his music rather in a western-style re-fitted with revolutionary lyrics (Pongweni 1982).

Sungura Music

Sungura is a genre of popular music in Zimbabwe that emerged just as local nationalists successfully fought for independence in 1980. Sungura, as Perman (2012) postulates means rabbit, and it is not a Shona word but it is Swahili. Sungura has remained the most popular style of music in Zimbabwe, yet it is still relatively unknown outside the country. Sungura emerged at a time of regional identity formation defined by patterns of migration, shared colonial and labour history, and a common sense of marginalisation shared between fans and performers (Eyre 2001). Zimbabwe's top selling pop music, *Sungura* is fast, punchy, electric guitar and vocal music, generally disparaged by urban intellectuals, but consumed passionately by rural farmers and labourers (Gambahaya and. Mutasa 2013; Eyre 2001).

Conclusion

Dance and music is an integral component of Zimbabwean culture and identity. The different types and dance and music though they have undergone various stages of transformation are still pivotal in moulding and defining ethnic identities. Some of the dances have transcended ethnic boundaries and have attained national and international recognition. Intermarriages amongst the different ethnic groups have resulted in culture cross fertilisation and as a result these dances and music are practiced in most parts of the country. According to Blacking (1981), in African societies music and dance are foundations of social life, which enable individuals to discover and develop their human potential and to reaffirm their relationships with each other. Music and dance help people remain intellectually alive and creative. Today, traditional dance and music has become a lived art that manifests philosophical and aesthetic traditions representing different tribal grounds. The acknowledgement in the existence of Zimbabwean traditional dances and music help make a template for in depth examination and exploration of our culture and traditions.

References

Allan, P. Merriam, A.P. 1982. *African Music in Perspective, Critical Studies on Black Life and Culture,* Vol. 6. Garland Publishing.

Asante, K. W. 2002. *Zimbabwe Dance: Rhythmic Forces, Ancestral Voices: An Aesthetic* Analysis, Library of Congress Cataloguing in-Publishing-Data.

Badejo, P. and S. Banerji. 2002. *African Dance,* Microsoft (R) Encarta (R) Encyclopaedia Microsoft Corporation, USA.

Berliner, P. 1993. *The Soul of Mbira.* Chicago, University of Chicago.

Blacking, J. 1981. *The Role of Music in National Development Programmes;* Lecture to students and staff of the Department of African Development Studies, University of Zambia.

Chauke, O. 2013. *Mbende –Jerusarema Dance*: National Arts Council of Zimbabwe (NACZ).

Chitando, E. 2002. *"Singing culture"*: *A case study of Gospel Music in Zimbabwe*, Nordiska Afrikainstitutet Research Report, No. 121.

Dadirai, A and Kwaramba. A.D. 1997. *The Battle of the Mind: International New Media Elements of the New Religious Political Right in Zimbabwe*, Oslo: University of Oslo.

Dance Africa. 2013. *Rhythms of Africa / Giya Africa / Mandingindira eAfrica*, The Harkness Foundation for Dance; The SHS Foundation BAM.

Eyre. B. 2001. *Playing With Fire Fear and Self-Censorship in Zimbabwean Music*. Handy-Print, Denmark. Freemuse.

Gonye, J. 2013. *Mobilizing Dance/Traumatising Dance: Kongonya and the Politics of Zimbabwe*, Dance Research Journal, Volume 45, Number 1, pp. 64-79.

Hassam, M.2012. *The Importance of Music in the African Culture: More than just a song*, Word Press.

Impey, A and Nussbaum, B. 1996. *Music and Dance in Southern Africa: Positive forces in the Workplace*; Struik Publishers, Zebra Press: South Africa.

Jenje-Makwenda, J. 2005. *Zimbabwe Township Music*, Harare, Story time Promotions, *Muziki*: Journal of Music Research in Africa, 3:1, 134-137.

Laws, K. 2002. *Physics and the Art of Dance: Understanding Movement*, Oxford University Press. 198 Madison Avenue.

Machingura, M, J. 2002. *The influence of Modernity on Zimbabwean Traditional Dances*, University of Zimbabwe, (Unpublished Thesis) pp 9-11.

Machingura, F and Machingura, M.J. 2011. *Women and Sungura music in Zimbabwe*: Sungura Music as a Culturally-Gendered Genre, *R and D Research and Discussion*, Vol. 4, No. 1.

Maonera, F. 2007. *Zimbabwe's Cultural Products – Deserving of Protection*, Trade and Development Studies Centre, Harare, Zimbabwe.

Meisner, N. 2006. *Dance, Microsoft* (R) Encarta (R) [DVD] Microsoft Corporation, USA.

Muwati, A. 2013. *A Potentially Dystrophic Era: Analysing the lyrical sociology of selected sungura songs in Zimbabwe in the 1990s and beyond,* Muziki: Journal of Music Research in Africa, 10:sup1, 107-121.

Nyathi, P. and Chikomo, K. 2012. *Zimbabwe's Traditional Dances, Volume 1,* Amagugu Publishers.

Perman, T. 2003. *Review of Ezra Chitando, Singing Culture, A study of Gospel Music in Zimbabwe,* H-Africa, H-Net Reviews Argyris, Chris in Schön, Donald, A. (1978): Organizational learning: A Theory of Action Perspective., Massachusetts: Addison-Wesley, Reading.

Perman, T. 2012. *Sungura in Zimbabwe and the Limits of Cosmopolitanism,* Ethnomusicology Forum, 21:3, 374-401.

Pongweni. A. J.C. 1982. *Songs that Won the Liberation War,* Collage Press.

Rutsate, J. 2007. *Performance of mhande song-dance: a contextualized and comparative analysis,* Master of Arts Thesis, Rhodes University, South Africa.

Rutsate, J. 2010. *"Mhande" Dance in the "Kurovaguva" Ceremony: An Enactment of Karanga Spirituality.* Yearbook for Traditional Music Vol. 42, pp. 81-99 Published by: International Council for Traditional Music.

Rutsate, J. 2011. Mhande dance in *kurovaguva* and *mutoro* rituals: An efficacious and symbolic enactment of Karanga Epistemology, Doctor of Philosophy, University of KwaZulu-Natal, South Africa.

Sheehan, S. 1993. *Cultures of the World Zimbabwe,* New York: Marshall Cavendish.

Tabex Encyclopaedia Zimbabwe, 1987. Quest Publishing (PVT) LTD, Harare, Zimbabwe.

Tracy, A. 1963. *Three Tunes for Mbira Dzavadzimu,* African Music, 3 (2); 23-26.

Tracy. H. 1969. The Mbira Class of African Instruments in Rhodesia, African Music 4 (3); 78-95.

Turino, T. 2000. *Nationalists, Cosmopolitans and Popular Music in Zimbabwe,* Chicago and London, University of Chicago Press.

Turino, T. 1998. *The Mbira,* Worldbeat and the International Imagination.

Vambe, M.T. 2011. *Rethinking the Notion of Chimurenga in the Context of Political Change,* In: Zimbabwe Muziki: Journal of Music Research in Africa, 8:2, 1-28.

Viriri, A. et al. 2011. *The influence of popular music in particular urban grooves lyrics on the Zimbabwean youth: The case of the Troika, Maskiri, Winky, D and Extra Large,* Muziki: Journal of Music Research in Africa, 8:1, 82-95.

Yuji, M.Y. 2009. *Jiti Music in Zimbabwe,* JSPS Research Fellowship, Nagoya University Graduate School of Letters, The 1st International Symposium at Nagoya University, Studies of Afro-Eurasian Inner Dry Land Civilizations Religious Dynamics of Contemporary Africa.

Zimbabwe Cultural Policy Document. 2000. *Dance and Music,* pp 19-20.

Zindi, F. 2003. *The Pop-Music Work Book-Zimbabwe Versus The World,* Zindisc Publications.

Dance-Mbira Dance, 2011. Zimfest.org/workshops/mbira-mbira dance/

The Zimbabwe Music Festival, 2007. http://www.zimfest.org/2007/Zimfest07RegGuide.pdf.

National Achieves of Zimbabwe, 2010. http://www.archives.gov.zw/downloads/category/4-books?download...archives./

Williams, M. 1997. Getting Started with Mbira Dzavadzimu, https://www.google.co.zw/?gws_rd=cr&ei=K_0rU56fKMf_ygP j9IGgCw#q.

Mbende Jerusarema Dance Traditional performing arts Social practices, 2005. http://www.unesco.org/culture/ich/doc/src/01857-EN.pd/Intangible Heritage Domain/

Kwaramba, A.D. 1997. M. Phil. *Traditional Music in Zimbabwe,* http://www.nai.uu.se/research/finalized_projects/cultural_imag es_in_and_of/zimbabwe/music/#sthash.WSaSjjCx.dpuf.

Chapter 8

Identities, Memoirs and Narratives: The dialectics of Rozvi ethnicity and power in Zimbabwe

Lesley Hatipone Machiridza

Introduction

The main objective of this chapter is to establish a firm foundation upon which readers can appreciate dialectics of Shona and Rozvi traditions. Since there is great variability in what is referred to as Shona, the Rozvi are singled out because their identities were situationally constructed from cultural traditions that were strategically drawn from the broader Shona culture. In addition, this paper attempts to correct the widely accepted misconception that the Rozvi were the sole builders of Great Zimbabwe and several other dry-stone walled monuments scattered throughout the Zimbabwean plateau and its immediate vicinities. The narratives of the Rozvi are interesting to pursue because to date, a fairly sufficient historical record about their past has been generated by the Portuguese, indigenous communities through their oral accounts, historians, ethnographers, and creative writers (Machiridza 2012). The data presented in this chapter was widely drawn from my MA dissertation and it shows that the Rozvi or Rozvi ethnicity was situationally and systematically constructed from ordinary Shona communities that were scattered throughout the Zimbabwean plateau (see Figure 1 below).

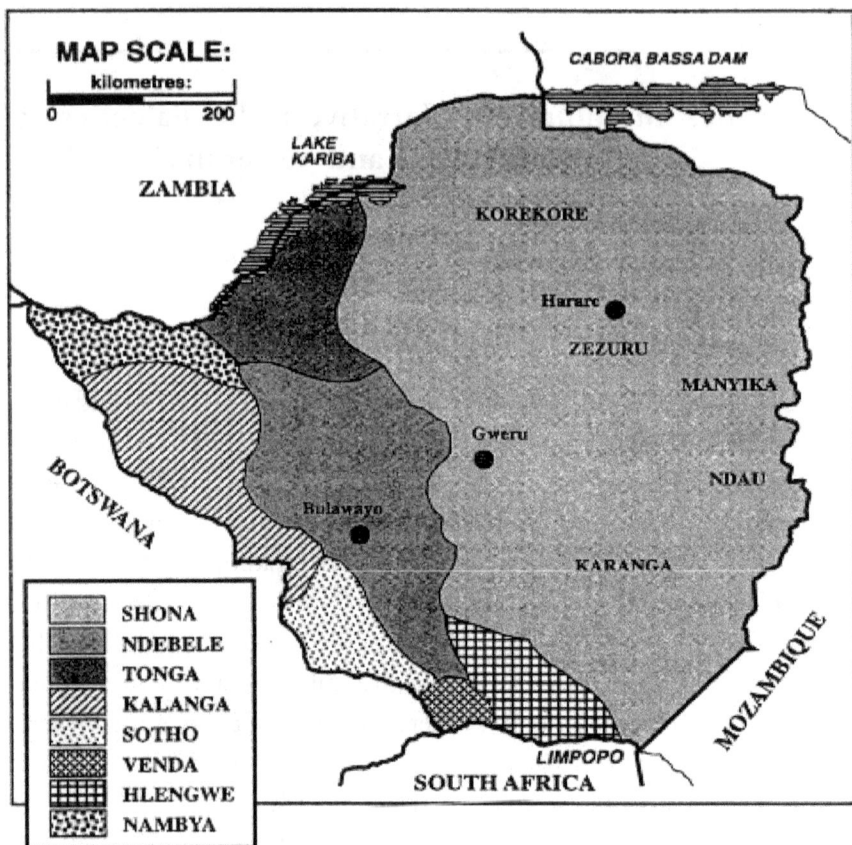

Fig. 1- Map of the Zimbabwean plateau showing the distribution of Shona and other ethnic groups that situationally became Rozvi (After Manyanga 2006).

As such their traditions and customs strongly resonate with some of the ethnic groups within the country such as the Karanga, Kalanga, Korekore/ Shangwe, Ndau, Venda, Ndebele and Nambya people. The Rozvi are believed to have originated in north-eastern Zimbabwe and their rise to power was closely associated with Changamire Dombolakochingwango (simply termed Dombo for short) of 1680-1696. Rozvi identities thus coalesced around political power, marriage systems, the *Mwari* religion, totemism, mythological versions, material culture and natural features like mountains and trees, dialects, performance of traditional roles like rain-petitioning

162

ceremonies, appointment of Chiefs, and awarding of land rights to newcomers (Machiridza 2012). However, in this chapter the Rozvi are only examined in terms of how they manipulated the institutions of marriage, totemism and taboos for social and political gain to the extent of becoming one of the most prominent ethnic groups in the history of Zimbabwe.

Who really was or is Rozvi?

The Rozvi are a complicated group to define in terms of their identity, ethnicity, history and archaeological signature. Numerous studies either directly or indirectly dealing with them have been conducted since the arrival of antiquarians in Zimbabwe during the late 19th century. Unfortunately, a corpus of literature has raised wide-ranging views, which are often conflicting, thereby mystifying the whole subject. According to Beach (1976:3) post-Rozvi groups found south of Rusape in Manicaland Province of Zimbabwe share traditions that Chikura Wadyembeu known as Changamire or Dombolakonachingwango (often shortened to Dombo) was the founder of the Rozvi. These traditions mention that this leader rose from somewhere around Murewa area (a district in Mashonaland East Province of Zimbabwe) before moving southwest to conquer Chiwundura and Tumbare pre-Rozvi occupants of Khami-type sites (see Figure 2 below). The warlike nature of the Rozvi is vividly depicted as marking their initial rise to power. Most importantly traditions about them highlight or emphasise the connection between particular historic events and the name Rozvi (see Machiridza 2005; 2008; 2012; 2013). This chapter shows that Rozvi as an identity was historically constructed. The Rozvi have, thus, been generally defined as a broad and dynamic ethnic group that rose to prominence during the 1670s in the north-eastern *moyo* nuclear area of the modern Mashonaland East Province of Zimbabwe under the leadership of ChangamireDombo (Machiridza 2005; 2012).

163

Fig. 2- Map showing the distribution of Khami type sites on the Zimbabwean plateau (After Machiridza 2012).

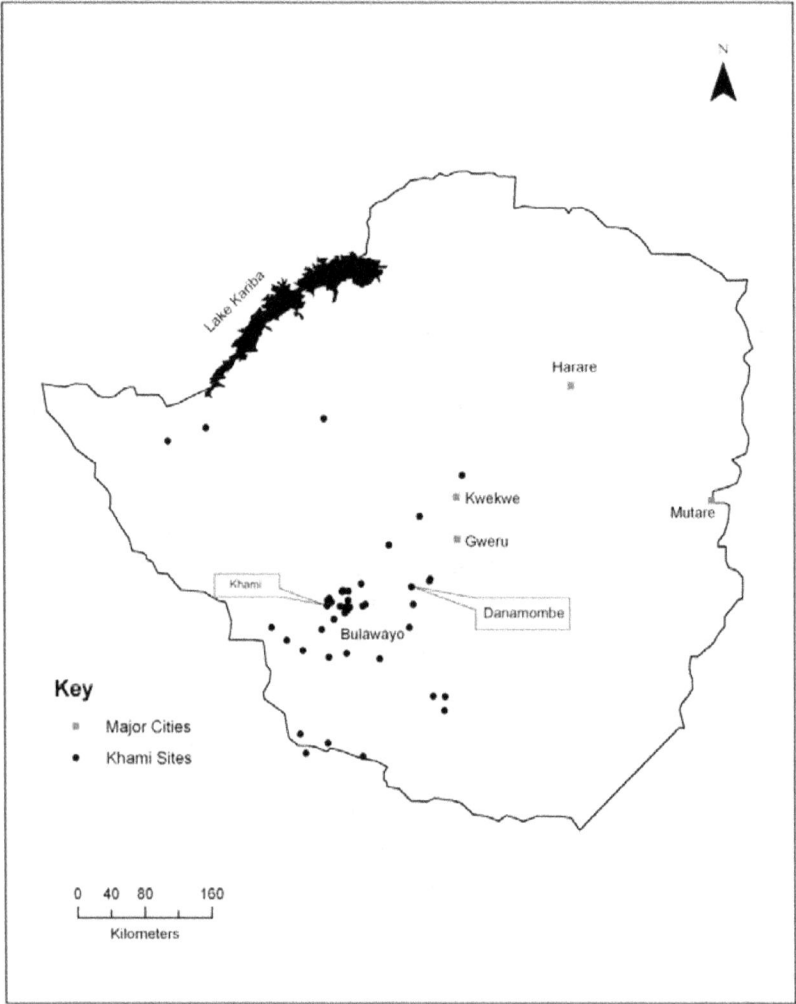

Marriage traditions and the Rozvi

Although several traditional methods of getting married like *kutizira* (eloping), *kuzvarira* (parent-organized child marriages), *kugara nhaka* (levirate marriage) and *kutemaugariri* (service marriage) among others, have been recorded ethnographically, currently marriages in

Zimbabwe are simply classified either as customary marriages or civil marriages governed under Act 5:11 formerly called Chapter 36. Despite so many variations inherent in ways to get married, the common denominator in most of these marriage unions among Africans is dowry/ bride price, which comes either in the form of money or cattle. According to Huffman (1982; 2007) among many Bantu speaking communities cattle played a very important role as a form of *lobola* (bride price). In the past, the more cattle one had, the more wives, children and wealth he had and often times the more political power he acquired. In the case of the Rozvi, their founder Changamire Dombo used cattle wealth to build his early political career by exploiting the *Nyai* clientele system (Beach 1983a; Machiridza 2013; Mazarire 2009).

The *Nyai* were groups of young men who established a dependent relationship with a 'host', 'principal baron', or 'influential head of houses' in order to get wives in exchange for their myriad services provided through a Shona custom called *kutemaugariri* (Machiridza 2012). Their services ranged from domestic activities to political tasks like guards, errand runners, spies, councillors, messengers or warriors (Beach 1983a; Mazarire 2009). These *vaNyai* could become anything depending on the aspirations of their baron. They could also accumulate wealth and power through time and eventually expand their baron's influence or even curve their own territories independently through similar *Nyai* clientele. Changamire was one of the most successful *Nyai* barons whose political power started as simply military power derived from his *Nyai* supporters. With the passage of time, *Nyai* was transformed to mean the elite Rozvi, while in some instances it remained as an identity for Rozvi subjects who were part of the confederacy system (Machiridza 2012).

On the other end, the institution of marriage was also manipulated by Rozvi elites in efforts to legitimise their ethnic identity and to negotiate power relations. The Rozvi used a Shona custom *kuzvarira* the diplomacy of giving their subject chiefs Rozvi girls as wives, but these wives represented the interests of their Rozvi family kin. Several chiefs appointed by the Rozvi were sometimes given young Rozvi girls as wives (see Beach n.d.; Bhila 1982; Mutasa 1990; 1991). This strategy served two fundamental needs for the Rozvi system of governance; firstly it promoted kinship ties by "blood." The word blood is in quotes because ethnicity is a social category that is hardly defined by such biological attributes (Machiridza 2012). In fact, the Rozvi manipulated *mitupo* (totems) using the *moyo* (heart) totem as the core referent to promote strong sentiments of kinship. This is why Loubser (1990) argues that totems should be seen as small scale ethnic units. Hence among the Rozvi, marriage ties and totems were objectified to justify a historically constructed identity.

Apart from that, inter-marriages between Rozvi women and distant chiefs naturally strengthened and legitimised Rozvi political influence in such areas (Bhila 1982). A Rozvi wife was expected to act like a secret agent by constantly giving political feedback to the Rozvi metropolis (Mutasa 1991). Thus through the manipulation of traditional institutions such as marriage, the Rozvi administration gradually became rooted in moral force and not coercion. This system worked well for their decentralised state which was made up of a number of ordinary dynasties. Since it is difficult to separate marriage from totemism and taboos among indigenous Zimbabweans, a much closer attention is drawn to these key concepts in the ensuing sections.

Totemism among Rozvi and their neighbours

Kinship ties among the Karanga communities have always been defined through clan names, *mitupo,* and sub-clan names, *zvidao,* often related to geographical areas suggesting common origins (Machiridza 2012). Bourdillion (1976:38) adds that '*mitupo*' and '*zvidao*' are often 'praise names', but they have religious and symbolic connotations, which make them more than just names. At times these names can be changed simply to conceal the identity of the group or to adjust its relations with other groups (Bourdillion 1976). Loubser (1988:303) elaborates that '*mitupo*' do not necessarily constitute corporate bodies, genealogically related people, or territorially defined units because members of the same '*mutupo*' can either be royals or commoners.

Oral traditions often mention status differences, and the status of each '*mutupo*' depends on political circumstances such that the history of status grades can be tentatively reconstructed through '*mitupo*' (Ralushai 1977:59). Thus oral traditions often identified pre-colonial groups such as the Rozvi through territorial regions, ruling houses, totems and sub-totems. These kinship attributes are well remembered in oral accounts and they are most effectively used in group identification as well as in distinguishing the 'major Rozvi' from the 'minor Rozvi' groups. Most oral traditions also point out that the titles 'Changamire' and '*Mambo*' were associated with Rozvi leaders who were largely of the *moyo* (heart) totem (Beach n.d.; 1976; 1983a; 1994a; Machiridza 2012; Mazarire 2009; Zachrisson 1978). Hence the *moyo* totem was commonly used to define kinship ties among the Rozvi.

Rozvi traditions centred on totemic identity

Beach (1994a) mentions that traditions collected during the late 19th century from a south-western perspective indicate that the Rozvi rose from an east to north-east direction that point towards Murewa. That area was a *moyo* nuclear zone (meaning a territorial region with a concentration of people bearing the *moyo* totem) this area was enclosed by non-*moyo* dynasties before Changamire broke away from the Mutapa to establish his power-base in the south-west around the 1690s. The Mutapa state was centred in the northern extreme parts of the Zimbabwean plateau after it succeeded Great Zimbabwe around AD 1450 as a major political force. By the late 17th century it was experiencing both internal and external political stress, which resulted in several socio-political adjustments, one of which was triggered by Changamire Dombo who broke away with a group of followers and migrated south-west wards. This migration triggered a series of other movements that further complicated the *moyo* totem identity as non-*moyo* groups were also assimilated by the prominent Changamire dynasties, while the weak *moyo* groups that either remained behind or migrated to other areas where they eventually got absorbed by non-*moyo* dynasties. Although the *moyo* totem was generally accepted as a common denominator for Rozvi identification, its value in that respect was only situational as other non-*moyo* houses took over senior offices in the Rozvi administration (Zachrisson 1978). Thus there are far too many *moyo* totem houses that are mentioned in oral traditions, but not all of them controlled power relations among the Shona.

The south-western Rozvi dynasties remained dominant, while the other *moyo* groups that remained in the north-east as well as those that migrated to the central plateau and south-eastern parts got submerged by different dynasties during the 18th century (Machiridza 2012). Oral traditions state that when the Rozvi arrived in the south-west, Chibundule, Chihunduro, Chiwundura or Chihunduru, Tumbare, Nichasike or Nichakadzike among others were the main ruling dynasties that were defeated and incorporated into the Rozvi leadership (Beach 1994a, 1976; Mazarire 2009; van Warden 1998; Zachrisson 1978). The Rozvi *moyo* totem became a fashion for some chiefs who strived to be identified with the Rozvi *Mambos* (Chiefs), as the case with Chihunduro-*shoko*, Tumbare-*bhebhe*, Mavhudzi-*shava*, Nerwande-*shoko* and Bepe-*dziva/mbedzi*, (see Beach 1994a; Mazarire 2009; Zachrisson 1978). These changed their *"zvidawo* (praise-names) to Mavhudzi-*shava/moyondizvo*, Tumbare-*moyo/bhebhe*, and Tumbare-*moyo/mitombo*, Chihunduro-*moyo/shoko*, Mangwende-*moyo/muzukuru*, and Svosve-*soko/moyondizvovhudzijena*respectively (Beach 1994a; Hodza and Fortune 1979; Machiridza 2012; Zachrisson 1978).

Thus Rozvi praise names and totems were never fixed or static; they always changed whenever the balance of power shifted as the case with Chihunduro-*shoko*, Tumbare-*bhebhe*, Mavhudzi-*shava*, Nerwande-*shoko* and Bepe-*dziva/mbedzi*. Some totems and praise names were invented or constructed as individuals sought to adjust to shifting power relations. Hodza and Fortune (1979:221) cited some of the Rozvi *'zvidawos'* that emerged when the Rozvi were integrating other chiefdoms and losing their grip on power as, Moyo *Sinyoro* (*senhor*), Moyo *Chirandu*, Moyo *Wakapiwa*, Moyo *Mutaurwa*, Moyo *Muturikwa*, Moyo *Shavamombe*, Moyo *Mupfuyiwa*, Moyo *Mushoriwa*, Moyo *Muvhimwa*, Moyo *Muzivikani*, Moyo *VarasaMugonderwa*, Moyo *Chipfuyamiti* and Moyo *Ndebele*. These shifting totemic identities reflect the fluctuating nature of Rozvi identities in varying socio-historical contexts and that clearly resonates with the notion of ethnicity (Machiridza 2012).

During the first third of the 19th century the south-western Rozvi disintegrated into several dynasties. Resultantly, Chihunduru, Tumbare, Mavhudzi and Nerwande retreated north-west to become *shoko* (monkey) among the Nambya of Hwange and *shava* (eland) among the Shangwe of Mafungabusi Plateau (Mazarire 2009). The Singo who settled among the Venda are also believed to have broken away from the south-west between 1750-1800 as some of their early chiefs had names like Lozi (Rozvi), Mambo, Dyambeu and Thoho-ya-Ndou (Loubser 1988). Oral traditions trace the Singo from Matangoni (Matonjeni) mountain (assumed as near Danamombe, the Rozvi capital), while others point towards Mberengwa mountain and some traditions emphasise the big lakes of Central Africa (Loubser 1988). Although they were Rozvi, their totem was not *moyo* but *singo*, which also indicates that the *moyo* totem was no longer the sole attribute for defining kinship among the Rozvi. Even the rest of Rozvi groups from the south-west were simply identified through house names, and not totems, showing that Rozvi kinship ties were no longer entirely defined through totemic attributes. Rozvi houses in south-eastern Bikita District of Zimbabwe were simply termed Jiri and Gumunyu, while those that set for Makoni in north-eastern Zimbabwe became Chiduku and Tandi, in upper Save there was the mention of house names like Tumbare, Nyashanu, Svosve, Chingombe, Mbava/Ruzane, Gwangwava-Musarurwa and Mutekedza among others as Rozvi (Beach 1976; 1983b; Machiridza 2012; Mazarire 2009).

Praise poetry and Rozvi totemic identities

This research also considered information from creative writers as crucial in the examination of the Rozvi. Of course, many particularly historians would doubt the value of these sources in any attempt to understand the past because of concerns surrounding imagination, mythology and distorted historical facts (Machiridza 2012). However, Shona praise-poetry constitutes an important component of African history because it celebrates clan/ societal origins, ancestors, memorable events and many other socio-economic qualities of past generations. In this case *nhetembo dzerudzi* literally "praises of the clan" are important because they are uttered to ancestral spirits *midzimu*, the whole lineage or clan/ societal group, and to the clansman who would have performed a good act (Fortune and Hodza 1974). The imagery by which thanks are conveyed varies from totems (animals or parts of living creatures) such as the zebra (*tembo*), eland (*mhofu/shava*), baboon (*mukanya*), monkey (*soko*), leg (*gumbo*) or heart (*moyo*) (Fortune and Hodza 1974). Usually praises follow the qualities of the animals such as its beauty, swiftness, and strength, but for the Rozvi the *moyo* (heart) is central to any living creature, hence it possibly signifies the central political role of the Rozvi in the past. Among the Shona, totems and clan/ societal group praise poetry constitute a genre of oral traditions that convey cultural messages, values and histories of clan members (Pongweni 1996). Even though clan/ societal group praise poetry is classified under creative or imaginative works, its role among the Shona has a very strong historical impression since it often addresses geographical origins, ancestral legends and political roles of particular clans/ societal groups (Kahari 1990).

The aforegoing connotes that totemism and praise poetry constitute complex traditions that promote sentiments of attachment among group members, ritualised collective consciousness and respect for symbolic objects of group identity (Pongweni 1996). Totemism and praise poetry also performs social functions among the Shona such as facilitating exogamy in marriages, acting as social lubricants emphasising respect, serving to distinguish 'them' from 'us' (ethnicity), which enhances respect, love, cooperation and support; they also act as oaths whenever there is need to demonstrate sincerity or truthfulness of a report or promise, and finally they act as taboos with magical sanctions that promote solidarity through sharing of food and showing commendable behaviour towards fellow kin-members (Pongweni 1996). Thus, both clan/societal group praise poetry (*nhetembo dzerudzi*) and sexual oriented praise poems (*zvireverevezvomugudza*) metaphorically depict attributes like a common descent and substance as socially defined and not biologically or genealogically imposed. In this chapter, I confine myself to examining totems and praise poetry associated with the Rozvi so as to make inferences on how they imagined themselves and how they were perceived by others. Kahari (1990:103) observed that the *moyo* totem was associated with praise names like *Moyondizvo/Bvumavaranda, Nematombo, Sinyoro, Wakapiwa, Muzukuru, Chirandu, Sithole, Wadyegora, Mavhudzi, Rwanza, Masukume, Dhewa, Tumbare* and *Zuruvi,* thus indicating the complexity of the *moyo* clan. Historically and even in contemporary circles, the names cited above are often widely used in identifying the Rozvi constituency. Hodza and Fortune (1979:223) adds that:

> Clan praises of the Rozvi recall their once extensive power and wealth. In them the function of the praises as propaganda and self-advertisement comes clearly to the fore ... The material of the praises is threefold, containing references to (i) the Rozvi wealth in cattle, (ii) their political power, and (iii) ancestral sites and names. Among the latter the names and praises of kings figure prominently.

The Rozvi political power is often vividly expressed through praise poetry, for instance Fortune and Hodza (1974:69) cited and translated the following Rozvi praise-poem:

171

Bvumavaranda,	'You, who receive the homage of your subjects,
Vakadzi vachizavomene;	women coming of their own accord;
Jengetanyika;	Keeper and master of the land;
Mwenewavanhu;	Lord of the people;
VaChuru-chamipfunde-manji;	Mound surrounded by abundant sorghum;
VaNyokahaisvosvwi.	Those who are known as A snake is not to be provoked.
Kuisvosva inoruma munhu.	If you provoke it, it will bite someone.

The above example summarises most of the important political qualities of the Rozvi as great leaders with many subjects. This praise-poem is acknowledging that the Rozvi were the major custodians of the land. If they were land custodians, then their ancestral spirits were the guardians of the land thus reinforcing Rozvi control of other groups. It also emphasises that the Rozvi were the rulers of the people, hence their authority was unquestionable. The imagery of the mound of sorghum depicts the Rozvi as care-givers of their many subjects and there are several versions of oral traditions that highlight the same qualities. Finally, the snake metaphor carries the skilful and dangerous qualities of the Rozvi, which largely befits the Rozvi army. Another poem highlights the Rozvi dialect, power, wealth and great ancestral heroes. Shoko (2001:19-20) recorded and translated the poem shown below:

Bhepe	Resident of the Royal capital
Nzinda	He who drapes in white apparel
Tumbare	Of the mountain
Wejila Jena VaChuluChaNhave	Possessor of red soils
VaChisavase VaChigalanakabhanga	He who carries his knife around
VaChichengetamunongolo	Keeper of an impala
Chilailochakanyeishomwe	Whose home supper is marulafruit Who dresses his wives in black
VaChilimamapfundemanji	Grower of plenty of sorghum
Aisava Tumbare	But for Tumbare
BwanabwomuRozvi Bwaisapera kutsva mumoto	The Rozvi offspring would have perished in fire (war)
Aiwa kani Tumbare	Yea Tumbare
Wejila Jena	He who dresses in white
Maita zvenyu *Bhepe*	Thank you

The poem above highlights a number of interesting aspects about the Rozvi; in particular it was recited in a Rozvi dialect. Tumbare, a former Rozvi military official is being praised on the basis of his dressing (white cloths also cited heavily in Moyo/*Sinyoro* praise poetry), weapons (knives), and history in warfare. His wives are said to have dressed in black clothes and this possibly signifies the value of cloth among the Rozvi in the past. Cloth as dressing material was rare when compared to animal skins, perhaps this scarcity made cloth a symbol of identity among the Rozvi back then. Unfortunately, it was difficult to determine the exact date when this poem became part of Rozvi traditions. Assuming that it dates to the times when the Rozvi were the prominent ruling class in pre-colonial times, it informs us about dressing styles or fashion preferences for the Rozvi. Fashion styles relate to ethnic identities, hence these stylistic aspects could be very crucial elements of Rozvi identities. The poem also emphasises special qualities associated with the Rozvi, and these include royal residences, land ownership and their ability to produce surplus food for their subjects. A related Rozvi praise poem comes from Mutasa (1991:5) and it goes as follows:

"Moyondizvo, Bvumavaranda!	"Moyondizvo, Bvumavaranda!
Vakadzi vachizavomene;	Women coming of their own accord;
Muti unokopa chirimo!	The tree which sprouts in the dry season!
Kukopa zhezha unokonze ndove;	In the rains it causes a swamp;
Mambo asingatandavari;	King who does not rest;
Kutandavara mvura inonaya mubvumbi,	If he rests, the rain would turn to mist,
Nyamusimiramombe!	One who pledges cattle!
Kusimira mbudzi nembukaurombo,	Pledging goats and animals is poverty,
Vakaperanenda!	Those who perished on towers to the moon!
Vagadzi voushe hwavaranda venyuisu!"	Those who ordain rulers among their subjects!"

The above Rozvi praise poem highlights several attributes of the group's identities. Firstly, it highlights the praise names, *"Moyondizvo/Bvumavaranda"*. It also emphasises the character of Rozvi

174

Mambos as dangerous if provoked. Again the Rozvi are portrayed as very rich in cattle. The stanza *"Vakaperanenda!"* has been interpreted in multiple ways, some argue it means those who were ravaged by lice, while others suggest it means those who were killed by spears. This study favours the one, which suggests 'those who perished on their way to the moon', when they built scaffolding using timber in attempts to get the moon as a present for their king or *Mambo*. This was a common myth that created strong sentiments of solidarity among the Rozvi.

Conclusion: Rozvi identity markers

The data shown above testifies that Rozvi was a consciously constructed identity that gradually acquired multiple meanings throughout the course of history. Initially, there was no mention of that name until the mid-18th century when a series of important socio-political events associated with ChangamireDombo and his followers had occurred. A review of the earliest written sources has proven that a great military leader called Changamire suddenly rose to power through a series of military campaigns backed by young fighters. In no time, that military formation was transforming itself into a formidable ruling dynasty popularly known as Rozvi. Eventually, Rozvi became a dynamic identity as it referred to Changamire Dombo's close kin, the co-opted (Torwa and other groups), core territories of the political entity, chiefs appointed by the Rozvi and the list goes on (Machiridza 2012). At some point in history, many Shona cultural traditions encompassing marriage, totemism and taboos acted as natural attributes or symbols of their ethnic identification. These ordinary cultural attributes were both systematically and strategically used to conceal, project, legitimise and reinforce Rozvi identities and power. Most importantly, various Shona traditional customs and material culture were subjectively objectified by Rozvi elites in order to signal their ethnic group identity. By and large, Rozvi manipulated customs and traditions are so diverse and complex to condense in a single chapter.

References

Beach, D. N. (n.d.) 'The Rozvi and the Changamire state: The origin of a myth: The historiography of the Rozvi', *Henderson Seminar paper, 34.*

Beach, D. N. 1976. 'The Mutapa Dynasty: A Comparison of Documentary and Traditional Evidence', *History in Africa*, 3: 1-17.

Beach, D. N. 1983a. Zimbabwe plateau and its peoples. In *History of Central Africa* 1, Birmingham D. and P.M. Martin (eds.), 248-277, New York: Longman.

Beach, D. N. 1983b. 'The Rozvi in Search of Their Past', *History in Africa*, 10: 13-34.

Beach, D .N. 1 994a.*The Shona and Their Neighbours,* Oxford: Blackwell.

Bhila, H.H.K. 1982. *Trade and Politics in a Shona Kingdom, The Manyika and their African and Portuguese Neighbours, 1575-1902.* London: Longman House.

Bourdillion, M.F.C. 1976. *The Shona Peoples: An Ethnography of contemporary Shona, with special reference to their religion,* Gwelo: Mambo Press.

Fortune, G. and Hodza, A. C. 1974. 'Shona-Praise Poetry', *Bulletin of the School of Oriental and African Studies, University of London,* 37 (1): 65-75.

Hodza, A. C. and Fortune G. 1979. *Shona Praise Poetry,* Oxford: Oxford University Press.

Huffman, T. N. 2007. *Handbook to the Iron Age: The Archaeology of Precolonial Farming Societies in Southern Africa,* South Africa: University of KwaZulu-Natal.

Huffman, T. N. 1982. 'Archaeology and Ethnohistory of the African Iron Age', *Annual Review of Anthropology*, 11: 133-150.

Kahari, G. 1990. *The rise of the Shona novel: A study in development, 1890-1984,* Gweru: Mambo Press.

Loubser, J. H. N. 1988. Archaeological contribution to Venda Ethnohistory, PhD Thesis, University of Witwatersrand, Johannesburg.

Machiridza, L. H. 2005. Setting the parameters for reconsidering the Rozvi archaeological identity in South-Western Zimbabwe: A Historical Archaeology Perspective, BA Honours dissertation, University of Zimbabwe, Harare.

Machiridza, L. H. 2008. Developing the Rozvi archaeological identity in south-western Zimbabwe, *Zimbabwean Prehistory 28*: 21-31.

Machiridza, L. H. 2012. Material Culture and Dialects of Identity and Power: Towards a Historical Archaeology of the Rozvi in South-Western Zimbabwe, MA Archaeology dissertation, University of Pretoria, Pretoria.

Machiridza, L. H. 2013. Insights into the meaning of Nyai, Rozvi and Torwa: a historical archaeology approach to identities, In *Zimbabwean Archaeology in the Post-Independence Era*, Manyanga, M. & S. Katsamudanga (eds.),199-212.Harare: Sapes Books.

Mazarire, G. C. 2009. Reflections on pre-colonial Zimbabwe, c.850-1880s, In *Becoming Zimbabwe: A history from pre-colonial period to 2008*, Raftopoulos, B. and A.S. Mlambo (eds.), 1-38, Harare: Weaver Press.

Mutasa, N. 1990. *NhumeYamambo*, Gweru: Mambo Press.

Mutasa, N. 1991. *Misodzi Dikita Neropa*, Gweru: Mambo Press.

Pongweni, A. J. C. 1996. *Shona praise Poetry as role negotiation: The battles of the clans and the sexes*, Gweru: Mambo Press.

Ralushai, V. N. M. N. 1977. *Conflicting accounts of Venda history in particular reference to the role of Mutupo in social organisation*, PhD Thesis, Queens University, Belfast.

Shoko, E. D. (ed.), 2001. Midlands State University: Inauguration and Installation Ceremony, 17 March.

Van Waarden, C. 1998. The Late Iron Age, In *DitswaMmung: The Archaeology of Botswana*, Lane P., Reid, D.A.M. and Segobye, A. (eds.), 115-160, Gaborone: Pula Press.

Zachrisson, P. 1978. *An African Area in Change, Belingwe 1894-1946: A study of Colonialism, Missionary activity and African response in Southern Rhodesia*, Gothenburg: Department of History in Gothernburg.

Chapter 9

Heritage typologies and organisation in Zimbabwe: Questions, insights and policy implications

Tapuwa Raymond Mubaya and Munyaradzi Mawere

Introduction

To neglect heritage is a cardinal sin, to invoke it a national duty (David Lowenthal 1998)

Heritage is one of the terms that have been used by almost all nations as a reference point of identity and unity (Eversole 2006). Every country has a collective identity grounded in past events and elements which are deemed significant to it, hence the term nation-states. Nation-states are unique and different from each other not only because of their geographical location and racial constitution, but ideology rooted in different socio-cultural and political backgrounds. This ideology is their common heritage. As David Lowenthal asserts in his quotation cited above, heritage resources, thus, constitute a crucial contribution to local identity and uniqueness. The protection and conservation of heritage, especially natural and cultural, is an international practice such that every nation has some system of cultural heritage management (Lee Long 2010). Zimbabwe like many other countries in Africa is gifted with varied and abundant forms of cultural and natural heritage. These forms of heritage are unfortunately fragile, finite and non-renewable. Once destroyed, they can never be recovered and replaced (Collet 1992). In fact, cultural and natural heritage are irreplaceable sources of life and inspiration.

From the foregoing, it is indubitable that natural and cultural heritage influence and shape our identity as a people. It is, therefore, imperative that such precious and priceless knotted heritage should be guarded strongly against any possible forms of threat and destruction so that it can be handed down to progeny untainted. This is one major reason why different countries have come up with legal instruments to conserve and protect cultural and natural heritage in their respective territories. At international level, Zimbabwe is a signatory to the 1972 World Heritage Convention concerning the Protection of the World's Natural and Cultural Heritage. At local level, Zimbabwe has got cultural heritage legislation in the form of the National Museums and Monuments Act Chapter 25.11 of 1972 which is administered by the National Museums and Monuments of Zimbabwe (NMMZ). The latter organisation is under the Ministry of Home Affairs and is mandated by NMMZ Act of parliament to look after the heritage of Zimbabwe on behalf of the people of Zimbabwe. The Act provides for the identification, documentation, research, preservation, presentation and management of the country's movable and immovable cultural and natural heritage of historical or scientific value or interest. NMMZ is also responsible for the establishment and administration of museums throughout the country (NMMZ Act chapter 25/11). In addition, to the above responsibilities, NMMZ also manages the country's liberation heritage within and outside the boarders of Zimbabwe. By Liberation War Heritage, we mean inheritance from the struggle against colonial rule from 1893 to the present. It comprises, tangible and intangible and movable and immovable vestiges of the country's liberation struggle (Mupira 2010).

On the other hand, the department of National Parks and Wildlife Authority (NPWA) manages and protects the fauna and flora natural heritage scientifically referred to as biodiversity. NMMZ and the NPWA are both government parastatal departments housed in two different ministries which are completely unrelated in terms of function and focus. In this chapter, we advance that the different visions of NMMZ and NRWA is one reason why in most cases these two institutions are involved in conflicts regarding the management of heritage sites with combined cultural and natural values.

The chapter seeks to broaden and deepen the reader's comprehension of the varied Zimbabwean cultural and natural heritage that gives it a unique cultural and natural identity. Drawing from local examples in Zimbabwe, the chapter explores the diverse heritage typologies in terms of their organisation, and with a view to generate insights and critical questions around policy making.

Conceptualising heritage

The discourse on heritage is mired with controversies compounded by the conceptualisation of the term "heritage" itself. This being the case, the concept of heritage has, over the years, received different interpretations from special interest groups, which makes it difficult to achieve a universally agreed definition. The complexity in the conceptualisation of heritage is further exacerbated by the fact that heritage is a dynamic and evolving term which keeps on changing meaning over time. Besides, some scholars (such as Smith, 2006) have revealed how heritage has always been associated with very old things though contrarily, heritage is not simply about old things and places but the past, present and future as human beings constantly create heritage every day. Yet, despites misconceptions, contradictions and disagreements on the conceptualisation of heritage, what different interest groups seem to agree is that heritage resources (whether natural or cultural) are invaluable assets that require special protection, conservation (or preservation) and attention from all concerned groups. Confirming this, UNESCO-ICCROM (2006) observes that although heritage is by no means uniformly desirable, it is widely viewed as a precious and irreplaceable resource, crucial to personal and collective identity and necessary for self-respect And, for this reason, people sometimes go to great lengths, often at huge expense, to protect and celebrate the heritage they already possess, to find and enhance what they feel they need, and to restore and recoup what they have lost. We should be quick, however, to underline that what appears to be at the centre of the conceptual confusion of the term "heritage" is the fact that the criterion employed in defining heritage resources vary from one country to another (see also Ndoro 2008). This means that what may be considered as heritage in one country may not be regarded as such in another. This brings to the fore the point that heritage is created and defined by the communities who uphold it. It is against this background that the concept of heritage has enjoyed sundry definitions, some of which are scholarly and others legally informed.

Besides, we underscore that though different definitions have been conjured in view of the concept of heritage, some working definitions have been proffered by scholars and different interest groups. The United Nations Educational, Scientific and Cultural Organisation (UNESCO) and the International Council of Monuments and Sites (ICOMOS) have been in the forefront in defining and championing common terminology and scope of heritage at international level since the 1960s. It was in 1965 that ICOMOS defined heritage as monuments and sites. Barely ten years later (in 1972), the World Heritage Convention Concerning the Protection of the World Cultural and Natural Heritage broadened the conceptualisation of heritage by considering it as cultural and natural property. In the same vein, Howard (2003) defined heritage as everything that people want to save (both cultural and natural). Narrowing it to inheritance, Neufeld (2000) defines heritage as everything people gain from their ancestors. This resonates with Graham's (2002: 1004) understanding of heritage – both tangible and intangible – as the continuous definition and re-affirmation of cultural identity, a screening of values, a use of memories of the past, a selective resource for the present.

From the preceding discussion, it is clear that heritage, whether cultural or natural, has to do with a legacy that people receive from their ancestors and pass on to future generations (UNESCO-ICCROM 2006). Sometimes, this legacy is created and re-created, affirmed and re-affirmed by concerned communities. We advance in this chapter that heritage is everything of value that people have inherited and wish to preserve for themselves and future generations: it encompasses all things that a society, group of people or even individuals deem necessary to retain for themselves and posterity. This means that heritage can be something transmitted or acquired from a predecessor, that is, a legacy shared now and passed on to posterity. It is possibly in the light of this understanding that the South African Heritage Resource Agency (SAHRA) (2005) claimed that heritage is our legacy from the past, what we live within the present, and what we pass on to future generations, to learn from, to marvel at and to enjoy.

However, the understanding of heritage as a legacy has led some scholars to argue that anything can be heritage. Howard (2003), for instance, argues that not everything is heritage, but anything can be heritage. He goes further to assert that heritage can be regarded as all the inherited resources which people value for the reasons beyond efficacy and utility. It is apparent from the preceding discussion that heritage goes beyond the physical remains from the past to include aspects of culture such as language, spiritual beliefs and many intangible aspects that can be used now and passed on to the next generation. This unpacking and conceptualisation leads us to yet another characterisation of heritage known as private heritage and public heritage respectively. Private heritage, also known as unofficial heritage, includes family heirlooms or photographs albums that are passed on from one generation to the next (Howard 2003). In Zimbabwe, private heritage is known as *nhaka* or *ilifa* as it includes the deceased's estate in the form of wealth, houses, domestic goods and their spouse and children. Public heritage (also known as national heritage or official heritage) is legacy that belongs to the entire nation and is protected by legislation. The NMMZ Act Chapter 25:11, for example, makes provisions for the compulsory acquisition of private heritage by the state in the interest of the public.

Yet, the different conceptualisations and characterisation of heritage, in itself, calls for further rigorous interrogation and scrutiny especially in view of policy making around heritage resources.

Heritage Typologies

The 1972 Convention Concerning the Protection of the World Cultural and Natural Heritage, commonly referred to as the World

Heritage Convention, makes a distinction in its classification of heritage into two broad categories namely; cultural and natural. At international level, there are basically three main types of heritage namely; cultural heritage, natural heritage, and mixed cultural and natural heritage. The third category implies that it is normal for heritage to fall into more than one category or field, hence the term mixed heritage. Mixed heritage contain both elements of cultural and natural heritage. Yet even the most commonly talked about heritage category, cultural heritage, can further be divided into tangible and intangible heritage. The tangible heritage can also be further sub-divided into moveable and immovable heritage. It is crucial to point out that these different types of heritage are intricately linked and cannot be completely divorced from each other. Below is a simplified diagram that shows the different heritage typologies in Zimbabwe.

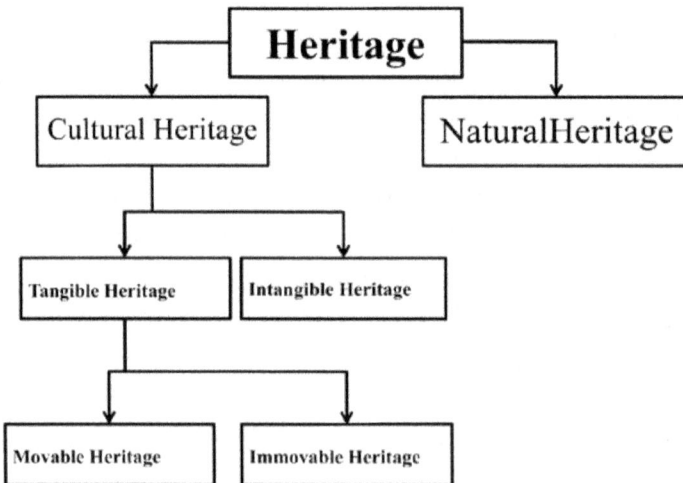

Fig. 1: Types of Cultural Heritage
Diagram designed by Dr.T.P.Thondhlana

What should be underlined in view of heritage typologies in Zimbabwe is our observation that heritage (both natural and cultural) is a medium through which identity, power and society are produced and reproduced (see also Munjeri 2003). This is because, as already highlighted in the preceding paragraphs, heritage is the legacy of physical and cultural artefacts and intangible attributes of a group or society that are inherited from past generations, maintained in the present and bestowed for the benefit of future generations. This holistic understanding of heritage (as with culture itself) has prompted the continual broadening of the scope of heritage over the years such that it now encompasses intangibles such as ethical values, social customs, belief systems, religious ceremonies and traditional knowledge systems (see also UNESCO 2003).

As is revealed in the heritage typologies in the diagram above (fig. 1), Zimbabwe's thrust on heritage is much focused on cultural heritage. This is not to undermine the importance of natural heritage, but to show that the value bestowed in culture goes a step further in corroborating the need to protect all heritage resources (including natural heritage). Cultural heritage tells us about the traditions, beliefs, achievements and existence of natural features (or biodiversity) in a country, including its people. Human beings use resources and they become important aspects of their culture, hence the term cultural heritage.

Just to elaborate further on the heritage typology in fig. 1, we reiterate that two types of cultural heritage can be distinguished namely; tangible and intangible. The former include material heritage (it can be physically touched) such as monuments, buildings, paintings, objects etcetera while the latter encompass immaterial heritage such as music, dance, literature, theatre, language, religious ceremonies, traditional performances and many others (see also UNESCO-ICCROM 2006; UNESCO 2008). For purposes of clarity and the scope of the book to which this chapter is part, in the ensuing sections, we discuss in detail the different forms of heritage in Zimbabwe as is shown in the heritage typologies in fig 1.

Forms of heritage in Zimbabwe revisited

(A) Cultural heritage

Cultural heritage can exist in many forms. As exemplified in fig. 1 above, two broad forms of cultural heritage can be distinguished namely; tangible heritage and intangible heritage.

(Ai) Tangible heritage

Tangible heritage is heritage that exists in material form. As the name implies, tangible heritage is physically verifiable, that is, it can be physically touched and seen. It includes, but not limited to monuments, buildings, sculpture, statues, bridges, walls, forts debilitation architectural works, mines, cultural landscapes, dresses, masks, shrines and cemeteries. Technically speaking, tangible heritage includes all works of arts and culture that can be seen and touched. As indicated in the diagram above *(fig 1)*, tangible heritage can further be sub-divided into movable and immovable heritage. Movable heritage can be easily moved from one place to another, for instance, objects such as the Zimbabwean birds, archaeological finds, museum collections, fossils and many others. Contrarily, immovable heritage cannot be moved from its place of origin for example, monuments such as Great Zimbabwe, Khami, Musimbira monument, Victoria Falls, Matobo cultural landscape etc. Examples of tangible cultural heritage include, but not limited to:

Archaeological heritage

Archaeological heritage include sites and places relating to all manifestations of human activity, as well as their associated cultural landscapes are prominent features of the cultural heritage of a people, in this case, Zimbabweans. It comprises all relics, objects and human traces from past periods of history on the surface, in the earth and in water bodies whose preservation and study contributes to the uncovering of the historical development of mankind and his links to the natural environment and for which archaeological research is the main source of information. Given that archaeological heritage is a human creation, it provides insights into the cosmology, epistemology and metaphysics of past societies as well as the way contemporary communities relate to the cosmologies and places designated as archaeological heritage (see also ICOMOS 1990). Ndoro (2001) supporting the same idea argues that some archaeological heritage such as rock shelters, rock art, or stone enclosures (for example, *madzimbabwe*) hold cultural and spiritual significance because the communities regard them as part of their cosmological environment. All remains and objects and any other traces of humankind from the past are considered elements of archaeological heritage. The notion of archaeological heritage includes structures, constructions, groups of buildings, developed sites, moveable objects, monuments of other kinds as well as their context, whether situated on land or underwater.

In the case of a country [such as Zimbabwe], archaeological heritage consists of the physical remains left behind by previous inhabitants. The remains may be as old as the beginning of mankind and as modern as yesterday (Collet 1992). Yet, whatever their age, archaeological remains are non-renewable; once destroyed they can never be replaced (Collet 1992). Archaeological sites fall into several categories which include:

Rock Art Sites

Zimbabwe has one of the highest concentrations of rock paintings in Africa. Nearly 4000 sites have been recorded and have some of the most skilfully executed rock art in the world (Garlake 1990; Mguni 2002). The artists who painted these works were late Stone Age Hunter-gatherers who lived in Southern Africa from about 20 000 years ago. Rock Art is reflective of the life of both Bantu communities and Hunter Gatherers as they lived thousands of years ago, depicting hunting scenes, religious beliefs, commercial life, ritual ceremonies, dancing and their everyday struggle to survive. This is some form of San rock art image that occurs in Zimbabwe in its thousands (Garlake, 1990; Mguni, 2002, 2004). Rock Art sites are scattered throughout Zimbabwe, with the largest concentration in

South Western Zimbabwe in the Matopos, and also in North Eastern Zimbabwe around Domboshava. Notable examples of Rock Art sites in Zimbabwe include Domboshava, Diana's Vow, Murehwa Rock Shelter, Chamavara, Dengeni, Nswatugi and Silozwane among many others.

Madzimbahwe (dzimbabwe tradition dry stone structures)
Zimbabwe tradition sites (which are part of dry stone walled heritage sites) are called *Dzimbabwe* (*dzimba dzamabwe* in Shona) which means owing to their structures that were constructed by piling stones one on top of the other generally without the use of any binding material. The stone walls were constructed by the indigenous people who are believed to be the ancestors of the Shona people who constitute the majority of the people in Zimbabwe. According to historical records, the walls were constructed between the eleventh and nineteenth centuries (see for example Garlake 1972, 1990). To date, there are over 400 recorded stone wall monuments dotted across the southern African *region of which Zimbabwe is part* (Ndoro 2001, emphasis original). Although these sites were abandoned for political, economic, environmental and social reasons, they continue to play a very important role to the current communities. They are highly valued to the extent that the biggest of these sites, Great Zimbabwe has given its name to the country. Two of the Zimbabwe tradition sites namely Great Zimbabwe and Khami monument are on the prestigious World Heritage list, twenty-six others are National Monuments, which is the highest status sites can have in the country (Chipunza 2005). Some of the examples include Dhlo-Dhlo and Naletale both in Gweru, Matendera in Buhera, Tsindi in Marondera, Kubiku in Gutu, Majiri in Masvingo, Chibvumani and Musimbira in Bikita, among many others.

Abandoned agricultural systems
A well-known example of abandoned agricultural systems in Zimbabwe is that of the Nyanga terraces, water furrows and settlements. Nyanga archaeological complex presents an impressive

landscape of stone built features, extending more than 7000 square kilometres in north-eastern Zimbabwe and constitute one of the largest agglomerations of stone structures in Africa (Soper 2002). Some of the features of the abandoned agricultural systems include widespread agricultural terracing and a variety of settlement structures and defensive works, as well as old water furrows and ridge-and-ditch cultivation works. These archaeological remains are a material manifestation of a Later Iron Age society and its agricultural practices which developed over a period of perhaps 600 years from around AD1300 (Soper 2002). As such, the Nyanga agricultural complex has an important place in the history and achievements of the peoples of Zimbabwe, demonstrating their appropriate adaptation to a range of local environmental and climatic change.

Grain bins

The invasion of Zimbabwe by the Ndebele in the late 1830s led to a political conflict between major ethnic groups (Shona and Ndebele) in the country. This period is usually referred to as *Nguva yeDzviti* (the 'Refuge' Period). The Ndebele raided the Shona in search of food, and to counteract this, the Shona built rough stonewalls and grain bins in hidden locations. The grain bins are dotted right round the country, but mostly in the South and Central parts of Zimbabwe where the Ndebele raids concentrated most. As National Monuments, grain bins are represented by Sibizini grain bins in Central Zimbabwe. By and large, there are several examples of archaeological heritage of this kind; hence the examples given above are not exhaustive.

Historic buildings

In Zimbabwe, historic buildings form another typology of heritage. According to NMMZ Act, all the buildings and structures that were constructed on or before 1910 are historic buildings that are worth conserving. These structures cannot be altered without the consent of the Executive Director of the NMMZ. Masvingo is the oldest town and has many historic buildings like Fort Victoria,

Meikles Building, Victoria Hotel, Italian Chapel, Bell and Curfew Towers. Most of these buildings were built during the colonial period and are also found in other towns of the country. These buildings are quite distinct and have been preserved as part of the heritage.

Old forts

A Fort is a defensive structure. In Zimbabwe, there are a number of forts built by the European settlers during the first uprising of the indigenous Africans against colonial rule. These are mainly found in Central and Southern Zimbabwe where the war was intense, and they include, Fort Tuli, Fort Victoria, and others. Fort Tuli is located 90km west of Beitbridge on the eastern bank of the Shashe River. The fort was built in July 1890 by the Pioneer Column. Until 1993, the fort was the main point of entry from South Africa into Zimbabwe. Africans also constructed some defensive forts like Chawomera and Nyangwe forts in Nyanga National Parks before the advent of colonialism.

Memorials and Shrines

Memorials and shrines are structures which were erected in honour of those who were mostly killed during the First Chimurenga War. Allan Wilson Memorial, which is a national monument, is one such example. Located at World's View at the Matopos, the memorial commemorates the men of the Shangani Patrol of 1893 led by Major Allan Wilson who were killed by the Ndebele troops on the 4th December 1893 near the Shangani River. The Shangani battlefield memorial was erected where the bodies were buried but the remains were transferred to Great Zimbabwe and in 1904 were again transferred to their respective resting places in the Matobo Hills. Allan Wilson was a member of the Pioneer Column who after the occupation of Mashonaland led the Pioneer Column which invaded the Ndebele state in 1893.

Liberation heritage

In Zimbabwe there is strong recognition of a new brand of heritage called liberation heritage. It is heritage in honour of the liberation war and the fallen and living heroes and heroines who died in and outside the country while on national duty. This heritage is relatively new in Zimbabwe. It was realised soon after independence and can be expressed through heroes' acres, provincial heroes' acres, guns, weaponry and regalia. Graves of victims of the liberation struggle are also considered as heritage. To this category, the Heroes Acre in Harare, where Zimbabwean heroes and heroines mainly those fallen comrades who were in the forefront during the liberation struggle against the colonial rule are buried, is one good example.

Colonial heritage

This is heritage that originates from a colonial past and is associated with the colonisation of the country by the European settlers. When the Pioneer Column conquered this country they erected a number of structures which served different purposes. Some of the structures were meant to perpetuate conquest and dominance. Others were erected to honour those who led the colonial process in Rhodesia (now Zimbabwe). For instance, Rhodes' grave at the World View in the Matopos is one such example. Though controversially viewed especially by Pan African scholars, this has nevertheless become part and parcel of the history and heritage of Zimbabwe. No wonder some scholars like Muringaniza (2002) claim that Rhodes' grave remains a source of inspiration to many white people in Zimbabwe. We underscore, however, that to many indigenous Zimbabweans, Rhode's grave is a reminder and symbol of economic, social, religious and political subjugation: It is a scar on the face of indigenous people of Zimbabwe who toiled and suffered in the hands of the colonial regime. The Providential Pass in Masvingo is another example of colonial heritage.

(Aii) Intangible cultural heritage

The UNESCO Convention for the Safeguarding of the Intangible Cultural Heritage (UNESCO: 2003) Article 2 consider Intangible Cultural Heritage as:

> The practices, representations, expressions, knowledge, skills – as well as the instruments, objects, artefacts and cultural spaces associated therewith – that communities, groups and, in some cases, individuals recognise as part of their cultural heritage. This intangible cultural heritage, transmitted from generation to generation, is constantly recreated by communities and groups in response to their environment, their interaction with nature and their history, and provides them with a sense of identity and continuity, thus promoting respect for cultural diversity and human creativity.

It is important to note that intangible heritage encompasses all forms and expressions of culture developed and handed down by word of mouth (oral tradition) and practice. To be more specific, this includes dance, drama, music, ceremonies, festivals, legends, myths, folktales, and all forms of verbal art (UNESCO 2003). In a general sense, these occur as events that may be perceived or heard while they last, but which cannot be touched or handled like objects. Put differently, intangible heritage is embedded in the minds and memories of the people who create and/or perform them. The "intangible cultural heritage" as defined in the paragraph above, is sometimes called living heritage and is manifested inter alia in the following domains; oral traditions and expressions, including language as a vehicle of the intangible cultural heritage, performing arts, social practices, rituals and festive events, knowledge and practices concerning nature and the universe and traditional craftsmanship (UNESCO 2003). In view of this, we underline that intangible cultural heritage can only be heritage when it is recognised as such by the communities, groups or individuals that create or re-create, affirm or re-affirm, maintain and transmit it.

Oral traditions and expressions

The oral traditions and expressions domain encompasses an enormous variety of spoken forms including proverbs, riddles, tales, legends, myths, songs, dramatic performances etc. Oral traditions and expressions are used to pass on knowledge, cultural and social values and collective memory (UNESCO 2003). They play a crucial part in keeping cultures alive and in shaping and preserving a particular people's identity. Some types of oral expression are common and can be used by entire communities while others are limited to particular [social] groups such as children, only men or women, perhaps, or only the elderly.

Performing arts

Performing arts range from vocal and instrumental music, dance to theatre. They include numerous cultural expressions that reflect human creativity and that are also found, to some extent, in many other intangible cultural heritage domains. Music is perhaps the most universal of the performing arts and is found in every society, most often as an integral part of other performing art forms and other domains of intangible cultural heritage including rituals, festive events or oral traditions (UNESCO 2003). In Zimbabwe, examples include *mbende/Jerusalema* dance, *mbakumba, chinyambera, ngororombe, jiti,* among many others.

Social practices, rituals and festive events

Social practices, rituals and festive events are habitual activities that structure and shape the lives of communities and groups and that are shared by and relevant to many of their members. They are significant because they re-affirm the identity of those who practice them as a group or a society and, whether performed in public or private, are closely linked to important events (UNESCO 2003). In addition, they are closely linked to a community's worldview and perception of its own history, memory and identity as a people. Social practices, rituals and festive events vary from small gatherings to large-scale social celebrations and commemorations. Rituals and festive events often take place at special times and places and remind a community of aspects of its worldview and history. In some cases, access to rituals may be restricted to certain members of the community. Initiation rites, rain petitioning ceremonies and burial ceremonies are examples of such rituals where some members of the society are restricted or excluded. Some festive events, however, are a key part of public life and are open to all members of society (UNESCO 2003).

(B) Natural heritage

According to ASE Report (2011:13), natural heritage designates outstanding physical, biological and geological features; habitats of threatened plants or animal species and areas of value on scientific or aesthetic grounds or from a conservation perspective. As further espoused in the same report, the following shall be considered as natural heritage; natural features consisting of physical and biological formations or groups of such formations, which are of outstanding universal value from the aesthetic or scientific point of view, geological and physiographical formations and precisely delineated areas which constitute the habitat of threatened species of animals and plants of outstanding universal value from the point of view of science or conservation and natural sites or precisely delineated natural areas of outstanding universal value from the point of view of science, conservation or natural beauty (see ASE Report 2011: 13).

From the foregoing, it is apparent that natural heritage involves all forms heritage that can be considered natural and that can exist or that came into being without the human input or alteration, including plants and animals. No wonder scholars like Pace (2003) argues that natural heritage sites must be outstanding examples that show major stages of the earth's history, or contain outstanding natural phenomena or are areas of exceptional natural beauty and aesthetic importance. In Zimbabwe, examples include landscapes, balancing rocks, rivers, fossil forests, animals, geological caves and natural falls. Due to the value accorded to these features, they (together with natural heritage sites) often serve as an important component in a country's tourist industry attracting many visitors from abroad as well as locally. In the ensuing paragraphs, we elaborate on some of the examples of natural heritage resources in Zimbabwe.

Chiremba Balancing Rocks

Geographically speaking, Chiremba Balancing Rocks is situated adjacent to Epworth community, some 15 km to the south-east of the city of Harare in Zimbabwe. It was declared a "national monument" in 1994. The balancing rocks are made up of rock formations perfectly balanced without other support. The balancing rocks contain impressive clusters of granite boulders, piled one on top of another, in some cases giving rise to small kopjes. Two sets of balancing rocks are of particular interest. As postulated by Maroyi (2011), the first set of the balancing rocks is referred to by the local community as "Domboremari" meaning literally "the money rock" because it appears on the former paper currency of Zimbabwe. It is worth noting as well that the geomorphology of Chiremba Balancing Rocks has also attracted the attention of the Standard Chartered Bank of Zimbabwe which has adopted the rock formation locally referred to as the "Flying Boat Formation" as a seal to represent financial and banking stability and strength (see also Maroyi 2011). As such, the Balancing rocks have assumed a symbolic importance as a seal of the Reserve Bank of Zimbabwe and, in this context; the natural stability represents financial, banking stability, and strength (Vumbunu and Manyanhire 2010).

Victoria Falls

Victoria Falls (also known as Mosi-Oa-Tunya) is one of the most spectacular features in Zimbabwe (and indeed the world-over). It was declared a World Heritage Site in 1989. The World Heritage Site and its environment covers approximately 30km radius from the falls. As one of the Seven Wonders of the World, it has attracted much international and local attention over the years. On the Zimbabwean site, National Parks and Wildlife Authority is administering and managing the area. Located on the Zambezi River, about 1000km from is source, the Victoria Falls are Zimbabwe's best known geographical feature and tourist attraction. With a width of 1708m and an average depth of about 100m, they form the biggest single curtain of falling water in the world.

Chinhoyi Caves

According to the National Museums and Monuments Act, a cave is a monument, and there are several of these features in Zimbabwe. Some of these features have already been discovered, but others are yet to be discovered. Of the already discovered caves in Zimbabwe, the Chinhoyi caves are the most spectacular ones. They are located in a range of hills some 10km west of Chinhoyi town. A labyrinth of limestone caves exists on an open sink-hole with vertical sides in which the water reaches a depth of over 100m. The caves are known to the local people as 'Chirorodziva' (pool of the fall), referring either to the fall or rock that created the sinkhole or to the use of the pool and its cliffs as a place of execution by the Nguni people in the 1830s. A former Chief Chinhoyi from which the area takes its name at one time reported that the caves were used as a refuge from raids by the Ndebele over 100 years ago.

Fossil Forests

Fossil forests are also one of the natural heritage resources in Zimbabwe. These are mainly concentrated in central Zimbabwe and Northern Zimbabwe where there are vast forests of different plant species. Some of these forest remains, which have fossilised over a long period of time, are also part of the Zimbabwean natural heritage.

Classification of heritage sites in Zimbabwe

In Zimbabwe, monuments have been categorised on the National Monuments Register into three classes for administrative purposes

(Chipunza 2005). The classifications are explicated in the table below (table 1).

Class 1	Characteristics	Examples
National heritage sites are those places/objects with qualities so exceptional that they are of special national significance.	i) have custodians in place; ii) have site museums; iii) are accessible through all-weather roads; iv) are provided with brochures, pamphlets, comprehensive research publications; **v)** include World Heritage Sites	i) Great Zimbabwe National and World Heritage Site (Masvingo) ii) Khami National and World Heritage Site (Bulawayo) iii) Domboshava Rock Art Site (Harare) iv) Ziwa National Monument (Nyanga) v) National and Provincial Heroes Acres vi) Matopos Rock Art Sites vii) Tsindi National Monument (Marondera) **viii)** Diana's Vow Rock Art site (Rusape).
Class 2	**Characteristics**	**Examples**
	i) are semi-public sites; ii) are partially accessible; iii) lack significant visitorship; iv) have literature available at some sites; v) have no site custodians; have no site museums	i) Chamavara (Masvingo) ii) Zinjanja (Gweru) iii) Majiri (Masvingo) iv) Alter Site (Mutare) v) Kagumbudzi and Matendera (both in Buhera).
Class 3	**Characteristics**	**Examples**

	i) are non-public sites; ii) are not easily accessible; iii) have very few specialist visitors; iv) lack amenities on site	i) Dambarare ii) Makaha	

World heritage sites in Zimbabwe

Throughout the world, there are cultural and natural heritage sites that are considered to have special importance to humankind. Among these sites, some are considered to be of outstanding value to all humanity in the world; hence they are known as World Heritage Sites. A site becomes a World Heritage site when it is inscribed on the United Nations Educational, Scientific and Cultural Organization's World Heritage List for its outstanding universal value. According to the *Operational Guidelines for the Implementation of the World Heritage Convention,* "Outstanding universal value means cultural and/or natural significance which is so exceptional as to transcend national boundaries and to be of common importance for present and future generations of all humanity" (*Operational Guidelines for the Implementation of the World Heritage Convention 1972).*

In Zimbabwe, there are five sites that have been declared as World Heritage Sites. We should underscore that what makes the concept of World Heritage exceptional is its universal application. This means that World Heritage sites belong to all the peoples of the world, irrespective of the territory on which they are located. In the table below (table 2), we elaborate on the five World Heritage Sites in Zimbabwe.

Name of site	Type of Site	Year Proclaimed
i) Mana Pools National Park	Natural Heritage	1984
ii) Great Zimbabwe monument	Cultural Heritage	1986
iii) Khami National Monument	Cultural Property	1986
iv) Victoria Falls	Natural Heritage	1989
v) Matobos Cultural Landscape	Mixed Heritage	2003

Heritage management in Zimbabwe: Questions, insights and policy implications

While it is almost universally agreed that heritage is an invaluable resource to humankind and so is worth protecting, its management in many parts of the world (for example in Zimbabwe) has met with challenges and even controversies. Though in most cases the source of the problems associated with heritage management range from community participation (or lack of participation) to ownership, the sources of the challenges vary from place to place and from time to time.

Emphasising on the universal interest by humanity to protect heritage, Hall and McArthur (1993) observe that apart from the fact that heritage is an integral component of sustainable development, four major reasons could account for the unprecedented interest in heritage conservation by different countries. The four reasons are listed below:

    i)   Rapid urbanisation has changed the world and people seek to keep buildings, townscapes and objects which help to maintain with the past and therefore build a sense of continuity in their lives.

    ii) Heritage creates individual, community and national pride and identities which enable people to define who they are.

iii) Heritage has scientific/educational and conservation significance and may be representative of certain natural and cultural environments.

iv) Heritage has assumed economic importance as people increasingly want to visit heritage sites and experience what has been preserved.

The four reasons elaborated above can be further simplified diagrammatically as is shown below:

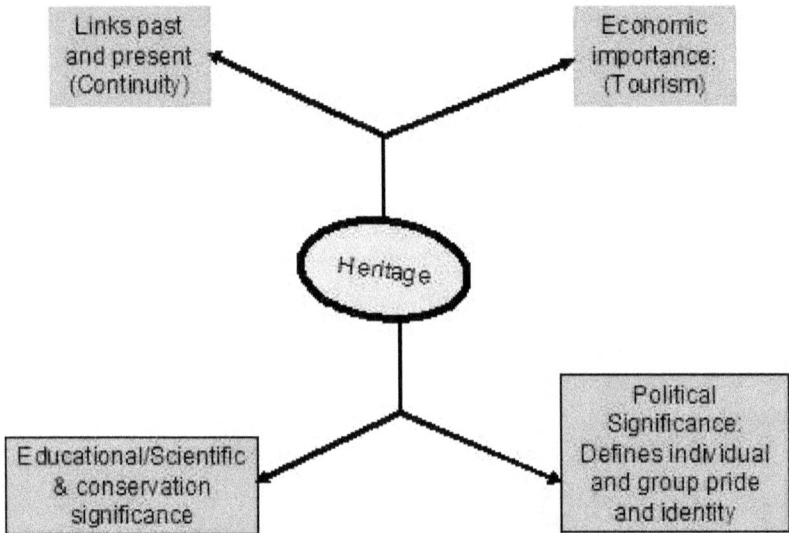

Fig 2: *Four major reasons for preserving heritage*
Source: Adopted from Hall and McArthur 1993.

The diagram above (fig. 2) illustrates the importance and value of heritage to people. Relating the diagram to heritage management in Zimbabwe, it is emphasised that there is need to link theory with practice (at social, political and economic levels) and the local with the national and the global. This is to say that in order for people, particularly the local communities where heritage resources are found, to appreciate and reap the benefits that accrue from the sustainable use of heritage resources, policies that support the conservation of heritage and seriously consider local communities input, should be crafted and formulated at national level. Such policies should complement the existing Conventions and Charters that protect heritage in its diverse forms.

Yet, though Zimbabwe has some laws crafted for the protection and conservation of cultural heritage, there is no policy and operational framework that has been developed to cater for the different types of heritage found in the country and even all the stakeholders involved in the management of heritage sites. This raises critical questions on why this scenario and how to go about the problem of exclusion in policy making and heritage management. We advance in this chapter that the problem of exclusion (of other stakeholders) could possibly be due to the fact that there is no professional independent board that lobbies and spearheads developmental issues in the heritage sector. Another contributing factor could be that Government departments dealing with heritage are scattered in different ministries, hence it is difficult to bring them together for the same cause.

Just to elaborate on the above, it could be noted that at national level, the governance of *arts* and *culture* activities in Zimbabwe is segmented to the following ministries: Education, Sport, Arts and Culture (the arts, arts education, the National Arts Council, the National Gallery, the National Library and Documentation Services), Home Affairs (Heritage sector – National Museums and Monuments of Zimbabwe, National Archives, Censorship Board), Justice, Legal and Parliamentary Affairs (copyright legislation), Information and Publicity (audio-visual industries – broadcasting, TV, film and music recording industry), Local Government (Chiefs and local authorities), Medium and Small Enterprises industries (national handcrafts centre), Environment and Tourism (cultural tourism), Higher and Tertiary Education (UNESCO and arts teacher education), Environment and Natural Resources Management (natural heritage sites), Health and Child Welfare (ZINATHA, traditional midwives), Agriculture (herbal medicine, Indigenous Knowledge Systems –

indigenous varieties) and Foreign Affairs (Cultural Diplomacy) (NPAAC 2012: 8).

In light of this scenario, it could be seen that there are no structures or committees put in place by government to harmonise the activities of government departments and parastatals in ministries with arts, culture and heritage and their positions on international cultural matters and developments. As a result, the absence of structures that relate to all institutions responsible for cultural heritage activities has led to a failure in the conception and formulation of a comprehensive national cultural heritage policy (see also NPAAC 2012).

The other problem is the one highlighted in the paragraphs above, that of exclusion. In Zimbabwe, the public is not meaningfully engaged in cultural heritage matters (Mawere et al 2013). As a result, most of them are ignorant about the laws that conserve and protect heritage. Add to that, most of the law enforcing agents (the Zimbabwe Republic Police) are ignorant about the existence of NMMZ Act Chapter 25/11. On the other hand, the private sector which is mostly instrumental in policy making and developmental issues are not as well engaged to participate and advice all stakeholders involved in heritage management. What then obtains is that NMMZ remains the only organisation responsible for initiating the drafting of policy documents related to heritage resources. The solo participation of NMMZ in heritage resource management partly explains the failure of NMMZ to sustainably manage most of the heritage resources in the country. In fact, more than three decades after attaining independence NMMZ has failed *not* only to review the legislation governing cultural heritage, but also to lobby for a cultural heritage policy. Owing to the current state of the economy in which the central government is failing to adequately fund the cultural heritage sector and other government departments and parastatals, NMMZ is finding it even harder to manage the heritage resources entrusted to its custody.

It is also interesting to note that in Zimbabwe there are three state universities namely, the University of Zimbabwe, Midlands State

University and Great Zimbabwe University all offering enterprising modules on archaeology, museums and heritage studies. The later specialises in culture and heritage studies. Instead of leading and spearheading the move, these universities have also folded their hands and unfortunately added their names to the list of institutions blaming NMMZ for its failures. The questions that continue lingering in the minds of critical observers especially in view of the above explained scenario are: Who is to blame for the problems haunting heritage management in Zimbabwe? Is it Zimbabwe or NMMZ? Is it the universities or the various stakeholders in the heritage sector? Who is supposed to initiate the move?

While it could be agreed that heritage management is currently facing serious problems, there is no agreement as to who should shoulder the blame. We argue in view of the challenges being faced and the failures by NMMZ that since heritage is a national resource, everyone concerned should play a part in its conservation and preservation. This should be a shared responsibility and priority for all Zimbabweans especially considering that Zimbabwe is perhaps the only country in the world to be named after a heritage site (Great Zimbabwe), a clear testimony of the importance of heritage.

Apart from questions and insights highlighted in the preceding discussion, the other equally probing questions which beg for serious responses are those to do with heritage typologies: Why is it that heritage is categorised into typologies? Also, is it feasible to clearly draw a line of demarcation between the different categories of heritage, say between the tangible and intangible? Is it not that separating the tangible from the intangible similar to separating the mind from the body or nature from culture? In view of these questions, we argue with Bouchenaki (2004) that tangible heritage is the spatial representation of culture while intangible heritage is the behavioural representation of culture, which may require non-intangible tools or locations to facilitate the behavioural representation. In fact, tangible and intangible heritage especially in an African context, and in particular Zimbabwe, are intricately interwoven such that separating them sometimes results in

203

conceptual problems. The question of heritage categorisation, as the question of heritage resource management raised in the previous paragraphs, thus, calls for a rethinking in the way heritage resources are viewed and categorised.

Conclusion

This chapter has discussed heritage typologies and organisation in Zimbabwe with a view to raise questions and insights for heritage resource management and policy making. Through critical questioning and penetrating analysis of the current heritage management in Zimbabwe, the chapter has registered a number of anomalies that for a long time now have been taken for granted in the heritage sector. These include but not limited to heritage typologies such as the tangible/intangible divide and the exclusion of some stakeholders in policy making and management of heritage resources. From the shortcomings and challenges confronting the current heritage sector in Zimbabwe, the chapter has called for a concerted effort by the Zimbabwean government (through its NMMZ) to engage all stakeholders in a manner that strives to foster and renders a vantage point for the nexus between quality management and sustainability of all heritage sites in the country.

References

Australia State of the Environment, 2011. Independent Report to the Australian Government Minister for Sustainability, Environment, Water, Population and Communities. Canberra: DSEWPaC.

Bouchenaki, M. 2004. *The interdependency of the tangible and intangible cultural heritage*. Paper presented at the Place-memory-meaning: preserving intangible values in monuments and sites, ICOMOS 14th General Assembly and Scientific Symposium, Victoria Falls.

Graham, G. J. Ashworth and Tunbridge, J.E. 2000. *A Geography of Heritage: Power, Culture, and Economy*, London.

Chikohomero, C. 2012. *The Crystal*, Black Crystal Consulting (Pvt) Ltd, Issue No. 6, Mount Pleasant, Harare.

Chipunza, K. 2005. Protection of Immovable Cultural Heritage in Zimbabwe: An evaluation. In: Ndoro W and Pwiti, G. (eds.), *Legal Frameworks for the Protection of Immovable Cultural Heritage in Africa*, ICCROM Conservation Studies 5, ICCROM.

Collet, P. 1992. *The Archaeological Heritage of Zimbabwe: A Master Plan for Resource Conservation and Development*, Harare, National Museums and Monuments of Zimbabwe.

Eversole, R. 2006. Heritage and Regional Development: A Process-and-outcomes Typology, *Australasian Journal of Regional Studies, Vol. 12, No. 3.*

Garlake, P.S. 1990. *Symbols of the paintings of Zimbabwe*, South African Archaeological Bulleting, 45: 17-27.

Garlake, P. S. 1972. *The hunter's vision: The pre-historic art of Zimbabwe*, Washington University Press: USA.

Hall, C. M and McArthur, S. 1993. *Heritage Management: an introductory framework* in: Hall, C. Michael and McArthur, Simon (eds.), *Heritage Management in New Zealand and Australia: visitor management, interpretation and marketing*, Oxford University Press, Auckland.

Heritage Festival, 2012. Harare, Zimbabwe.

Howard, P. 2003. Heritage: Management, Interpretation, Identity, London: Continuum.

ICOMOS, 1990. *Charter for the Protection and Management of the Archaeological Heritage*, International Council of Monuments and Sites.

Katsamudanga, S. 2003. The Dilemma of Preserving Intangible Heritage in Zimbabwe, In: *ICOMOS Scientific Symposium: Place-Memory-Meaning: Preserving Intangible Values in Monuments and Sites*, p.337-342. Paris: ICOMOS.

Lee Long, D. 2010. Cultural Heritage Management in Postcolonial Polities: Not the Heritage of the Other, International Journal of Heritage Studies, 6:4, 317-322.

Lowenthal, D. 1998. *The Heritage Crusade and the Spoils of History*, Cambridge University Press.

Maroyi, A. 2011. Protection of an archaeological site: A case study of Chiremba balancing rocks, Epworth, Harare, Zimbabwe, Scientific Research and Essays, Vol. 6(27), pp. 5718-5725, 16.

Mawere, M., Mubaya, T., and Sagiya, M. 2013. Challenges, dilemmas, and potentialities for poverty relief by heritage sites in Zimbabwe: Voices from Chibvumani heritage site stakeholder, *Journal of Sustainable Development in Africa*, 15 (1): 186- 198.

Mguni, S. 2002. Continuity and change in San belief and ritual: Some aspects of the enigmatic 'formling' and tree motifs from Matopo Hills Rock Art, Zimbabwe, MA dissertation, Johannesburg: University of the Witwatersrand, South Africa.

Mguni, S. 2004. Cultured representation: Understanding 'formlings', an enigmatic motif in the Rock Art of Zimbabwe, Journal of Archaeology, 4: 181-199.

Munjeri, D. 2003. Anchoring African Cultural and Natural Heritage: The Significance of Local Community Awareness in the Context of Capacity-Building, *World Heritage Papers, 13*: 76-81.

Mupira, P. 2010. A framework for managing Zimbabwe's liberation war heritage, First Draft, Unpublished, National Museums and Monuments of Zimbabwe, Harare, Zimbabwe.

Muringaniza, S. 2004. Heritage that hurts: The case of the grave of Cecil John Rhodes in the Matopos National Park, Zimbabwe, In: Cressidda, F, Hubert, J and Turnbullp (eds.), The dead and their possession, Repatriation in Principle, Policy and Practice, London: Routledge.

National Museums and Monuments of Zimbabwe. 1972. *NMMZ Act Chapter 25:11,* Harare.

Ndoro, W. 2001. *Your Monument our Shrine: The Preservation of Great Zimbabwe, Studies in African Archaeology, 19*, Uppsala.

Ndoro, W, Mumma, A. and Abungu, G. (eds.), 2008. Cultural Heritage and the Law, Protecting Immovable Heritage in English Speaking Countries of Southern Africa, ICCROM Conservation Studies 8, Rome: ICCROM.

NPAAC, 2012. Research on Legal Instruments on Arts and Culture in Zimbabwe, Nhimbe Trust, Bulawayo, Zimbabwe.

Pace. A. 2003. Heritage: Notes from a Small Place, Workshop Presentation on Cultural and Natural Heritage, The Superintendent of Cultural Heritage, Government of Malta.

UNESCO, 2003. "The Convention for the Safeguarding of the Intangible Cultural Heritage," available online at unesdoc.unesco.org/images/0018/001897/189761e.pdf.

UNESCO-ICCROM 2006. Introducing Young People to the Protection of Heritage Sites and Historic Cities: A Practical Guide for School Teachers in the Arab Region.

UNESCO. 2008. *Operational Guidelines for the Implementation of the World Heritage Convention*, Paris: UNESCO.

SAHRA, 2005. *South African Heritage Resources Newsletter,* 1, (1).

Smith, L. 2006. *Uses of Heritage,* Oxon. Routledge.

Soper, R.2002. Nyanga: Ancient Fields, Settlements and Agricultural History in Zimbabwe, British Institute in Eastern Africa, London.

Throsby, D. 2002. Paying for the Past: Economics, Cultural Heritage and Public Policy.

Vumbunu, T, and Manyanhire, I. O. 2010. Tourists Arrivals at Chiremba Balancing Rocks in Epworth Zimbabwe. *Journal of Sustainable Development in Africa, 12*(8), 241-253.

Chapter 10

Theories of culture: Juxtaposing cultural relativism, ethnocentrism and determinism in contemporary Zimbabwe

Francis Muchemwa, Tapuwa R. Mubaya and Munyaradzi Mawere

Introduction

The discourse on culture is highly historic and has sustained controversies of epic proportions in African anthropological and other such disciplines. The controversies have largely been a result of the nebulous nature and complexity of the concept of culture coupled with the different interpretations evoked by the study of the concept across different disciplines. The complexity of culture as a concept has been precipitated by the fact that different societies have different cultures that distinguish them from one another. In fact, human beings are unique species in the universe given their special communication and thinking capacities besides their locally humanly unique culture that distinguishes them from other animals. This is to say that human beings are identified by their respective culture which also separates human beings from other kinds of existence (Tomlinson 1999). This is despite the fact that the world is gradually becoming a single village through the processes of modernity and globalisation that that continually emphasises oneness and homogeneity across societies.

Taking the instance of the current inevitably irreversible wave of globalisation, one realises that the wave has in many ways, removed cultural boundaries between different countries of the world thereby increasingly bringing people of different cultures in closer interaction with each other. The kind of interaction that has resulted from the process of globalisation has been characterised by some as positive while others have considered it as negative depending on the level of sensitivity and respect people from the centre have for other cultural groups. This connotes that the consequence of the interactions between different cultures vary from cultural exchange to cultural diffusion, cultural assimilation to cultural conflict and in some cases cultural extinction (Tomlinson 1999).

Throughout history, humans have replaced or altered customary behaviours and attitudes as their needs have changed: cultures have changed as societies change and respond to their needs. Just as no individual is immortal, no particular cultural pattern is impervious to change, and the change in cultural norms and values is a gradual process which is inevitable. While cultural exchange has always been cherished in many societies throughout the world, the problem is that through the process of globalisation some cultures have dominated others resulting in the extinction (of some cultures) or cultural conflict. This is not to say that cultures have always been static, but the dominance of one culture by another should always be expected whenever two cultures that consider themselves unequal encounter each other. In Zimbabwe for example, when the culture of the indigenous people of Zimbabwe encountered that of the European settlers, the culture of the former was dominated. The colonial settlers imposed their cultural beliefs on the indigenous people, a process that could be described as cultural imperialism (as opposed to cultural relativism) and sometimes ethnocentrism which even undermines cultural determinism).

This chapter problematises the concept of culture before examining cultural theories such as cultural determinism, cultural relativism and ethnocentrism and position them in a Zimbabwean context. The chapter further explores the applicability of the aforementioned theories while analysing the extent to which they differ and at the same time coexist in contemporary Zimbabwean society.

Unpacking the term culture

Culture is a common word these days but one of the most contentious and often misconstrued concepts across disciplines. While the conceptualisation of the word *"culture"* have been explored by many scholars across disciplines, it could be generally traced to as far back as 1871 when the English Anthropologist Edward B. Taylor, in his book, *Primitive Culture* explained. In fact, the term 'culture' was introduced into anthropology as a technical term by Tylor (see White and Dillingham 1972: 21). Tylor saw culture as 'that complex whole, which includes beliefs, art, law, morals, customs and any other capabilities and habits acquired by man as a member of society' (quoted in White and Dillingham 1972: 21; see also Keesing 1974). Due to its complexity, the concept of culture has been defined and re-defined over the years by scholars from different socio-political and cultural orientations. This accounts for the multiplicity of definitions of culture as a concept. Part of the difficulty in defining the concept of 'culture' lies in its multiple meanings as is understood by scholars across disciplines. Realising this, the American anthropologists, Kroeber and Kluckhohn, reviewed different conceptualisations and definitions of culture and compiled a list of 164 different definitions (see also Spencer-Oatey 2012). Other scholars like Apte (1994:45), writing in the ten-volume Encyclopaedia of Language and Linguistics, summarised the problem of defining culture as follows: 'despite a century of efforts to define culture adequately, there was in the early 1990s no agreement among anthropologists regarding its nature.' We underscore in this chapter that much of the difficulty [of understanding the concept of culture] stems from the different usages of the term from time to time. It is, therefore, important to note that culture is a slippery and ubiquitous concept. To be more specific, culture is a complex concept and no universal single definition of it has achieved consensus in the literature. However, attempts to offer a technical definition of the concept 'culture' have been made, of course with little success, throughout human history. Hofstede (1980:21-23), for instance, defines culture as 'the collective programming of the mind which distinguishes the members of one group from another', and which is passed from generation to generation. For Mulholland (1991), culture is a set of shared and enduring meaning, values, and beliefs that characterise national, ethnic, or other groups and orient their behaviour. Huntington (2006) also defined culture as the set of learned behaviours and ideas (including beliefs, attitudes, values, and ideals) that are characteristic of a particular society or other social group. Apart from that, the Culture Policy of Zimbabwe (2007:6) defines culture as the totality of a people's way of life, the whole complex of distinctive spiritual material, intellectual and emotional features that characterise a society or social group and includes not only arts and literature, but also modes of life, the fundamental rights of the human being, value systems and traditions and beliefs. It went further asserting that a people without a culture are a people without identity. This is because a people's culture gives them the reason to live as it guides them to make correct and beneficial choices in life (Culture Policy of Zimbabwe 2007: 6). Culture therefore bestows identity to a people. This means that people create, develop and perpetuate culture. In more or less the same way as the Culture Policy of Zimbabwe, Spencer-Oatey (2008: 3) opines that 'culture is a fuzzy set of basic assumptions and values, orientations to life, beliefs, policies, procedures and behavioural conventions that are shared by a group of people, and that influence (but do not determine) each member's behaviour and his/her interpretations of the 'meaning' of other people's behaviour.' Considering the complexities surrounding the definition of culture what becomes clear instead is that the word culture is an all-encompassing word which can mean everything and not clarify anything.

Following from the preceding discussion, one could note that culture is the totality of both the material and non-material expressions and communications of particular group of people that evolve over time as the people respond to their life challenges. No wonder Adesina and Adetoro (2000) comment that culture gives order and meaning to the socio-economic, political, religious and value system of a people. As is captured in our understanding of culture and of course in the definitions paraded above, it is clear that culture is always changing given that each generation adds something of its own before passing it on; hence culture is never static but is always dynamic. The other central feature of culture as is revealed in the preceding discussion is that it [culture] influences the way people perceive, think and behave in any given context. Above all, culture identifies and distinguishes one group of people from another. This means that when a group of people loses its culture, it has also lost its identity. For this reason, we argue in this chapter that it is highly unacceptable for any group of people to impose its own culture on another even if those whose culture is being suppressed will gain materially or otherwise. In fact, the importance of culture in any society across the world cannot be underestimated. This explains the reason why people have gone to war in the name of defending their culture against imperialism. A good example is the Meccabbean revolt against Antiochus Epiphanes when Antiochus tried to impose Hellenistic culture on the Jewish people.

Having problematised the concept of culture and shown its different dimensions, we move on to juxtapose three theories of culture (cultural relativism, ethnocentrism and cultural determinism), theories that appear to be commonplace in the current Zimbabwean context. In fact, guided by Geertz Clifford's (1973: 5) advice that "if you want to understand what science is, you should look in the first instance not at its theories or its findings, and certainly not at what its apologists say about it; you should look at what the practitioners of it do", we examined what practitioners of culture do and different scholars say about culture before examining the same in view of cultural theories.

Juxtaposing cultural relativism, ethnocentrism and determinism in the Zimbabwean Context

With several UNESCO World Heritage Sites, Zimbabwe is endowed with a variety and depth of historical, religious, natural and cultural riches that are yet to be fully discovered and recognised by the African continent and indeed the world-over. All of the Zimbabwean riches especially the cultural and religious ones are found among the different ethnic groups that scattered all over the country. These include but not limited to the Shona, Ndebele, Tonga, Kalanga, Ndau, Nambya, Korekore and Venda. Although coming from different, all these various ethnic groups share considerable common cultural traits, hence the term Zimbabwean culture. The Shona constitute one of the largest communal-cultural groups in Zimbabwe as this group is an aggregate of small ethnic groups who are all classified as Shona for the simple reason that they each speak a dialect of what the linguists call the Shona language (see Gelfand 1973).

Zimbabwean culture like any other cultures in the world is constantly evolving and changing to suit and adapt to the changing needs and values of society. This is to say that culture is never static, but always porous and dynamic to the extent that it evolves in order to conform to the factors affecting and influencing society. Culture is porous in the sense that it can easily donate to other cultures and accommodate new elements from other cultures which in turn will be modified to suit the new context and realities. It is, therefore, apparent that all cultures are susceptible to change. This means that the culture that was practiced hundred years ago in Zimbabwe is no longer compatible with some (though not all) of the current socio-cultural norms and values of today. It is in view of the dynamism, flexibility and porosity of culture that different theories have been postulated in attempt to understand and explain what culture is and how it operates in different contexts. While we acknowledge that culture has many theories that have been postulated over the years to try to unpack and understand it, this chapter only focuses on three theories namely; cultural determinism, cultural relativism and cultural ethnocentrism. The choice of these theories is not accidental but premised on our observation that the aforementioned have a closer link and could be easily related to the Zimbabwean society than any other theory that one can think of. As such, the abovementioned theories are, in this chapter–explained in view of the Zimbabwean context and ascertain their applicability and relevance thereof.

Cultural Determinism

This theory is premised on the pretext that people are what they are because of how and where they were brought up. Put differently, one's background and cultural orientation determines how he or she perceives and make sense of the world around him/her. This is to say that it is through social interaction that people learn, perceive and believe things to be what they are (whether right or wrong, good or bad). This theory relates considerably with the cultural context of Zimbabwe as elsewhere in the African continent and beyond. From the ethnographic researches we have carried out in different parts of Zimbabwe, we observed that if one is born and bred in a family that believes in African Traditional Religion where the veneration of ancestral spirits is an issue, such a person is likely to believe that life and fate of the living is controlled and determined by the dead. And, in fact for the reason that traditionally the Shona have a spiritual hierarchy of existence with God at the top followed by the ancestors in their perking order of seniority and down to the living beings on earth (Mawere 2005; Viriri and Mungwini 2009; Mawere 2010), many of the people who are born and bred in the Shona culture believe in life after death and the power of disembodied bodies and that of God. As has been stressed by many scholars (Mawere 2010; Viriri and Mungwini 2009), there is amble evidence among the Shona people which shows that the activities of ancestral spirits affect people in various ways whether positively or otherwise. This connotes that spiritual beings are very much counted, among the lives of those in the physical world, as important participants in shaping everything that may (and may not) happen. This is because by their very nature, ancestral spirits or the 'living dead' (Mawere 2010), occupy a better position than the living in determining events and influencing them, as they are no longer susceptible to the restrictions and limitations of space and time. No wonder scholars such as Minkus (1984) has argued that ancestral spirits hold their descendants

215

and successors responsible for the proper conduct of lineage affairs, maintenance of the customs they established and proffering the ritual attention they require. Based on such beliefs, followers of African Traditional Religion in Zimbabwe as elsewhere on the African continent are made to believe that the dead have a special role to play in the peoples' politics and survival to the extent that during droughts they engage in ceremonies such as *mukweerera* (rain petitioning). By rain petitioning ceremony, we mean the ritual by which the living people ask for rains from God through the ancestral spirits (Mawere 2013). This ceremony has been misunderstood by earlier Anthropologist on Zimbabwe and Africa in general as rain making ceremony. As one linkage between cultural determinism and the realities in Zimbabwe, rain-petitioning ceremonies are still being practised in many parts of the country despite criticism from science and Christianity which respectively consider the ceremonies as irrational (and unscientific) and heathen.

Further viewing (and perhaps applying) cultural determinism in relation to the Zimbabwean context, one would observe that the proponents of African Traditional Religion also believe that there is a spiritual explanation to death such that whenever death of a person in the society it is normal that they carry out *gata*. As espoused by Masaka and Chingombe (2009), *gata* is done when someone has died and the elders of the family go out to consult a traditional healer to account for the death or to ascertain the causes of death of the deceased. *Gata* is "a *traditional* ceremony [that] is held to determine *and establish* the cause of the death" of a person (Mandaza 1970:58, emphasis original) This is not to say that among the Shona traditionalists death is not always considered as natural, but the cause is always associated with some evil acts of enemies or understood as a curse from the ancestors. The main purpose of *gata*, thus, is to find out the cause of the death as well as putting in place corrective measures to safeguard the remaining societal (or family) members from a related mishap. This resonates with Gundani's (2004: 94) observation that "the original idea behind the '*gata*' ritual was for the family to adopt corrective measures by way of spiritual fortification, which often required the *n'anga*'s [traditional healer] involvement." While the intention for *gata* is normally to safeguard the remaining members from a related mishap, the *n'anga* also discloses the culprit responsible for the death of the deceased. This is premised on the understanding that to Africans in general, the Shona people included, the concept of causality is central to their metaphysics and epistemology. Thus for [traditional] Africans everything (including death) has a cause: nothing happens on its own accord and without a cause.

In the Zimbabwean context, determinism as a cultural theory is also evident in the way the Shona people conceive the idea of *ngozi* (avenging spirit) besides many other issues in the realm of life. The notion of *ngozi* is pervasive among the Shona and many other ethnic groups in Zimbabwe. Technically, *ngozi* is the spirit of a person who has been murdered and then comes back to seek revenge in the family of the murderer by causing unfathomable sorrow through illnesses, misfortunes or a series of deaths until the perpetrator pays reparations to the offended family (Mawere 2005, 2010). It should be emphasised, therefore, that among the Shona people, it is not always the case that the wrongdoer is the one who gets killed or cursed by *ngozi* but any person who is a blood relative of the wrongdoer is subject to the anger of *ngozi* (Mawere 2010: 573). In fact when the guilty family has failed, deliberately or otherwise, to pay reparations, *ngozi* strikes viciously and harshly by not only targeting the perpetrator of the crime but his kinsmen as well. As Bourdillon (1976:233) remarks, "*ngozi* is fearsome and terrifying because it attacks suddenly and very harshly". This belief in *ngozi* among the different ethnic groups in Zimbabwe relates well with the theory of determinism in view of the people's metaphysical and epistemological worldviews. In the Shona people's metaphysical understanding, for example, "*munhu haafi zvachose*/a human being does not die forever" (Mawere 2010:572). This means that the Shona people believe in the metaphysical realm of life after death as for them the end of bodily life marks the beginning of spiritual life – "life in disembodied body" (Mawere 2010: 572). For this reason even the morality of the Shona people is endorsed by the spiritual world –"the world beyond" (Mawere 2010) where 'the departed forebears' *(vadzimu)* in their disembodied forms reside but still with the power to communicate, act and influence the lives of those in the physical world. This is one reason why traditionalists in the Shona culture claim that they communicate with their *vadzimu*, in the spiritual world, and scholars such as John Mbiti (1969) and Bourdillon (1993) refer to the *vadzimu* as 'the living-dead' and 'ancestor spirits' respectively.

Cultural Relativism

The other cultural theory explicitly applicable to the Zimbabwean context is cultural relativism. Cultural relativism is, however, highly a contentious term such that many definitions and characterisations have been conjured over the years. Benedict (1934) offered five insights which could be used to summarise cultural relativism. These are;

- Different societies have different moral codes.
- The moral code of a society determines what is right within that society; that is, if the moral code of a society says that a certain action is right, then that action is right, at least within that society.
- There is no objective standard that can be used to judge one society's code as better than another's. There are no moral truths that hold for all people at all times.
- The moral code of our own society has no special status; it is but one among many.
- It is arrogant for us to judge other cultures. We should always be tolerant of them.

In line with Benedict's insights, Herskovits (1973:15) explains that cultural relativism is "the idea that each culture or ethnic group is to be evaluated on the basis of its own values and norms of behaviour and not on the basis of those of another culture or ethnic group." This means that cultural relativism pays more attention to the culture to which one group or individual belongs such that culture is

218

considered as the springboard of the group or individual's beliefs and behavioural patterns. Herskovits (1973: 31) further explains that cultural relativism as a theory that does not imply that there is no system of moral values to guide human conduct. Rather, cultural relativism suggests that every society has its own moral code to guide members of that society, but that these values are of worth to those who live by them, though they may differ from those of the people who do not belong to that culture. This, in itself, means that the terms and values of one culture should not be used to prove right or wrong other cultures since the universe has many societies with different cultures which should be appreciated and respected as they are.

Somewhat following Herskovits' understanding of cultural relativism, Nkeonye (1994) argues that a culture can only be understood in its own terms, and that standards from other cultures cannot be applied to it. Drawing from the aforementioned scholars, it is clear that cultural relativism stresses the idea that culture moulds individuals' personality, and that what is regarded as normal by one culture may be regarded as abnormal by another. In the light of this theory, people from different cultural backgrounds are obliged to respect each other's culture.

In Zimbabwe, some traits of cultural relativism could be observed if one is to consider–the coexistence and conviviality of different cultural and ethnic groups. A case in point is that of rites of passage such as the rite of male circumcision among the Shangani people (of Chiredzi and Mwenezi) and the Varemba people (of Gutu and Mberengwa), which in itself like many other rites of passage, is deductive and transformative. Emphasising the former, Atkinson (1999:112) argues that the rite of circumcision is significant because it is a repository of the broad scheme of traditional education in which parents plan to impart the needs of their children and also pass on the traditions or heritage of society. The rite of circumcision is performed in a faraway *enhoveni* (the forest area), which lies about ten kilometres from the rest of the community. There, *madzenga* (the boys at the forest) and their *vadzabi* (accompanying elders) erect some temporary huts to sojourn (Maposa 2011) while being taught about adult life of a male person. And, emphasising the transformative role of circumcision Whitehead (2004) argues that it [circumcision] facilitates the transition from one state to another. Among the Shangani people, for example, male circumcision is part of a traditional initiation school that transforms boys into men. Generally, the Shangani males are circumcised at between 13 and 17 years of age although older participants may exist. For any traditional Shangani male, traditional male circumcision is indispensable if one is to be accorded full respect of personhood and identity, what Sibanda (2013) describes as 'scars of identity' and 'scars of sacrifice' that represent 'going back to the roots'. This is to say that, among the Shangani people, no matter what age one might be, without undergoing the male circumcision he would not be considered as a full adult. Yet, this is different in other ethnic groups across Zimbabwe such that the significance of circumcision becomes relative with people born and bred in cultural environments such as those of the Shangani likely to embrace circumcision rites. The way they are raised is, therefore, a determinant factor for their perception of circumcision rites.

Cultural Ethnocentrism

Cultural ethnocentrism is a theory that involves judging other ethnic groups in relation to one's own cultural background and contains an inherent element of viewing one's own culture as superior to another (Hooghe 2008). This means that cultural ethnocentrism has a superiority complex in it: it is more of an elitist theory that has could be blamed for the undesirable habits of "Othering" and "Saming" in many societies – habits that cultivate "hierarchical and stereotypical thinking" (Lacan 1964; Mawere 2013: 5). This theory has greatly been applied in many African societies and particularly in Zimbabwe as elsewhere beyond the African continent. In view of the pervasiveness of ethnocentrism in Africa, Kasomo (2011: 2) had this to say:

Ethnocentrism has a long history in Africa and its manifestations are based on the origins of various ethnic groupings, preferences, attitudes, politics, colonialism, evangelism with its economic and social implications. With time, certain stereotype behaviours have been formed consequently leading to the present realities facing Africa.

Yet, while ethnocentrism has always been present among the African societies, it was intensified by Western evangelism and subsequent colonialism. Hans van Doome (1993) was apt to advance that it was thought the people living outside of Europe or North America, as it were, lived a previous stage of the development of mankind thus were regarded as underdeveloped and following pagan religion and, therefore, devilish and their cultures inferior. Kasomo (2011) seconds this view as he argues that some African communities during missionaries' evangelisation were given conditional baptism because the Europeans could not ascertain if they were human beings because they were too black. In fact most of the earliest anthropological and philosophical works on Africa were biased to prove that African cultures were inferior to the European ones – one reason the Europeans used as a justification to colonise and impose their cultures on the African peoples (see also Kumbirai 1977; Fanon 1969; and Asante (2000) who argue the same).

However, cultural ethnocentrism should not be confused with racism. As Germov and Freij (2009) point out, ethnocentrism differs from racism (overt discrimination), as it does not *directly* involve a negative vision of other ethnic groups; rather, it entails a difficulty in understanding other cultures, as the beholder applies his or her own perspective to the world, thereby inherently ignoring the validity of other perspectives. We argue, however, that despite what Germoy and Freij explain, it should be understood that where ethnocentrism is bluntly applied, it leads to racism as was the case during the colonial era in many parts of Africa (including Zimbabwe).

In contemporary Zimbabwe, the theory of ethnocentrism still applies in many circles and parts of the country. Following Hooghe's

221

(2008) understanding of ethnocentrism, one observes that some ethnic groups (especially large ethnic groups such as the Shona and Ndebele) in Zimbabwe still perceive themselves as superior to others. In this case, some cultural elements of smaller ethnic groups such as the Tonga, Ndau, Shangani and many others are often looked down upon. This is quite explicitly in the way how some small ethnic groups in Zimbabwe are often caricatured by members of larger ethnic groups. A case in point is that of the Ndau people of Eastern Zimbabwe who are normally referred to as *Vana Wasu* by members of the larger group, Shona following their way of speaking. In fact following their way of speaking, the *Vana Wasu* are often laughed at and sometimes looked down upon by members of the ethnic group, Shona who think their accent is superior to that of the Ndau people. On a similar note, the Tonga people of Northern Zimbabwe are often ridiculed for their matrilineal culture by larger ethnic groups such as Shona and Ndebele who are patrilineal. This is because some members of the Shona and Ndebele perceive matrilineality as an inferior cultural element, hence despise the Tonga culture as a whole.

The above is also true and more visible in the Zimbabwean education system where some indigenous languages such as Shona and Ndebele are taught and examined at school (at Ordinary and Advanced levels) while others such as Shangani, Venda, Kalanga and others are not. Besides, the use of English as the *lingua franca* (international language) does nothing more than perpetrating ethnocentrism. English language is considered as a superior language to all other languages spoken in Zimbabwe. In order for a student to advance from Ordinary level to Advanced Level or to enrol for a course in any academic institution (such as University or College), he/she should pass English Language at Ordinary Level. As a result, many parents, especially those in the elite strata of the Zimbabwean society prefer that their children speak English as they believe that this is the only suitable linguistic vehicle in the modern world. To this end, many ethnic languages are being suppressed to the extent that most of the people are no longer comfortable speaking them. This clearly shows that some languages are being considered more superior to others. We, therefore, argue that with the passage of time this will consequently lead to the extinction of those languages being looked down upon. This is likely to happen despite the fact that nature languages should be preserved because any language reflects the culture, tradition and identity of its people.

Conclusion

Using different examples and cases studies from across the Zimbabwe, this chapter has explored the concept of culture. It has been made clear that the concept of culture is notoriously contentious such that several definitions and characterisations have been conjured throughout history. More importantly, the chapter has discussed cultural theories, particularly cultural determinism, cultural relativism and ethnocentrism, in view of the contemporary situation in Zimbabwe. The choice to discuss these theories has not been accidental but premised on the fact that Zimbabwe is home to multiple ethnic groups and, therefore, a melting pot of people from different cultural and political persuasions. As a result, these different ethnic groups sometimes converge and differ in so far as their customs and values are concerned. We conclude that considering the diverse cultures existent in Zimbabwe, there is need to understand the nuances of culture so as to foster tolerance, conviviality, co-existence and sensitivity between people of different cultural backgrounds.

References

Asante, M. K. 2000. *The philosophers of Egypt: Ancient African voices from Imhotep to Akhenaten*, African American Images, Chicago: USA.

Adesina, S.A. and Adetoro, R.A. 2000. Harnessing over-positive culture for national progress and development. In *Nigerian Journal of Curriculum and Instruction*, 9 (1), 32-36.

Apte, M. 1994. Language in sociocultural context, In: R. E. Asher (Ed.), *The Encyclopaedia of Language and Linguistics, Vol.4,* (pp. 2000-2010), Pergamon Press: Oxford.

Atkinson, N.D. 1999. *Issues in Education: A Philosophical Perspective,* Harare: Zimbabwe Open University.

Bannerman, J.H. 1978. Towards a History of the Hlengwe People of the South of Rhodesia, NADA, Vol. XI (5), pp. 483-496.

Benedict, R.1934. *Patterns of Culture,* Houston-Mifflin, Boston.

Bourdillon, M.F.C. 1976. The Shona Peoples: An Ethnography of the contemporary Shona, with Special reference to their Religion, Gweru, Mambo Press.

Bourdillon, M.F.C. 1993. Where are the Ancestors? Changing culture in Zimbabwe, Harare, University of Zimbabwe Publications.

Culture Policy of Zimbabwe. 2007. Ministry of Education Sports and Culture, Harare, Zimbabwe.

Den Van, P.G. 1970. Race and Ethnicity: Essays in Comparative Sociology, Orbis Book, New York.

Fanon, F. 1968. *The wretched of the earth* (translated by Richard Philcox), Grove Press: New York, USA.

Geertz, C. 1973. *The interpretation of cultures: Selected essays,* Basic Books: United States of America.

Gelfand, M. 1973. *The Genuine Shona: Survival Values of an African Culture,* Mambo Press, Gweru.

Germov, J. and Freij, M. (2009). On Line Case Studies, Second Opinion, (4th Edition).

Giddens, A. 1997. *Sociology,* London: Polity Press.

Gundani, P. H. 2004. "Continuity and change in the Zimbabwean religio-cultural landscape in the era of HIV/AIDS", in Barry, H (ed.), *Zimbabwe: The Past is the Future,* Harare, Weaver Press, pp. 87-105.

Herskovits, M. J. 1973. *Cultural Relativism: Perspectives in Cultural Pluralism,* New York: Vintage Books.

Hofstede, G., 1980. *Culture's Consequences: International Differences in Work-related Values,* London: Sage Publications.

Hooghe, M. 2008. *'Ethnocentrism', International Encyclopaedia of the Social Sciences,* MacMillan Reference, Philadelphiawww.kuleuven.be/citizenship/_data/etho_iess.pdf

Huntington, S. P. 2006. *Kampf der Kulturen, Die Neugestaltung der Weltpolitik im 21, Jahrhundert,* Hamburg, Spiegel.

Kasomo, D. 2010a. Grabbing Independence from British Colonial System: An African is Deeply Religious, Berlin: VDM Verlag.

Kasomo, G, 2011. *An assessment of ethnic conflict and its challenges today,* In African Journal of Political Science and International Relations Vol., 6(1), pp 1-7.

Keesing, R. M. 1974. Theories of Culture, *Annual Review of Anthropology , 73-97.*

Kumbirai, J. 1977. Kurova guva and Christianity. In M. F. Bourdillon, *Christianity South of the Zambezi, Vol.2 (pp, 123-130),* Gweru: Mambo Press.

Kyeyune, D. 1997. New Trends for the Empowerment of the People (ed.), Paulines, Nairobi.

Lacan, J.1964. *The four fundamental concepts of psychoanalysis,* Hogarth Press: London.

Mandaza, D. M. 1970, "Traditional Ceremonies Which Persist", in C. Kileff and P. Kileff (eds.), *Shona Customs: Essays by African Writers,* Gweru, Mambo Press, pp.54-60.

Maposa, R.S, 2011. 'Going under the Traditional Knife': Linking African Traditional Education and the Ethic of Identity through Shangani Culture, Zimbabwe, Journal of Emerging Trends in Educational Research and Policy Studies (JETERAPS) 2 (6): 479-484.

Masaka, D. and Chingombe, A. 2009. The Relevance of 'Gata' among the Shona of Zimbabwe in the context of HIV/AIDS Pandemic, Journal od Pan African Studies, Vol.3, No, 1.

Mawere, M. 2005. 'Life after Bodily Death: Myth or Reality?' Zambezia J, Humanit, 32(2):26-46.

Mawere, M. 2010. "Peeping into the world beyond": Metaphysical Speculations on the Nature of Life in Disembodied Bodies, Educational Research, Vol.1 (11) pp.568-576.

225

Mawere, M. 2013a. *Rain petitioning and step-son play*, Langaa Publishers: Bamenda, Cameroon.

Mawere, M. 2013b. Rethinking the epistemological divide between knowledge and other knowledge forms in environmental studies: An Anthropological review, *The International Journal of Humanities and Social Studies*, 1 (2): 1-6.

Mbiti, J. 1969. African Religions and Philosophy, 2nd ed., Heinemann.

Minkus, H. K. 1984. 'Causal theory in Akwapim Akan Philosophy' in Wright, R. A. (ed.) African Philosophy: An Introduction. New York: University Press of America.

Mulholland, J. 1991. *The Language of Negotiation*, London: Routledge.

Nkeonye, O. 1994. *Cultural Relativism: Some Comments*. Philosophic a 53, pp. 57-71.

Sibanda, F. 2013. Beyond Identity Scars: Reflections on the Vitality of Shangani Male Circumcision in the Context of HIV and AIDS in Zimbabwe, *Journal of Emerging Trends in Educational Research and Policy Studies (JETERAPS) 4(1): 1-7*.

Spencer-Oatey, H. 2008. *Culturally Speaking, Culture, Communication and Politeness Theory*, 2nd edition, London: Continuum.

Spencer-Oatey, H. 2012. What is culture? A compilation of quotations, *GlobalPAD Core Concepts,* GlobalPAD Open House.

Tilley, J. J. 2000. *Cultural Relativism*, Human Rights Quarterly, 22: 501–47.

Tomlinson, John 1999, *Globalization and Culture*, Cambridge, UK: Polity Press lash.

Viriri, A. and Mungwini, P. 2009. 'Down But Not Out': Critical Insights in Traditional Shona Metaphysics, *The Journal of Pan African Studies*, vol.2, No.9.

White, L. A. and Dikkingham, B. 1972. *The content of culture: Basic concepts in anthropology*, Minneapolis: Burgess Publishing Company.

Whitehead, C. 2004. "Religious Experience and the theory of Anti-Structure", Downloaded from: http://www.socialmirrors.org/cms/images/downloads/ RE_and_antistructure.pdf, Accessed: 10 June 2012.

Chapter 11

Marriage in a globalised world: The effects of globalisation on traditional marriage systems in Zimbabwe

Genius Tevera and Tapuwa Raymond Mubaya

Introduction

In the course of history, Africa as an entire continent has at one period or the other become a battle ground for external socio-political, economic and even cultural forces struggling for her soul (Chinwe 2010). This was most evident during the colonial adventure of European imperialists in Africa. Colonialism was about empire building, finding raw materials and opening up new markets. To do this effectively, some colonisers used religion to undermine the rich cultures of the colonised people. At the same time, many people were displaced from their cultural lands to pave the way for settlers and for development; cultural objects and artefacts were plundered and carried away from the colonised countries (Mazrui 2001).

Today, Africa is confronted by yet another irresistible phenomenon called globalisation which is viewed by some as a "societal plague" (Doran 2000: 6). It has been viewed as such because globalisation has swept like a flood tide through the world's diverse cultures, destroying stable localities, displacing peoples, bringing a market-driven, 'branded' homogenisation of cultural experience, thus obliterating the differences between locality-defined cultures which had constituted our identities (Tomlison 1999). Globalisation is an elusive and contentious term whose meaning remains obscure often even among those who invoke it (Scholte 1995). Generally globalisation may be referred to as the widening, deepening and speeding up of world-wide interconnectedness in all aspects of contemporary social life, from the cultural to the criminal, the financial to the spiritual (Held 1999).

As a result of globalisation, Western cultures have been forced onto the peoples of Africa as 'the culmination of all human progress' (Ajayi 1966: 606), a model to be followed without equivocation or reservation. Supposedly universalistic and achievement-oriented, Western cultures are expected to penetrate the back-ward looking cultures with their values through a uni-linear process of inter-cultural communication (Himmelstrand et al 1994:3). In other words, there is no question why the rules of existence elaborated in the West, could not be applied in exactly the same way, in others parts of the world with different backgrounds and experiences. Africans have thus been invited to devalue themselves, their institutions and their cultures by cultivating an uncritical empathy for Western economic, cultural and political values which are glorified beyond impeachment (Nyamnjoh 2000). The perpetuation of Western cultures as the standard of measure not only dispossessed Africans of their own cultures, it infantilised and dis-empowered them by forcing them to learn afresh, under the guidance of condescending and overbearing Western overlords, new ways of seeing, doing and being (Nyamnjoh 2000).

Against this background, it is a verity that globalisation has affected the African people's cultural life in various ways and has inevitably altered their beliefs at personal levels. The advent of globalisation has caused a shift from the traditional marriage customs and beliefs to a new cultural approach where women are not necessarily compelled to engage in matrimonial relations as they feel that they are independent and their existence is not dependent on man. While globalisation has many facets namely economic, political and cultural, this discussion focuses on cultural globalisation. Cultural globalisation refers to "the emergence of a specific set of values and beliefs that are largely shared around the planet" (Castells 2009 p. 117). In this regard globalisation is seen as colonisation and imperialism thus it has been stated in some quarters that colonialism can be viewed as the first stage of globalisation (Saul n.d.). In the same vein, Waters argues that globalisation is the direct consequence of the expansion of European culture across the planet through settlement, colonisation and cultural mimesis (Waters 1996). Cultural dislocation and loss are inevitable consequences of the rapid social change of globalisation. It is vital to note that all change, no matter how seemingly beneficial, involves elements of loss and the universal human response to loss is to experience grief (Maris 1996).

In light of the above, the impact of globalisation especially on African cultural values weighs heavily in favour of the negative and it is these negative impacts that constitute the biggest challenges to Africa (Chinwe 2010). There is no doubt that Africa is facing a lot of challenges on account of the phenomenon of globalisation especially the institution of marriage. As a result of globalisation, there has been a continuing shift and transformation in traditional patterns of social and cultural organisations, among others. To this end, traditional marriage systems in Zimbabwe are undergoing these transformations. One of the major transformations is the way people especially women perceive marriage. This has greatly changed due to the discourse of human rights that places women at par with their male counterparts. The proliferation of Non-Governmental organisations focusing on the welfare and empowerment of women has rendered the marriage institution unpalatable. In traditional Shona society marriage is considered an achievement, failure to do so results in social pressure upon the incumbent. In this chapter we argue that while culture change is normal, the rate at which marriage customs and beliefs are changing in Zimbabwe is horrendous. Though many traditional cultural forms are still very much in place in many rural communities, such traditions have been seriously eroded, weakened, and/or replaced by new or completely foreign usages especially in urban settings. These cultural practices are no longer adhered to as they are considered incompatible with the ethos of globalisation.

An overview of traditional Shona marriage systems

Marriage and family constitute foundational institutions in virtually all known human societies from primitive ancestors to present day societies (Adei 2003). African societies attach a lot of importance to their respective traditions, customs and cultural values because they serve as a means of expressing individual and group feelings and thoughts and act as storerooms for history and traditions while also serving, at the same time, as an integral part of their cultural heritage (Graham et. al 2000). Marriage can therefore be regarded as one of the most important social customs of traditional African societies because through it, kinship is formed, the lineage is maintained and expanded, and new households and units are formed. Thus, marriage is said to be amongst the most significant life events in most Shona societies as it signals the beginning of adulthood. Thus Mbiti (1990) submits that for Africans, marriage is the focus for existence. He went further arguing that it is the point where all the members of a given community meet; the departed, the living and those yet to be born. Chavunduka (1979) and Geifand (1984) also observed that despite the changes brought about by colonialism and capitalist development among the Shona, marriage is a social commitment that establishes a social relationship not just between two people, but also among families and friends.

In view of the above, marriage is seen as a union between two families and not between two individuals (Hendrix 1998:734). This is what makes marital breakdown very difficult because problems are settled not between two persons but between the two families of the couples concerned. Mbiti (1990 p.104), notes that "marriage is looked upon as a sacred duty which every normal person must perform." Add to that, in an African context marriage has a primary and secondary purpose. The primary purpose of marriage is procreation and the education of offspring while the secondary purpose is mutual help in all aspects of life, which builds and promotes that unity. Procreation is so important that most people consider it to be the fundamental purpose of marriage within traditional African settings. Marriage and procreation is a unit, without procreation, marriage is incomplete. More so, procreation is significant since in the Shona culture one's own being is believed to be immortalised, that is, 'the person does not only live in the present, but in the future' (Gonese in Mawere and Mawere 2010). The legacy bequeathed to the individual by his ancestors is continued after his/her death through procreation. The family name is perpetuated and the link between ancestors and the living is assured. Without children, therefore, the family genealogy and identity ultimately die off. In view of this, a childless marriage is considered a misfortune or a curse from the ancestors or God.

It is thus evident that children are central to marriage and if a woman fails to bear children, her family would be expected to compensate the husband by giving him another wife (in most cases the younger sister of the wife) to do that which the first wife has failed to do. In the case that the wife's family has no other woman to give to the husband, they are obligated to give him back the bride price. However, where the situation is reversed and it is the husband who is sterile, the woman can be impregnated by any man from her husband's lineage on behalf of the husband but this was done secretly. In short, in traditional Shona society if a marriage fails to produce children measures are taken to correct that anomaly. Marriage customs such as *kupindira* (using a substitute husband) and *chigadzamapfiwa* (substitute wife) are meant to ensure that a marital union 'produces' children (Chigidi 2009 p180). This is because procreation is not only a profound function of a marital relationship but guarantees societal regeneration to ensure its continued existence (Mawere and Mawere 2010).

On the other hand, the traditional Shona marriage system is based on patriarchal and gives a husband exclusive sexual right over his wife. The wife has no rights to expect fidelity from her husband but rather has rights to sexual satisfaction, meaning a husband can engage in extra marital affairs as long as he is able to please and satisfy his wife. Extra marital affairs on the part of the husband only become a problem when he fails to satisfy his "official" wife or wives (Holleman 1974).

Types of marriages among the Shona people

Zimbabwe has a pluralistic marriage system. It is one of the countries where choices of the type of marriage are wide and varying. One can choose to co-habit *(kuchaya mapoto)*, to get married in an unregistered customary law union, to be in a registered customary marriage, or to be in a registered civil marriage (Dube 2013). Customary marriages are governed by customary law while civil marriages are governed by general law. All marriage systems under traditional customary marriage are anchored on the payment of *lobola* (bride wealth) by the bridegroom's family to the bride's family. Traditionally, the Shona considered *lobola* as a noble custom that functioned as a safeguard against marital dissolution because it generally needs to be repaid upon divorce (Meekers 1993 in Mawere and Mawere 2010).

Basically, there are two recognised registered marriages under customary marriage. The first one is termed monogamy. Monogamy is a form of marriage in which an individual chooses and is permitted by law to have only one spouse at any given point in time. This means that a man will only have one wife, while a woman will have one husband (Dube 2013). Under Zimbabwean law, this marriage is provided for in the Marriages Act [Chapter 5:11] formerly known as Chapter 37. Such a marriage can be presided over by a legally designated marriage officer, who can be a religious minister such as a priest or pastor, or by a marriage officer at the Magistrates Court. Marrying a second wife or husband is strictly prohibited under this marriage regime, and anyone who does so will be committing the crime of bigamy. Bigamy is punishable by a prison sentence of just one year or a fine or both (Dube 2013).

The second type of registered marriage is the Customary Marriages Act: Chapter 5:07 which used to be called Chapter 2:38. This type of marriage is called a potentially polygamous marriage because it allows a man to marry more than one wife. Although a man can then decide not to marry more than one wife, should he do so then he will be acting within the parameters of the law (Dube 2013). There are two types of potentially polygamous marriages both of which are guided by customary law. The first is a registered customary marriage prescribed under the Customary Marriages Act [Chapter 5:07], formerly known as Chapter 231, or in vernacular '*muchato wekwamudzviti*' (Dube 2013). Such a marriage allows a man to marry more than one wife. This marriage is recognised as a marriage at law. A man in such a marriage is not obliged under any law to notify (inform) his wife of his intention to marry a second wife. Neither does he have an obligation to request the consent of his first wife or other wives before marrying other women (Marriage Act of Zimbabwe).

There is also a third type of customary marriage which is not registered and actually in terms of the law it is called an Unregistered Customary Law Union. This type of marriage is limited to the cultural practice of the payment of bride price (*roora/lobola*) by the man to the woman's family. Although all the other types of marriages may be preceded by the payment of *lobola*, their uniqueness lies in the registration of the marriage. For an unregistered customary law union, once the *lobola* process is done, then the two are considered married and can live together. Under the unregistered customary marriage, a man can marry as many wives as he wishes. Although traditionally all subsequent marriages were entered into after notification to the other wives, in modern times that is seldom the case. For most Zimbabweans who follow a patrilineal structure in which descent is through the male line, after marriage a woman moves into her husband's home (Dube 2013).

Some of the defining characteristics of Shona marriage

The payment of lobola (*roora*)

Roora/lobola is a significant element of marriage among the Shona of Zimbabwe (Ansell 2001). It is a custom that has stood the taste of time. The concept of *roora/lobola* is translated into English as bride wealth or bride price (Chireshe and Chireshe 2010). According to Zvobgo (1996) *lobola* is a custom in which the husband (or his family on his behalf) delivers or promises to deliver to the father (or guardian) of the wife, stock or other property, in consideration of which the legal custody of the children born of the marriage is vested in their father (or his family) to the exclusion of any member of the mother's family (Chireshe and Chireshe 2010). Traditionally, the payment of lobola validates marriage and is an essential requirement for entering into customary marriage. Normally, the bride price is paid in the form of cattle, money and clothes to the bride's parents and these are meant to cement the relationship between the two families. The bride price is paid as a token of appreciation and normally translates to that. It is taken only as a way of formalising relationship with the other family and normally all family members would chip in assisting the groom to pay for his bride as starting up a new family was communal in nature (Bourdillon 1997; Mangena and Ndlovu 2013).

Levirate Marriages

According to Shona custom, when one's husband dies the widow is married off to a male relative of her deceased husband usually a younger brother. This emanates from the concept that a woman is not married to one man but rather is married to the whole family so in the event that the husband died she was given to another man from the same lineage. Traditionally, a woman who refused to marry her late husband's relative faced the threat of being sent back to her patrilineal home and this must have worked to persuade them to agree to the marriage as it was always a disgrace for a women to leave her matrimonial homestead and go back to stay with her parents. With the coming of globalisation this culture is no longer very prevalent. Today, most women once their husbands pass away would rather take care of their families on their own or they prefer to find their own partners who are not necessarily related to their deceased husbands. Apart from that, families no longer stay in compounds with the rest of the extended family and members of the extended family no longer have control over the running of their kinsman's family.

Child bearing

For the Shona people, every marriage is supposed to be fulfilled through child bearing which is the landmark of parenthood. This is affirmed by (Bourdilion 1976) who notes that, parenthood is fulfilled through childbearing and rearing, which establishes status among the Shona people. That is why a multiplicity of intervention strategies is employed to avoid the tagging of the couple and families concerned if infertility is suspected. Children are crucial in any marriage contract among the Shona people. In fact, children are a determinant factor in one's social status, respect and honour. Children give a marriage some form of stability and dignity [*kupa mhuri chiremera nerutsigo*] (Chingombe et al 2012 p.3). One of the foremost traditional values of the African is love for large families. For an African the primary purpose for marriage is children and to have as many of them as possible. This is the reason why polygamy or the union of one man with several women still holds supreme attraction for most Africans. This is also explains why the birth rate in Africa is among the highest in the world. The fact is that the African still counts his blessings by the number of children he has whether they are educated or not, rich or poor, healthy or sick, well-fed or hungry (Jacques 1972).

Challenges of traditional marriage systems in the global era

Women's empowerment

The changes in awareness, and policies including the emancipation of women was brought about by the efforts of many such as activists, women's movements, national governments and international donor organisations (Jahan 1996). Women empowerment is not only about participation in decision making but is also a process that should lead people to perceive themselves as able and entitled to make decisions. The social implication of empowerment is that women today have attained some economic power and are not necessarily dependent on their husbands. In Africa, such women empowerment initiatives have resulted in a situation where African women are increasingly questioning traditional patriarchal practices including traditional marriage (Esere 2003; Mapala 2004). The empowerment of women can result in some men feeling that they are losing control over their wives. These men often become insecure which manifests in a very authoritarian attempt to keep things under control. The empowered women in these situations may assert themselves by securing a protection order from the courts.

Gay couples and marriages

The Shona people condemn homosexuality as it is an alien practice among them. The term 'homosexuality' was coined in the late 19th century by a German psychologist, Karoly Maria Benkert to refer to what Palen (2001: 273), described as "a sexual orientation toward, and sexual activity with, members of the same sex." Today, the most common term that is used to refer to male homosexuals is *gays*; and for female homosexuals is *lesbians*, (a term derived from the inhabitants of the Greek island of *Lesbos*) Chemhuru 2012). Zimbabweans frown upon same sex relationships as they view this practice as a possible origin of the HIV and AIDS scourge (Panos 1988). Some churches notably the Anglican Church have actually solemnised gay marriages. This is anathema to the Shona people yet they are being forced to accept it as something normal. In addition, some Human Rights activists who are donor funded by the West even want these to be recognised constitutionally. This shows the extent to which western cultural imperialism is going in the name of globalisation and human rights protectionism (Mazuru and Grand 2013).

According to Cock (2003), the assertion of a public gay identity is problematic in the African context. One of the most powerful voices against homosexuality was by the President of Zimbabwe, Robert Gabriel Mugabe who in mid-1995 proclaimed homosexuality as unAfrican, and branded gays and lesbians as 'worse than pigs and dogs' (Dube 2013). It is crucial to note that Zimbabwe's new constitution makes same-sex marriage a criminal offence as section 4.78 of the new constitution prohibit persons of the same sex from marrying each other. It is this social stigma that has driven many African gays to operate in secrecy (Castells 1997). In South Africa, there is a legislation which supports gay marriages and all these unethical activities have cropped up as a result of the influence of globalisation.

The increasing problem of HIV and AIDS

According to UNAIDS (2008), Sub-Saharan Africa accounts for two-thirds (67%) of the total of 33 million people living with HIV and AIDS. The statistical figures also show that hetero-sexual transmission between couples is still the predominant mode of HIV and AIDS spread in sub-Saharan Africa. The other problem that has accelerated the HIV and AIDS pandemic is the use of condoms which have somehow licensed immorality and gave people the impression that HIV and AIDS can be prevented by the use of condoms.

The use of contraceptives

The West encourages the use of contraceptives such as male and female condoms yet acknowledging that they are not hundred percent effective and abstinence is articulated as a secondary thing. This legitimises promiscuity as one would be protected and sex with multiple partners becomes inevitable. The culture of wanton sexual engagement is typically of the West where morality has been relegated to the periphery and immorality is eulogized as the paragon of virtue (Mazuru and Grand 2013). Sex, which among the Shona had been primarily for procreation is now for personal physical gratification as many youths now engage in it before marriage as is common in Western countries (Bohannan 1985). In traditional Shona marriage women were using traditional ways of child spacing. With the advent of globalisation, women are now using various contraceptive methods most of which have detrimental effects to their health. These contraceptives are also used to regulate the number of children in a family. A general observation by the researchers shows that most married couples prefer to have two to four children on average.

The increase in divorce cases

In the olden days marriage was highly respected to the extent that they were very few cases of divorce. This was due to the fact that the extended family had a pivotal role in moulding and counselling men and women. Today there are countless cases of divorce and these mainly border on infidelity. In traditional African society divorce was not a common occurrence because of the cultural practices, like wife inheritance and "lobola" that cemented relationships and promoted the institution of marriage.

Early marriages

Early marriage refers to any form of marriage that takes place before a child has reached 18 years. It is disheartening to note that children as young as thirteen years are getting married. This is mainly due to the fact that they are taught sex education at elementary stages. Coupled with obscene films and videos that they watch on television and internet, these children would in turn want to enact and practice what they see thereby falling prey to sexually transmitted diseases and HIV and AIDS. Apart from that, pornographic material abundant on the parallel market influence youngsters to engage in sexual activities at tender ages.

Individualism

The traditional parenting practices of the Shona people in Zimbabwe were premised upon the extended family system. Children grew up among relatives who, together with own parents would direct the child along the parts the child should go. Grandparents, uncles and aunts, elder brothers, sisters, cousins and nephews would all make an input in the upbringing of the child. Nowadays people prefer to teach and educate their children without interference from the extended family which used to decide and preside on issues affecting the broader community. Marriage is no longer a contract between two families. Instead it is a contract between the two concerned partners. The role of the auntie *(vatete)* is no longer considered.

Single parenting

Women today have full control over their choice of partners as well as the nature of their relationship with those partners. The gradual erosion of traditional marriage has been observed in many African societies especially among the better educated and urban segments of the population. Nowadays, women who are educated or those who are engaged in wage labour often challenge their husbands' authority and want a greater influence in decision making. Thus, the tendency to avoid marriage is visible visible among professional, better educated, urban and wealthy women. Rather than contracting a formal marriage, these women prefer unmarried cohabitation or to have lovers who do not live with them because this allows them a greater amount of liberty.

Commercialisation of lobola

The transition from communalism to capitalism, from traditional to modern, has seen the payment system of *lobola* also adopting exploitative tendencies. In this regard we are forced to accept May's proposition that: "such a system is, of course, liable to abuse in an increasingly commercial society. Fathers demand unduly high amounts for educated daughters as a recompense for the money they have invested in educating their girls". (May 1984:48). An educated girl attracts more money for two reasons; it's a compensation for the money invested in her education and it is believed that she would be of more value to the husband than an uneducated one. Some Shona communities now have a separate charge for a girl who gets married soon after University graduation. This particular girl attracts a high charge because she possesses what is called *chitupa chinyoro*; which can

239

be loosely translated into "a fresh educational certificate (Mangena and Ndlovu 2013 p.476). Lobola today is so capitalistic that the money paid determines the woman's condition in marriage.

Contrary to the way it was done before, the paying of lobola has been transformed into a commercial transaction with cash forming the larger component of the transaction. Daughters are now treated as part of the family assets which can easily be translated into cash for economic gains. This change in patterns of *lobola* payment is a result of globalisation as people have become individualistic and materialistic seeking economic gains rather than family ties. Globalisation has re-oriented people's values resulting in people being concerned more about what they stand to benefit economically from a relationship rather than seek true happiness. Interestingly some women are against the issue of paying lobola. They argue that the practice objectified them as women giving man the impression that like any other material object women are at their disposal to do with whatever they wanted. They further argue that payment of *lobola* portrays women as objects on the commercial market that can be bought and disposed of as and when the owner saw it fit.

Intercultural marriages

In cases where the world has shrunk into "a global village", boys and girls get married to people from other cultures that do not necessarily value bride price payment. Even the concept of marriage itself seems to be losing its traditional value (Mangena and Ndlovu 2013 p.476). Consequently, Africans get exposed to other cultures including instances of intercultural marriages. Such marital arrangements may lead to problems as a result of the different orientations of the couple in areas like values, religion, language, communication and male-female sex roles (Romano, 2008).

Cohabitation

Cohabitation has become another thorny issue as youngsters stay with their partners as if they are married when they are actually not. This has been exacerbated by the age of majority act, which is also a western invention. Cohabitation has become the norm as according to the western, global culture marriage is an issue between two consenting adults (Mazuru and Grand 2013). This exposes the woman to divorce anytime the partner deems fit and the same applies for them. So these unsanctioned marriages of convenience approved by the West instead of being liberating are actually oppressive and have sentence many unsuspecting women to death by exposure to the HIV and AIDS virus (Mazuru and Grand 2013).

Conclusion

There have been radical changes in the life of the Shona over the past decades. It would not be proper to assume that what was permissible those hundred years or so back still obtains today. Mainly the changes witnessed were due to external influences globalisation being the major one. The challenges of globalisation to Zimbabwean marriage institutions are enormous and varied. The concept of globalisation has affected Zimbabweans in both positive and negative ways. The wave of globalisation is affecting all facets of life and as such traditional Zimbabwean families and communities that have remained intact through their various cultural and traditional set ups run the risk of breaking their necks in order to adjust to the whims of globalisation. In fact, globalisation is putting the traditional marriage institution in peril. The result is that traditional marriage is being diluted to the extent that it is being degraded and will ultimately atrophy. In short, globalisation is creating a world in which cultural values and traditions are being eroded. However, the preservation of the traditional family values within the prevailing circumstances cannot be achieved by a total rejection of modernity and globalisation nor can they be achieved by an open-ended and unquestionable acceptance of change in the name of modernity, advancement, and civilisation and information technology. We conclude, therefore, that the discourse of globalisation must be approached with caution if Zimbabwean traditional communities wish to preserve family values in an ever-changing world.

References

Adei, S. 2003. *African Traditional Marriage and Biblical Patterns: The case of the Ashantis of Ghana*, Masters of Theology Thesis, University of South Africa.

Ajayi, J.F.A. 1966. The Place of African History and Culture in the Process of Nation-building in Africa South of the Sahara, In: I. Wallerstein (ed.) *Social Change: The Colonial Situation*. John Wiley and Sons: New York. pp.606-16.

Ajayi, O.O. 2005. *Globalisation and the Politics of Marginality*. In Globalization and Marginalization, Eds., Vaughan, O., M. Wright and C. Small, Ibadan: Sefer Books, pp: 201.

Ansell, N. 2001. "Because it's our culture!' (Re)negotiating the meaning of *lobola* in Southern African secondary schools,' *Journal of Southern African Studies* 27(4) 697-716.

Bohannan, P. 1985. *All the Happy Families: Exploring the varieties of Family life*: McGraw-Hill Book Co. New York.

Bourdillon, M.F.C., 1997. *Where are the ancestors? Changing culture in Zimbabwe*, Harare: University of Zimbabwe Publications.

Bourdillon M.F.C. 1998. *The Shona Peoples* (Revised edition). Gweru: Mambo Press, In: Mawere, M and Mawere, A.M. 2010. The Changing Philosophy of African Marriage: The relevance of the Shona customary marriage practice of *Kukumbira,* Journal of African Studies and Development Vol. 2(9), pp. 224-233.

Castells, M. 1997. *The power of identity,* Cambridge, MA: Blackwell.

Castells, M. 2009. *Communication Power, New* York: Oxford University Press.

Chavhunduka, G. L. 1979. *A Shona Urban Court,* Gweru, Mambo Press.

Chemhuru, M. 2012. *Rethinking the legality of homosexuality in Zimbabwe: a philosophical perspective*, International Journal of Politics and Good Governance, Volume 3, No. 3.3.

Chigidi, L.W.2009. *Shona Taboos: The Language of Manufacturing Fears for Sustainable Development,* The Journal of Pan African Studies, vol.3, no.1.

Chingombe, A., Mandova, E and Nenji S. 2012. *Perception and management of human fertility: a shona landscape*, International Journal of Management and Sustainability 1(1):1-12.

Chinwe, A.F. 2010. *Africa and the challenges of globalization: A critical appraisal of the relevance of Pan-Africanism*, Enugu State University of Science & Technology, Enugu, Nigeria.

Chireshe, E and Chireshe, R. 2010. *Lobola: The Perceptions of Great Zimbabwe University Students, The Journal of Pan African Studies*, vol.3, no.9.

Cock, J. 2003. Engendering gay and lesbian rights: The equality clause in the South African constitution. *Women's Studies International Forum, 26*(1), 35–45.

Doran, Charles F. 2000. *Globalization and Statecraft, SAISPHER,* p. 6.

Dube, R, 2013, Till death do us part? Marriage in Zimbabwe, Research and Advocacy Unit (RAU).

Esere, M. O. 2003. Resolving Conflicts in Marriages: A Counsellor's Viewpoint, *in Journal of Education, 22*(1), 26 - 41.

Gelfand, M. 1984. *The Genuine Shona*, Gweru, Mambo Press.

Graham, B, Ashworth, G.J & Tunbridge, and J.E, 2000. *A Geography of Heritage: Power, Culture and Economy,* London.

Gonese, G. 1999. *The Three Worlds*, COMPAS Newsletter Number 1.

Held, D & Megrew, A. Global, D & Perraton, J. 1999. *Global Transformation: Politics, Economics and Culture*, Stanford University Press, Stanford California.

Hendrix, L. 1998. 'Marriage.' In: *Encyclopaedia of Cultural Anthropology.* Vol. 3.

Himmelstrand, U, Kinyanjul, K, Mburugu, E. 1994. *'Introduction: In search of New Paradigms?'* in: Ulf Himmelstrand, Kabiru Kinyanjul and Edward Mburugu (eds.), African Perspectives on Development: Controversies', Dilemmas and Openings. James Currey: London. pp. 1-15.

Holleman J.F. 1975. *Shona Customary Law: With Reference to Kinship, Marriage, the Family and the Estate.* (Cape Town: Oxford University Press).

243

Jacques, M. 1972. *Africanity, the Cultural Unity of Black Africa*, New York: Oxford University Press, pp. 124-125.

Jahan, R. 1996. The Elusive Agenda: Mainstreaming women in development, *The Pakistan Development Review, 35*(4), 825–834.

Mangena, T and Ndlovu, S. 2013. *Implications and complications of bride price payment among the shona and ndebele of Zimbabwe*, International Journal of Asian Social Science, 3(2):472-481.

Mapala, M. M. 2004. *Traditional marriage counsellors and HIV/AIDS: A study of Alangizi National Association of Zambia in Lusaka* (Unpublished doctoral dissertation), Southern and Eastern Africa Regional Centre for Women's Law, University of Zimbabwe, Zimbabwe.

Marriages Act [Chapter 5:11] Acts 81/1964, 6/1967 (s. 15), 35/1967.(s. 32), 20/1968, 42/1971 (s. 5), 37/1972, 21/1973 (s. 66), 41/1978 (s. 4), 17/1979 (s. 7), 29/1981 (s. 59), 15/l982 (s. 3), 18/1989.(s. 37), 22/2001 (s. 4); 23/2004 (s. 282); S.I's 213/1982, 666/1983.

Marris, P. 1996. *Loss and Change*. Routledge: London.

Mawere, M. and Mawere, A.M. 2010. The changing philosophy of African marriage: The relevance of the Shona customary marriage practice of *Kukumbira*, Journal of African Studies and Development Vol. 2(9): 224-233.

May, J. 1984. *Zimbabwean women in colonial and customary law*, Gweru: Mambo Press.

Mazrui, A. 2001. *Pan-Africanism and the origins of globalization.* http://igcs.binghamton.edu/igcs_site/ dirton12.htm. Accessed 3 January 2007.

Mazuru, M and Grand, N. 2013. *HIV and AIDS, Globalisation and the Shona Indigenous Knowledge Systems: the Impact of HIV and AIDS on the Shona Culture*, Greener Journal of Social Sciences, Vol. 3 (4), pp. 171-179.

Mbiti, J.S. 1990. *African Religions and Philosophy*, 2nd Ed. Oxford, Heinemann Meekers D. 1993. The Noble Custom of Roora: The Marriage Practices of the Shona of Zimbabwe', J. Ethnol. 32 (1): 35-54.

Morgan, J. 2013. *Zimbabwe's new constitution makes gay marriage a 'crime'*, Gaystarnews.

Nyamnjoh, F.B. 2000. "For many are called but few are chosen": Globalisation and Popular Disenchantment in Africa, African Sociological Review, 4, (2), pp. 1-45.

Palen, J.J. 2001. *Social problems for the 21st Century*, New York, McGraw Hill.

Panos Institute, 1988. *Blaming others: Prejudice, Race and Worldwide AIDS,* Sabbatier: London.

Parpart, J. L., Rai, S.M., & Staudt, K. 2002. Rethinking Empowerment, Gender and Development: An introduction. In: J .L. Parpart, S. M. Rai., & K. Staudt (Eds.), *Rethinking empowerment: Gender and development in a global/local world* (pp. 3–21). New York, NY: Routledge.

Romano, D. 2008. *Intercultural marriage: Promises and pitfalls,* Boston, MA: Intercultural Press.

Scholte, J. A. 1995. "Globalisation and Modernity," Paper presented at the International Studies Association Convention, San Diego.

Saul, S. n.d. *Colonialism.* University of Montreal, Quebec, Canada.

Tomlinson, J. 1999. *Globalization and Culture.* Cambridge: Polity Press.

UNAIDS. 2008. *Report on the global AIDS epidemic,* Geneva, Switzerland: UNAIDS.

Waters, M., 1996. *Globalization.* London: Routledge, pp: 2.

Zvobgo, C. J. M. 1996. *A history of Christian missions in Zimbabwe.* Gweru: Mambo Press.

www.ingramcontent.com/pod-product-compliance
Lightning Source LLC
Chambersburg PA
CBHW060032030426
42334CB00019B/2290